Lancastrians, Yorkists and the Wars of the Roses   1399–1509

ROGER TURVEY

SECOND EDITION

HODDER
EDUCATION
AN HACHETTE UK COMPANY

The Publishers would like to thank Robin Bruce, Nicholas Fellows, David Ferriby and Sarah Ward for their contribution to the Study Guide.

The Publishers thank OCR for permission to use specimen exam questions on pages 73, 182, 204 and 206 from OCR's A Level History A specifications H105 and H505 © OCR 2014. OCR have neither seen nor commented upon any model answers or exam guidance related to these questions.

The Publishers thank Pearson Education Ltd for the exam questions reproduced on pages 118 and 194 (taken from Level 3 GCE History Advanced Paper 3, paper reference 9HI0/30). Pearson Education Ltd accepts no responsibility whatsoever for the accuracy or method of working in the answers given on pages 197–8.

The Publishers would like to thank the following for permission to reproduce copyright material:

Photo credits: p5 TopFoto; **p31** Roy 20 E VI f.9v Marriage of Henry V to Catherine of France in 1420, c.1375 (vellum), French School, (14th century)/British Library, London, UK/© British Library Board. All Rights Reserved/Bridgeman Images; **p39** World History Archive/TopFoto; **p46** The Marriage of Henry VI and Margaret of Anjou, engraved by Freeman (engraving), English School, (19th century)/British Museum, London, UK/Bridgeman Images; **p79** Portrait of King Edward IV of England (oil on panel), English School, (15th century)/Private Collection/Bridgeman Images; **p82** Photograph reproduced with the kind permission of Northampton Museums and Art Gallery; **p92** http://upload.wikimedia.org/wikipedia/commons/f/f7/MS_Ghent_-_Battle_of_Tewkesbury.jpg; **p107** Liszt Collection/TopFoto; **p122** Portrait of King Richard III (oil on panel), English School, (15th century)/Private Collection/Bridgeman Images; **p126** The Princes Edward and Richard in the Tower, 1878 (oil on canvas), Millais, Sir John Everett (1829–96)/Royal Holloway, University of London/Bridgeman Images; **p142** Apic/Getty Images; **p153** TopFoto.

Acknowledgements: Alan Sutton, *Henry V and the Southampton Plot* by T.B. Pugh, 1988. *BBC History Magazine*, 'Henry V: The Cruel King' by I. Mortimer, 2009. Cambridge University Press, *The Tudor Revolution in Government* by G.R. Elton, 1953. Longman, Green & Co., *Recueil des Croniques et Anchiennes Istories de la Grant Bretaigne* (*Account of the Chronicles and Old Histories of Great Britain*) by William Hardy, editor, 1864. Methuen, *Henry V* by C.T. Allmand, 1992. Oxford University Press, *Tudor England* by John Guy, 1990; *The Earlier Tudors* by J.D. Mackie, 1987. Palgrave Macmillan, *The Wars of the Roses* by A.J. Pollard, 2001. Routledge, *The Transformation of Medieval England 1370–1529* by J.A.F. Thompson, 1983. Williams & Norgate, *The History of England: A Study in Political Evolution* by A.F. Pollard, 1912.

Every effort has been made to trace all copyright holders, but if any have been inadvertently overlooked the Publishers will be pleased to make the necessary arrangements at the first opportunity.

Although every effort has been made to ensure that website addresses are correct at time of going to press, Hodder Education cannot be held responsible for the content of any website mentioned in this book. It is sometimes possible to find a relocated web page by typing in the address of the home page for a website in the URL window of your browser.

Hachette UK's policy is to use papers that are natural, renewable and recyclable products and made from wood grown in sustainable forests. The logging and manufacturing processes are expected to conform to the environmental regulations of the country of origin.

Orders: please contact Bookpoint Ltd, 130 Milton Park, Abingdon, Oxon OX14 4SB. Telephone: +44 (0)1235 827720. Fax: +44 (0)1235 400454. Lines are open 9.00a.m.–5.00p.m., Monday to Saturday, with a 24-hour message answering service. Visit our website at www.hoddereducation.co.uk

First published in 2010 by
Hodder Education
An Hachette UK Company
Carmelite House, 50 Victoria Embankment
London EC4Y 0DZ

Impression number	10	9	8	7	6	5	4	3	2	
Year		2019	2018	2017	2016					

Cover photo © Print Collector/Getty Images
Produced, illustrated and typeset in Palatino LT Std by Gray Publishing, Tunbridge Wells
Printed and bound by CPI Group (UK) Ltd, Croydon CR0 4YY

A catalogue record for this title is available from the British Library

ISBN 978 1471838224

Contents

Dedication

Keith Randell (1943–2002)

The *Access to History* series was conceived and developed by Keith, who created a series to 'cater for students as they are, not as we might wish them to be'. He leaves a living legacy of a series that for over 20 years has provided a trusted, stimulating and well-loved accompaniment to post-16 study. Our aim with these new editions is to continue to offer students the best possible support for their studies.

CHAPTER 1

Henry IV and the origins of dynastic crisis 1399–1413

Medieval England was a wild, sparsely populated country of peasants ruled by a king supported by his landowning nobility and gentry. It is a period in history which has long fascinated historians because of its drama, intrigue and bloody conflict. Much has been written about Henry Bolingbroke's usurpation of his cousin, King Richard II, not least how it led to a dynastic conflict that dominated the later part of the century. This introduction provides an essential background by examining four themes:

★ Introduction: fifteenth-century England

★ England and Europe in the fifteenth century

★ The deposition of Richard II

★ The troubled reign of Henry IV

Key dates

1399	Henry IV usurped the throne by removing Richard II	**1405**	French invaded England through Wales
1400–10	The Glyndŵr rebellion in Wales	**1408**	Battle of Bramham Moor
1403	Percy rebellion and Battle of Shrewsbury	**1413**	Henry IV died

 1 ## Introduction: fifteenth-century England

▶ *What was fifteenth-century England like?*

Government and administration

The fifteenth century was a period when personal monarchy stood at the centre of government. The king took a personal interest in the running of the kingdom and in the machinery of government. The most vital cogs in that machine were the **king's council** and departments of state such as the Court of Exchequer (finance) and Court of Chancery (law) that made up central government. As an aid to government the monarchy also had **Parliament** at its disposal to offer advice, pass laws and raise revenue. Unlike the departments or courts that made

 **KEY TERMS**

King's council Elite body of councillors, drawn mainly from the nobility, who met the king regularly to frame policy and govern the country.

Parliament Institution of government representing English landowners, consisting of the Houses of Lords and Commons. It had the power to grant taxes and to pass laws.

up central government, Parliament was not a permanent feature of royal rule but it played a vital if occasional role in governing the kingdom. At the very least, the election of representatives from the privileged class in localities across England to sit and meet together in Parliament in London had the effect of bringing the kingdom together.

The fifteenth century witnessed the development of central and local government. Local government had long been focused on the county as a unit of administration with its own officials appointed by the Crown. However, by the second half of the century a new tier of administration had developed to sit

Figure 1.1 The location and relationship of central government and regional councils.

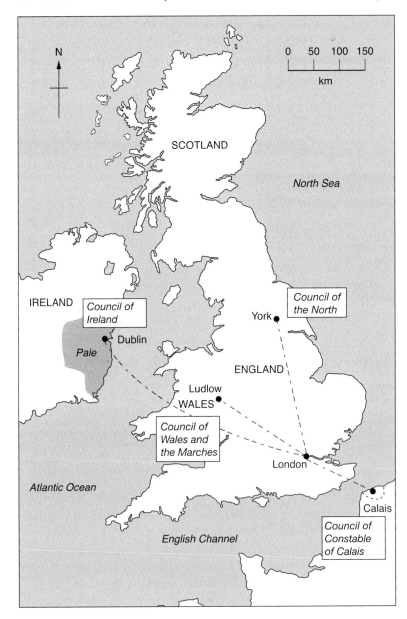

between central and local government: the regional council. The councils of the North and of Wales (the latter included the westernmost counties of England) were established to function as extensions of the king's council. In this way, the reach, power and authority of the Crown were beginning to be felt in even the remotest regions of the kingdom. By binding the outlying regions of the kingdom together in partnership with the Crown at the centre, the government of the kingdom became more effective and, in time, more efficient.

The maintenance of law and order

English kings had no police force to enforce law and order. However, fear of what the Crown, as a God-given institution, could do was a potent weapon in the struggle to maintain law and order. The monarchy communicated its orders by means of **royal proclamations** that were carried by royal messengers to various parts of the kingdom. Although not everyone was able to read these proclamations, word soon spread, thus making known the monarch's will to a great number of people. The monarchy also relied on the unpaid services of the local **gentry** and nobility, who were expected to uphold and enforce the law by means of the powers vested in them through the offices of **sheriff** and **justice of the peace (JP)**. The holders of these offices had no supporting enforcement agencies but relied on their wealth, status and influence in the community to exert their authority.

Unlike its counterparts on the Continent, the English monarchy did not have the financial means to maintain a regular, professional army. The only professional forces available to the monarch were the 300 men that garrisoned Berwick to guard the border with Scotland and the 4000 men maintained in the Calais garrison.

The Crown also exercised its authority in more informal but equally effective ways. Royal imagery was used to impress both the people and visitors alike. For those wealthy and influential enough to be invited to attend the monarch in one of the many royal palaces, the sheer scale and size of the buildings themselves would have been impressive, let alone the paintings and portraits that hung within. Even the majority of the population who might be fortunate enough to view the palaces from afar would have been impressed. There were also frequent royal progresses in which the king and his **court** toured the kingdom. This served to overawe those who witnessed them and to remind the people of the might and majesty of the monarch. However, if the people needed reminding of the power of the Crown they had only to reach for their coins, every denomination of which carried pictures of the ruling monarch.

Society and economy

At the beginning of the fifteenth century England was a relatively prosperous, if sparsely populated, kingdom of between 2 million and 3 million people. The population had barely begun to recover from the effects of the **Black Death**

KEY TERMS

Royal proclamations Royal commands that had the same authority in law as acts of Parliament.

Gentry Class of landowners below the nobility. They were divided into three strata: knights, esquires and gentlemen.

Sheriff Chief law officer in the county who arrested and detained criminals, some of whom were dealt with in the sheriff's court or passed on to the justices of the peace. The sheriff also supervised parliamentary elections.

Justice of the peace (JP) Local law officer and magistrate at county level. JPs also governed the county by enforcing acts of Parliament and acting on decisions taken by the Crown and central government.

Court The royal court acted as a public place for people to come and meet the king. The court was attached to whichever palace the king happened to be living in.

Black Death Plague that spread across the British Isles between 1347 and 1351, killing up to half of the population.

KEY TERMS

Bloody flux Refers to dysentery, an inflammatory disorder of the intestine that results in severe diarrhoea accompanied by fever and abdominal pain.

French pox Refers to an outbreak of syphilis (a sexually transmitted disease) that spread through the ranks of the French army and also infected the English.

Sweating sickness A virulent form of influenza.

Infection-resistant Constant exposure to infection enabled some people to develop natural immunity.

in the mid-fourteenth century before it was struck again by disease, pestilence and death. The plague returned in the 1420s and 1430s, killing large numbers of people before it disappeared, only to be replaced by equally deadly outbreaks of the '**bloody flux**' in 1472 and the so-called '**French pox**' of 1475. Following another bout of plague in 1479–80 and the '**sweating sickness**' of 1483, the increasingly **infection-resistant** population first stabilised and then began to rise quite dramatically from the 1490s. Little wonder that the fifteenth century has been described as 'the golden age of bacteria'.

England was a mainly rural kingdom in which the lives of nearly 90 per cent of the population revolved around the cycle of the seasons and the harvesting of the crops. Arable or crop farming went hand in hand with pastoral or animal husbandry, with cattle, pigs and sheep the three most significant livestock in the agricultural economy. Of these, sheep were probably the most important insofar as their wool was the mainstay of England's largest industry – cloth. It has been estimated that the cloth trade employed over 35,000 people, around three per cent of the working population, and accounted for nearly 80 per cent of England's exports. Between 1462 and 1508 the average annual export of cloths rose from 25,000 to 90,000. This helps to explain why nearly half the statutes passed by Parliament during the Yorkist period, 1461–85, dealt with commerce and industry.

A society dominated by agriculture depended on the success of the harvest to survive. Harvest failures invariably led to a sharp increase in the death rate and to social unrest, due to deprivation, starvation and disease. W.G. Hoskins (writing in 1976), a specialist in social and economic history, calculated that in an average decade around one in every four harvests would be deficient, with one in six being seriously bad. Unfortunately for Edward IV, it is known that England suffered three bad harvests in a row between 1481 and 1483. Nor did it improve much in the following seven years, 1484–90, with only one really good harvest in 1485 and the rest merely average. Fortunately for Henry VII, the 1490s were something of a 'golden age', witnessing six plentiful harvests, with only one being seriously deficient.

Peasant, priest and parish

If farming dominated the lives of the overwhelmingly peasant population, so did the borders of the parish in which they lived. The local church and parish priest guided and shaped the lives of those who faithfully followed their teachings. Peasants looked to the priest for leadership, advice and comfort, and to satisfy their spiritual needs. The cycle of life was represented by the Church, in its form of worship, and in the way it regulated baptism, marriage and burial. The Church was an ever-present part of daily life and it served as a reminder of God's plan for man: to work, to worship and to obey. The preacher and the pulpit exerted a powerful influence over all sections of society but they were at their most persuasive with the largely uneducated mass of the population.

Social order and the Great Chain of Being

The Church was able to exert so much authority over the people because of a concept known as the **Great Chain of Being** (see Source A). This was the belief that every man was born to a specific place in the strict hierarchy of society and had a duty to remain there. It conveyed the contemporary idea of God punishing those who rebelled against their prince – treason – or who questioned the Great Chain of Being – heresy. However, it also emphasised that those in authority held their power for the good of those below them, and were subject to those above them. The concept was clearly expressed in Church doctrine and it was ordered to be taught as a normal part of the church service. Thus, by means of the weekly sermon preached from the pulpit, the Church aided the Crown in its endeavour to govern and control the people.

KEY TERM

Great Chain of Being
The belief that every man was born to a specific place in the strict hierarchy of society and had a duty to remain there. It conveyed the contemporary idea of God punishing those who rebelled against their prince (treason) or who questioned the Church's teachings (heresy).

SOURCE A

Study Source A. What does this illustration reveal about the thinking of late medieval minds?

The Great Chain of Being. Late fifteenth-century illustration showing animals and plants at the bottom, topped by God and the angels. The people in the middle represent the various social classes.

Nobility and gentry

There had been little structural change by the beginning of the sixteenth century. The three social hierarchies of monarchy, nobility and gentry stayed broadly unaltered in size and in their relationship to each other:

- The nobility and gentry made up less than three per cent of the population but they, along with the Crown and Church, possessed over 95 per cent of the wealth of the kingdom. Their wealth came primarily from the ownership of land, but the profits of war and the revenue derived from royal service also contributed to their financial power. The maintenance of law and order was as vital to the survival of a medieval king as it was to the survival of the nobility and gentry. Discontent, disorder and rebellion were ever-present threats. To help the Crown maintain the peace and security of his kingdom, the king made use of, and controlled, the richest and most powerful ruling classes in England: the nobility and gentry. The source of their wealth and power, and that of the king, was the ownership of land.
- Besides the ownership of land, titles also defined the upper levels of society. For example, a duke was the premier noble title in England, followed by marquis, earl, viscount and baron. The most powerful, the noble elite, were those who could claim a blood relationship with the king or had secured a regular place at court, or, more significantly, in the **royal household**. They were men who were well known to the king and who personally served him in government and in war. Although the nobility were comparatively few in number, between 55 and 65, the king relied on them to provide him with the means to govern and police the provinces.
- The gentry made up the class below and are sometimes referred to as the lesser nobility because they, too, were landowners and members of a politically and economically privileged elite. Like the nobility, the gentry, were classed according to title but in a less formal sense. For example, the knight occupied the highest rank of gentry but this was a title conferred by the king for life and did not descend to the heir. Below the knights were the esquires and gentlemen, the last rank being adopted in the fifteenth century to take account of the growing numbers of smaller or lesser landowners who had gained their wealth by trade.

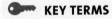

KEY TERMS

Royal household
The retinue and servants who looked after the monarch's personal needs and his financial and political affairs.

Doctrine The rules, principles and teachings of the Church.

The English Church

Apart from the king, the Church was by far the largest landowner in the kingdom. The fifteenth-century English Church was part of the Roman Catholic Church and its first allegiance was not to the English Crown but to the Pope in Rome. Although the Pope had no control over the day-to-day running of the Church in England, he had the spiritual authority to determine how the people worshipped and how Church **doctrine** was to be understood.

The Pope also had the power to influence a kingdom's domestic and foreign politics by either offering or withholding his support for the ruler.

The Church was a powerful organisation that consisted of:

- **regular clergy** – some 10,000 strong
- **secular clergy** – numbering around 35,000.

It formed a state within a state, with its own system of law courts and privileges available for the clergy, which rivalled the authority of the king. These courts dealt with religious crimes and crimes committed by churchmen. Although this relationship had the potential to be awkward, Crown and Church normally managed to exist side by side in relative harmony.

Despite its size, power and wealth the Church did have internal problems. The chief abuses were poverty, **pluralism**, non-residence and ignorance. Many parish priests were poorly educated, some were illiterate, and their poverty contrasted with the wealth of the bishops. For example, by the end of the fifteenth century, 75 per cent of parish priests earned less than £12 a year (£5500 in today's money) while two-thirds of bishops earned more than £400 (£180,000 in today's money). The average annual wage for unskilled farm labourers at this time was between £2 and £3. In order to survive, many priests tried to serve more than one parish (in the worst cases as many as five), which affected the quality of religious worship. It has been calculated that of the 10,000 parishes in England and Wales a quarter were likely to be without a resident clergyman. Nevertheless, in spite of its flaws, the Church was generally popular with the people, whom it served well.

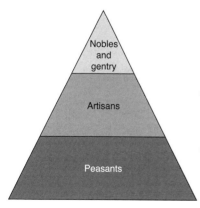

- At the top of this hierarchy were the elite groups: the Lords spiritual and temporal, knights, esquires and gentlemen.

- Next were those distinguished by their occupations: the clergy, lawyers, merchants and master craftsmen.

- Finally came the lowest and the largest group – those with neither wealth nor status: labourers, ordinary soldiers, paupers and vagrants.

Figure 1.2 Social pyramid showing the classes in society from the highest to the lowest.

KEY TERMS

Regular clergy Monks and nuns who devoted their lives to prayer and study in monasteries, sheltered from the outside world.

Secular clergy Parish priests, chaplains and bishops who lived in the outside world. They performed tasks such as marriage, baptism and burial.

Pluralism The holding of more than one parish by a clergyman.

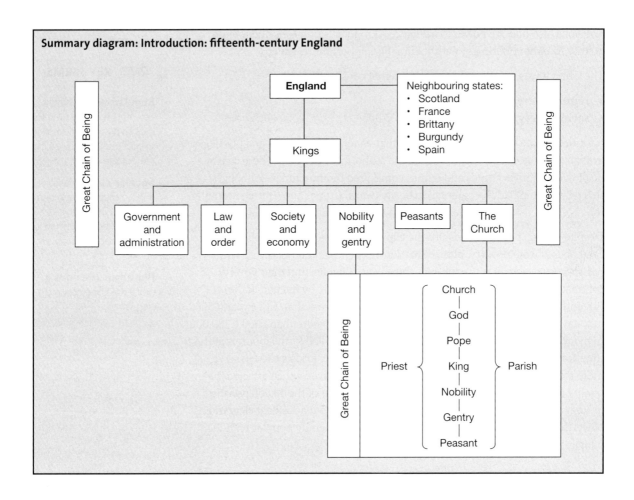

Summary diagram: Introduction: fifteenth-century England

2 England and Europe in the fifteenth century

▶ *What was the nature of England's relationship with continental Europe in the fifteenth century?*

The kingdom of England

The kingdom of England embraced the greater part of the British Isles, stretching as far north as Northumberland and Cumberland on the Scottish border, and as far west as the **Marcher** counties of Cheshire, Shropshire and Herefordshire bordering Wales. The rest of the kingdom bordered the sea and laid claim to the outlying territories that consisted of the Isle of Wight, the Scilly Isles and the Isle of Man. Beyond the territorial confines of the kingdom, the authority of English

 KEY TERM

Marcher A French word used to describe the border region between Wales and England.

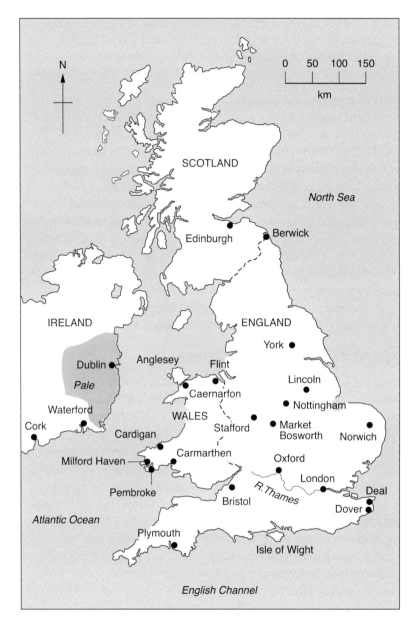

Figure 1.3 Fifteenth-century Britain with key towns and cities.

kings extended further afield to the whole of Wales, a significant slice of eastern Ireland, the Channel Islands and Calais in France. Indeed, until 1453 the English Crown exercised its authority over great swathes of northern and south-western France.

The struggle against the French and the consequent loss of these continental possessions in the so-called **Hundred Years' War** (1338–1453) contributed to a growing sense of Englishness and of nationhood that evolved into an early form of English nationalism. In the opinion of many Tudor historians and writers, the

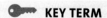 **KEY TERM**

Hundred Years' War
Historical term used to describe the intermittent conflict between the kings of England and France for possession or control of the French crown and kingdom of France.

playwright William Shakespeare prominent among them, the key event that defined Englishness was the Battle of Agincourt of 1415. Henry V's victory over the French in that battle was used to help create 'a spirit of Agincourt', a feeling of unity within the realm where Englishmen could feel pride in being English.

Yet fifteenth-century England was a divided land, being much more regionalised than it is today. In terms of their customs, culture and mode of life, the north-country people were very different from southern folk. Even as late as the 1530s, John Leland, Henry VIII's librarian, described his visit to Lancashire as if he were entering 'a wild, foreign land'. The west country, too, was thought to be a strange land, especially as it bordered Cornwall, in which more than half the people spoke the Celtic language Cornish, and did not think of themselves as being English. The difference between the English and their Celtic neighbours, the Irish, Scots and Welsh, was more pronounced, with the latter being considered more foreign than even the French. Scotland remained an independent kingdom, but whereas Wales had been conquered and ruled by the English for over 100 years (except for the decade-long Glyndŵr rebellion, 1400–10), Ireland continued to resist complete assimilation, yielding only **the Pale**, a territory with Dublin at its heart, to English rule.

England and its continental neighbours

People preferred to live in peace. They believed this was the way of life that God had ordained for man. As God's representative on earth, the king was expected to maintain this ordered existence. However, if a ruler were challenged in an aggressive manner by a foreign power, then war was acceptable as a form of defence. In such circumstances, kings were expected to win great victories for the honour of their subjects. Obviously, this was an oversimplified view of the relations between states, which were far more complex in reality because they sought to avoid war, particularly by the late fifteenth century. Diplomacy in this period had become more subtle and wide-ranging than before. This was because communication was swifter, there were better roads and faster ships, and decisions were being taken by increasingly powerful and ambitious rulers who, because of better maps, knew much more than their predecessors of the world outside their immediate localities.

France, Burgundy and Brittany

English kings had been gaining and losing territory in France ever since William the Conqueror had first linked England with the Duchy of Normandy in 1066; consequently, bitter rivalry existed between them. The latest contest had been the Hundred Years' War (1337–1453), which had resulted in the loss of all English lands in France except Calais. France had finally been able to drive the English out because of the increasing strength of its monarchy, which had ended

KEY TERM

The Pale Territory in eastern Ireland occupied and ruled by English kings since the thirteenth century. The capital of this English-controlled region was Dublin.

Table 1.1 The kings of England. Between 1399 and 1509 the kingdom of England was ruled by six monarchs.

King	Years of reign
Henry IV	1399–1413
Henry V	1413–22
Henry VI	1422–61, 1470–1
Edward IV	1461–9, 1471–83
Richard III	1483–5
Henry VII	1485–1509

Figure 1.4 The kingdom of England and its territorial authority in Wales, Ireland and northern France, *c.*1430.

civil conflict and absorbed all but one of the semi-independent **feudatories**, such as Burgundy and Normandy, into a large and prosperous kingdom. Only Brittany remained, but not for long. By the late fifteenth century, France's resources in terms of manpower and revenue were about three times those of its English neighbour across the Channel. England could no longer exploit France's weaknesses, nor compete on equal terms with this enlarged kingdom. England's continental ambitions would have to be reassessed by Henry VII.

 **KEY TERM**

Feudatories Territories with feudal lords who owed allegiance to the king of France.

? Why might Source B prove useful to a historian studying the Hundred Years' War between England and France?

SOURCE B

Thomas Walsingham, a monk from St Albans, kept a chronicle of events between 1376 and 1422. Adapted from an entry in Walsingham's *Chronica Maiora* dated June 1377.

At dawn on 29 June, five thousand Frenchmen in fifty ships, both large and small, attacked the town of Rye [in Sussex], which they captured with ease, although the townspeople, confident of their own strength, had decided to forbid anyone taking their possessions away from the town. Love of worldly goods would encourage everyone to hold out more vigorously in battle. Yet though they were armed and carrying bows they turned back on the day of battle. Because of their foolishness, the town was taken and all their possessions with it.

Scotland

Scotland was an independent kingdom but it was smaller and less wealthy than England. As a consequence, Scottish kings were often subjected to English pressure to recognise the superior authority of the king of England. This occasionally resulted in war but never conquest. For example, Edward I's failed attempt to conquer Scotland at the beginning of the fourteenth century served as an example to his successors. There were often arguments over where the border between the two states lay, but the most pressing point of conflict was the frequent cattle raids into the richer northern counties of England by the poorer Scottish clansmen. To defend themselves, Scottish kings had traditionally allied themselves with the kings of France. This 'auld alliance' was a constant source of anxiety for English kings.

Spain and the Holy Roman Empire

Another factor which came to play an important part in influencing the way in which English kings pursued their diplomacy in the second half of the fifteenth century was the unification of Castile and Aragon in 1479. The marriage between the rulers of Castile and Aragon, Ferdinand and Isabella, led to the creation of Spain, a new power that quickly established itself as a powerful player in international affairs. As the theatre of conflict changed from northern to southern Europe, with England being relegated to the status of a second-rate power, Spain assumed England's traditional position as France's main rival. Not that this deterred the emperors of the Holy Roman Empire (centred mainly on Germany and the Low Countries) from seeking an alliance with the English when the European situation demanded that allies be found in war. England's links with the Empire had grown as a result of trade. This was mainly conducted by way of the **Hanseatic League**, a group of north German port towns that dominated trade in the North Sea and Baltic, sponsored by the emperor. However, as England's trade and commerce grew, its kings came into conflict with such commercial monopolies.

🔑 KEY TERM

Hanseatic League
Merchants from the mainly German city ports on the Baltic and North Sea who came together to form a trading union and thus dominate trade in northern Europe.

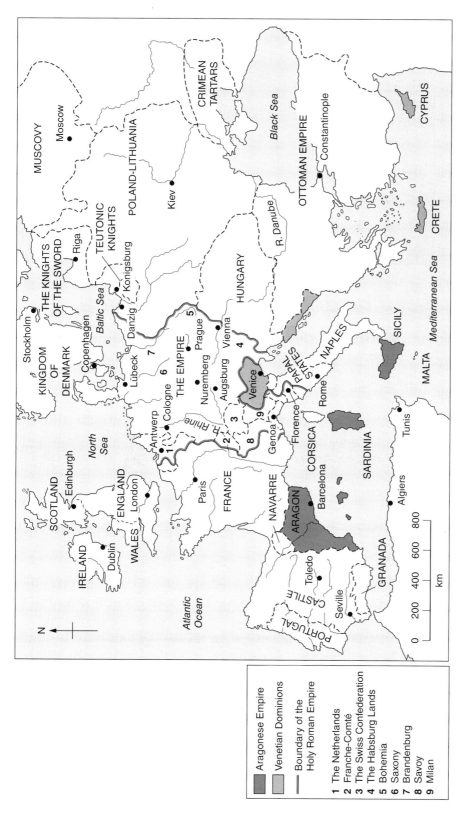

Figure 1.5 A political map of Europe in c.1490.

Aragonese Empire

Venetian Dominions

Boundary of the
Holy Roman Empire

1 The Netherlands
2 Franche-Comté
3 The Swiss Confederation
4 The Habsburg Lands
5 Bohemia
6 Saxony
7 Brandenburg
8 Savoy
9 Milan

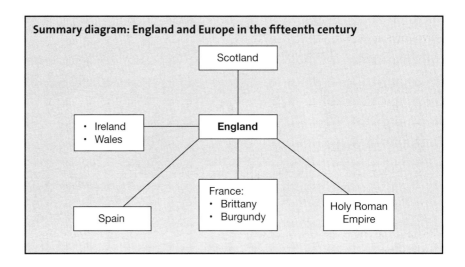

Summary diagram: England and Europe in the fifteenth century

③ The deposition of Richard II

▶ *Why was Richard II forced to abdicate?*

Richard II

KEY TERMS

Divine right Belief that monarchs were chosen by God to rule the kingdom and that their word was law. To challenge their right to rule was the same as challenging God's.

King's peace The idea that, as the king was appointed by God, his law was the highest authority which brought order and protection to the people.

Usurpation The seizure of the throne without authority or in opposition to the rightful line of succession.

By the fifteenth century, monarchy had acquired an almost mystical quality. To their subjects, kings were not like ordinary men and claimed God-given power to govern and make laws. This **divine right** to rule enabled the monarch to command the respect of the people, who were constantly reminded of the Crown's privileged status by the Church. The monarchy's strength lay in the combination of traditional respect for its authority and power to dispense patronage and reward. People were expected to abide by the law and for those who disturbed the '**king's peace**' there was arrest by the Crown's officers, trial in the royal courts of justice and punishment by fine, imprisonment or death.

The power of monarchy was such that even a boy of fourteen was able to project sufficient authority and confidence to disperse a violent mob. When the peasants rebelled in 1381 and stormed London, the boy-king, Richard II, acted courageously and decisively in confronting the rebel leaders, Wat Tyler and John Ball. Richard's impressive display of God-given royal authority led to the collapse of the Peasants' Revolt but it also convinced the young king that he was a strong and capable leader. Youthful confidence evolved into adolescent arrogance, which conspired to produce in adulthood a cruel tyrant. Richard was to find that the power of monarchy was only as strong as the support it received from the nobility.

Richard II had ruled England for over twenty years when, in 1399, he was **usurped** from the throne. His rule had been autocratic and despotic and by

1399 many in the nobility had turned against him. By promoting some noble favourites at the expense of others, some of whom were stripped of their titles and exiled, Richard contributed to a growing sense of discontent and resentment. Chief among the exiled nobility was Richard's cousin, Henry Bolingbroke, Duke of Hereford (1397) and Earl of Derby (1377), who had a distant claim to the throne. Denied his inheritance, the Duchy of Lancaster, Bolingbroke returned from exile and gathered enough support to win the crown from Richard.

The deposition of Richard II

English kingship was, in part, a religious office. Through his anointment at his coronation, Richard II received God's blessing allied to divine power. As king, Richard was expected to set an example of piety and to protect the Christian faith and Church. However, Richard's increasingly autocratic rule alienated some senior clerics in the Church, who claimed that the king had betrayed the principles of kingship by ignoring the promises he had made in his coronation oath. The Church abandoned Richard to his fate and although its senior clerics were divided over the rights and wrongs of his usurpation, none was prepared to support him.

In the summer of 1399 King Richard surrendered to Henry Bolingbroke at Flint Castle. Outnumbered by the enemy, the king had no choice but to negotiate with Henry Bolingbroke, who offered him generous terms. In return for restoring Bolingbroke to his Lancastrian inheritance and for surrendering selected members of the royal council for trial, Richard would be released and free to continue his rule. Persuaded by the Archbishop of Canterbury to accept the terms, Richard surrendered to Bolingbroke and accompanied him to London. However, Bolingbroke had no intention of keeping faith with the king, whom he deposed and imprisoned in the Tower of London. Richard was later removed to Pontefract Castle, where he died in captivity in February 1400 (see Source C). Although some of the nobility were opposed to Richard's deposition, they did nothing to stop it.

SOURCE C

Adapted from an entry in Walsingham's _Chronica Maiora_ dated February 1400.

Richard, the former king was distraught. He killed himself by voluntary starvation it is said, ending his days at the castle of Pontefract, on 14 February. His body was displayed at the more populous places that lay on the road from the castle to London, wherever they stopped for the night. After the last rites had been said at St Paul's cathedral in London, it was ordained that Richard's body should be carried to be buried. The bishop of Chester, the abbot of St Alban's and the abbot of Waltham performed the last rites in the absence of the nobles and the people.

Study Source C. What evidence is there in the source to suggest that Richard may not have killed himself?

When the news of Richard's death became known a number of nobility and gentry began to question the new king's right to rule. Some thought they had exchanged one tyrant for another, while others wished to revenge themselves on the man they blamed for the late king's death. On the other hand, just as many supported the new regime and were content to be rid of Richard. In this increasingly unstable and uncertain atmosphere, Duke Henry assumed power. According to the chronicler Thomas Walsingham, 'Henry Bolingbroke was crowned King Henry IV at Westminster by Thomas, archbishop of Canterbury, on 13 October [1399], a year to the day after he had been sent into exile. This was thought to be a miracle sent by God.' Henry IV was to find that the crown was more easily won than held.

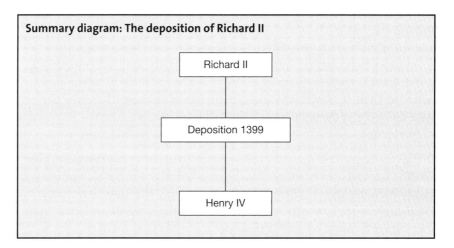

Summary diagram: The deposition of Richard II

Richard II → Deposition 1399 → Henry IV

 # The troubled reign of Henry IV

▶ *Why was Henry IV's reign so troubled?*

Henry IV

Henry IV was the son of John of Gaunt, Duke of Lancaster, who in turn was the youngest son of Edward III. This royal connection did not protect Henry IV from those who sought to challenge his kingship. By usurping the throne Henry had set a dangerous precedent. Other ambitious noblemen might do as he had done and mount a challenge for the crown. Henry's action had led to the throne losing some of its mystique, its majesty and more importantly, its authority. Henceforth, the power and authority of the Crown would come to rely heavily on the skill, strength and personality of the monarch. Henry possessed the attributes necessary to rule effectively but he was hamstrung by the consequences of his usurpation. Although many nobles were opposed to Richard, few were wholeheartedly for Henry.

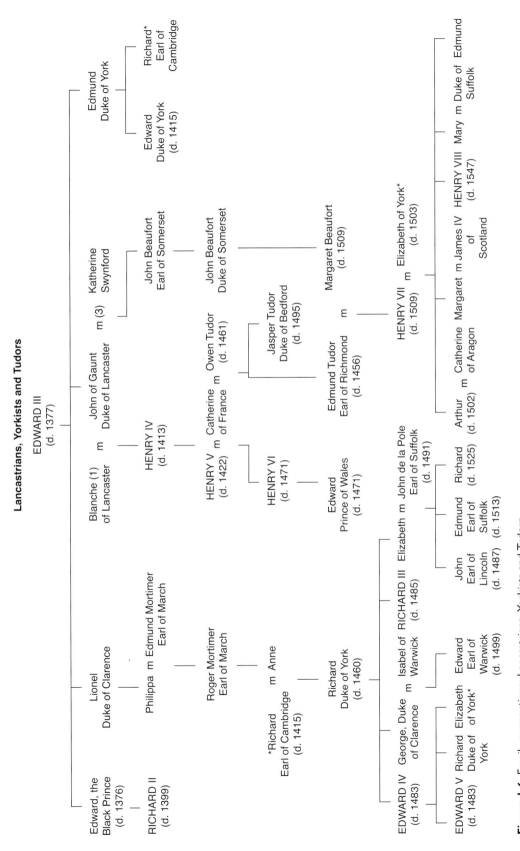

Figure 1.6 Family connections: Lancastrians, Yorkists and Tudors.

Challenges to Henry IV

The deposed Richard II proved an immediate focus of opposition to the usurper. The death of the king did not deter the ambitious from pursuing their dreams of wealth and power. Among the first to conspire against the new regime were those nobles who had been closely linked to Richard and whom Henry had demoted on his accession to the throne:

- John Holland, Duke of Exeter, was demoted to Earl of Huntington.
- Thomas Holland, Duke of Surrey, was demoted to Earl of Kent.

John and Thomas Holland, half-brother and nephew, respectively, of Richard II, were joined in the conspiracy by former supporters of the former king, John Montacute, Earl of Salisbury, and Thomas le Despenser, Earl of Gloucester. The conspiracy was quickly quashed by Henry IV, who had the nobles involved tried and executed. Henry had successfully overcome the first serious threat to his kingship but he would face many more.

Besides complaints from Parliament over his extravagant spending, Henry endured a decade-long rebellion (1400–10) by the Welsh under their charismatic leader, Owain Glyndŵr (see page 19). The most serious opposition to his kingship came from a number of powerful noble families such as the Percy Earls of Northumberland and the Mortimer Earls of March. These families kept the flame of rebellion alive in England between 1403 and 1408. To add to his troubles, Henry also suffered periodic bouts of ill health; from 1410 he ceased to rule effectively after a series of strokes incapacitated him.

Conflict with France, Scotland and Wales

The difficulties facing Henry IV encouraged the French and Scots to try their luck against what they thought was a weakened England, led by an unpopular monarch. Before the Scots had a chance to invade England, Henry led an army north to confront his enemies. His invasion, in the autumn of 1400, proved successful and he reached Edinburgh but he failed to bring the Scots to battle. Having made his point and unable to sustain an occupation of the country – he lacked the funds and resources to do so – Henry returned to England.

Henry's successful military expedition to Scotland deterred the French from mounting an attack on English territory in France. Apart from demanding the return of Richard's widow, Queen Isabella, whom Henry was keeping in 'honourable confinement', the French simply confirmed the truce they had signed with Richard II. Unfortunately for Henry, his triumph in ensuring there would be no resumption of the Hundred Years' War was short lived. On his way back from Scotland news reached him that the Welsh had risen in rebellion. To make matters worse, Parliament refused to grant Henry the additional monies he had requested to equip and sustain an army in the field. Fearing a popular rebellion if he tried to raise taxation without Parliament's approval, Henry decided to try to live within his means. Shortage of money was to be an enduring problem for Henry throughout his reign.

SOURCE D

Adapted from an entry in Walsingham's *Historia Anglicana* dated September 1402. Walsingham describes the invasion of England by the Scots and the resulting Battle of Homildon Hill.

At that time the Scots, made restless by their usual arrogance, entered England in hostile fashion; for they thought that all the northern lords had been kept in Wales by royal command; but the Earl of Northumberland, and Henry his son, with an armed band and a force of archers, suddenly flung themselves across the path of the Scots who, after burning and plundering, wanted to return to their own country, so the Scots had no choice but to stop and do battle. They chose a hill near the town of Wooler, called Homildon Hill, where they assembled with their men-at-arms and archers. When our men saw this, they left the road in which they had opposed the Scots and climbed a hill facing the Scots. Without delay, our archers, shot arrows at the Scots to provoke them. In reply the Scottish archers directed all their fire at our archers; but they felt the weight of our arrows, which fell like a storm of rain, and so they fled.

> Study Source D. What evidence is there in the source to suggest that the Scottish invasion of England was not intended to conquer the kingdom?

Owain Glyndŵr

The Welsh rebellion, begun in the autumn of 1400, proved to be the most enduring problem facing Henry throughout his reign. Led by the accomplished and charismatic Welsh prince, Owain ap Gruffudd Fychan (known as **Owain Glyndŵr**, a name taken from the district in which he was born), the Welsh fought a long campaign that lasted for over a decade. Beginning as a guerrilla campaign, the Welsh gained in strength and confidence and within eighteen months of the start of the rebellion they were able to challenge the English in open combat. Two early battles, at Hyddgen in 1401 and Pilleth in 1402, cemented Glyndŵr's reputation as a brilliant military strategist and commander when he defeated superior English forces. Further victories and the capture of the strategically important castles of Aberystwyth and Harlech meant that by 1404 Glyndŵr was in control of virtually the whole of Wales. Successive royal expeditions led by Henry IV failed to find, let alone defeat, the Welsh leader. As English-held castles and garrison towns such as Carmarthen fell to the Welsh, Henry IV appeared powerless to help.

> **🔑 KEY FIGURE**
>
> **Owain Glyndŵr (c.1359–c.1415)**
>
> A descendant in the direct male line of the Princes of Powys Fadog, Glyndŵr was one of the wealthiest native landowners in Wales. He was educated in the Inns of Court in London and had fought for Richard II in royal campaigns in Scotland and Ireland.

SOURCE E

Adapted from an entry in Walsingham's *Historia Anglicana* dated August 1404.

All through the summer, Owain Glyndŵr and his Welshmen looted, burned and destroyed the lands of the English. He captured and killed many Englishmen, took many castles and razed them to the ground through treachery, ambush or open warfare, and kept some for himself as protection. John Trevor, bishop of St Asaph, when he saw that the Welsh cause was prospering, became a traitor and went over to Owain's side.

> Study Source E. What evidence is there in the source to suggest that Walsingham was hostile to Glyndŵr?

Mortimer, Percy and the Battle of Shrewsbury

The repeated failure to crush the rebellion led some disaffected English nobles, particularly those with extensive estates in Wales, to desert Henry. Among the first to do was Sir Edmund Mortimer, uncle of the young Edmund, Earl of March, who, as the great-grandson of King Edward III, had a claim to the throne. Mortimer's defection in 1402 sent shockwaves through the English establishment, the ripples of which encouraged other noblemen to challenge Henry. In 1403 **Henry Percy** (known as Hotspur), the son and heir of the Earl of Northumberland, and his uncle, Thomas, Earl of Worcester, rebelled against Henry IV. Their defeat and death at the Battle of Shrewsbury in July 1403 gave the king a breathing space but he was soon confronted by an even bigger problem. Encouraged by the success of the Welsh against Henry IV, the French decided to intervene and they forged an alliance with Glyndŵr.

The Franco-Welsh alliance

In the summer of 1405 a French army landed in Wales and joined a Welsh army under Glyndŵr. Later that year the Franco-Welsh army, some 13,000 strong, invaded England and confronted the royal army, led by Henry IV, north of Worcester. Fearful of the consequences of defeat, the armies did not engage in battle, and after a week the Welsh and their French allies retreated back to Wales. Undeterred by this setback, Glyndŵr and Mortimer planned future campaigns against Henry IV. They were joined by Henry Percy, Earl of Northumberland, who rose in rebellion against the king. In 1405 the allies signed the **Tripartite Indenture** whereby they agreed to partition England and Wales between them following the defeat and death of Henry IV. In the event, nothing came of the plan and thereafter the Welsh rebellion began to falter, Glyndŵr suffered a number of heavy defeats in battle and his French allies returned home. Nevertheless, it took the English nearly a decade to finally suppress the rebellious Welsh, who had returned to employing guerrilla tactics after the recapture of Aberystwyth and Harlech castles in 1409. The successful campaigns against Glyndŵr after 1406 were led by Henry IV's son and heir, the future Henry V.

Further conspiracies and rebellion

As Henry dealt with the French invasion of England through Wales, he received news that Hotspur's father, Henry Percy, Earl of Northumberland, together with Thomas Mowbray, Earl of Norfolk, and Richard Scrope, Archbishop of York, had risen in rebellion in the north of England. The rebellion was suppressed and Mowbray and Scrope were tried and executed. Percy escaped to Scotland. Following the beheading of Archbishop Scrope at York, Henry IV fell ill with what was rumoured to be leprosy. Many contemporaries regarded this as a sign from God that the usurper king was being punished for his many sins. In 1408 Percy returned from exile in Scotland and joined Thomas, Baron Bardolf, in leading an army to confront the king. They were overtaken by a force led by the

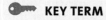

KEY FIGURE

Henry Percy (1364–1403)

The son and heir of the Earl of Northumberland, Percy had earned a reputation for his courage and military skills. His father, Henry, and uncle, Thomas Percy, Earl of Worcester, had helped Henry IV to seize the throne but had become discontented with his rule, hence their rebellion in 1403.

KEY TERM

Tripartite Indenture
An agreement signed by Mortimer, Percy and Glyndŵr to partition England and establish an independent Wales.

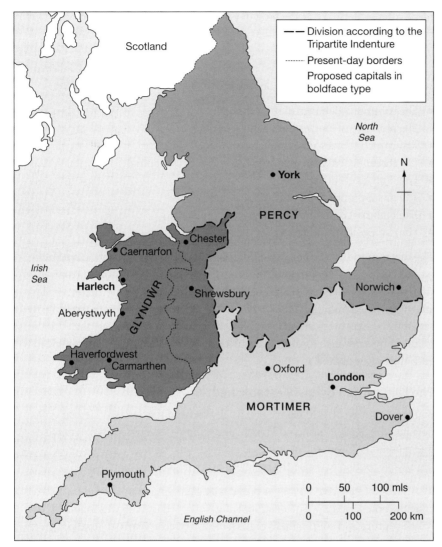

Figure 1.7 The intended partition of Henry IV's kingdom following his death. Why might this plan to partition the kingdom encourage the nobility to support Henry IV?

sheriff of Yorkshire, Sir Thomas Rokeby, who defeated and killed them at the Battle of Bramham Moor.

The Parliament of 1406

In the midst of his problems coping with conspiracies, rebellions and the French invasion, Henry IV endured a difficult relationship with his Parliaments. The Parliament of 1406, known as the Long Parliament, was the most contentious. It lasted, with two adjournments from March until December, longer than any other Parliament in Henry IV's reign. It also witnessed one of the most sustained confrontations between king and commons in English medieval history. Having made a generous grant to the king in the Coventry Parliament of October 1404, neither the financial nor the military situation showed any significant signs of improvement during the subsequent year. A frustrated Commons was unwilling to subsidise a king who appeared unable to defend the kingdom. The following issues were cited by the Commons and presented to the king in a petition:

- The continued defiance of the Welsh.
- The presence of French troops in Wales.
- The French threat to the English province of Gascony.
- The threat posed by pirates terrorising English shipping.
- The high levels of taxation.
- The misappropriation of Crown revenues.
- The high cost of maintaining the royal household.
- The composition and powers of the royal council.

The real importance of the Long Parliament lies not in its legislation but in the political achievement of the Commons, which was arguably more substantial than that of any other medieval Parliament. The triumph of the Commons in 1406 was the culmination of several years of bitter wrangling with the king. By refusing to grant taxes until Henry IV had agreed to acknowledge the petition, followed by a promise to address their concerns, the Commons had managed to curb the power of the Crown.

The Lancastrian dynasty established

By the beginning of 1410 Henry had finally secured his dynasty. He had defeated the Scots, Welsh and French, and suppressed numerous conspiracies and rebellions. Given the obstacles that faced him, Henry IV's achievements are impressive, but he was also the recipient of some good fortune:

- After 1404 the Scots no longer posed a threat owing to political differences within the kingdom. The death of King Robert III in 1406 was followed by the capture and confinement of his heir, the twelve-year-old James I, by Henry IV. James I was held captive in England for eighteen years before he was released by Henry VI on payment of a £40,000 ransom (nearly £19 million today).
- After 1407 the French were in no position to threaten Henry IV because of political infighting at court. Owing to the weak rule of the mentally ill Charles VI, the kingdom descended into civil war between two rival groups: the Duke of Orléans (Armagnac faction) and the Duke of Burgundy (Burgundian faction).
- By 1408 the English nobility had been cowed into submission, and there were to be no more conspiracies or rebellions after the defeat of the Earl of Northumberland at Bramham Moor.
- By 1410 the Glyndŵr rebellion was all but over. Although the Welsh continued to fight the English using guerrilla tactics for another two or three years, they no longer posed a threat to the English crown.

Death and succession

Despite Henry's achievements, the stresses and strains of ruling such a dangerous and unstable kingdom had taken their toll on his health. A sick Henry withdrew from public life and he invested his son and heir, Prince Henry, with the power to rule the kingdom. For nearly two years Prince Henry ruled with the assistance of a group of close advisers, chief among them was Henry Beaufort, Bishop of Winchester. Winchester suggested that, given the seriousness of the king's debilitating illness, the prince should persuade his father to abdicate. When Henry IV heard this he roused himself from his sickbed and, in November 1411, returned to take charge of the government. Prince Henry and Bishop Beaufort were dismissed from the royal council and replaced by men trusted by the king. Henry ruled for a further fourteen months before he finally succumbed to his illness and he died in March 1413. Shortly before he died Henry IV confirmed Prince Henry, the eldest of his four sons, as his successor.

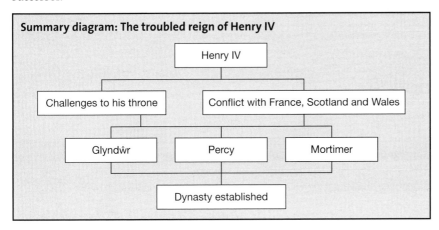

Summary diagram: The troubled reign of Henry IV

Chapter summary

England's relationship with Europe developed significantly during the fifteenth century. Trade, diplomacy and war dominated this developing relationship, especially with France, which witnessed a century-long conflict for control of the kingdom. The usurpation of Richard II was a significant event that ended the succession of the direct line of Plantagenet kings. The usurper, Henry IV, endured a troubled reign. Besides complaints from Parliament over his extravagant spending, Henry endured a decade-long rebellion (1400–10) by the Welsh under their charismatic leader Owain Glyndŵr. The most serious opposition to his kingship came from a number of powerful noble families who wished to remove him from the throne. The Percy Earls of Northumberland and the Mortimer Earls of March kept the flame of rebellion alive in England between 1403 and 1408. To add to his troubles, Henry also suffered periodic bouts of ill health; from 1410 he ceased to rule effectively after a series of strokes disabled him. Yet, in spite of the considerable obstacles placed before him, Henry IV succeeded in firmly establishing the Lancastrian dynasty on the English throne by the time of his death in 1413.

Refresher questions

Use these questions to remind yourself of the key material covered in this chapter.

1 What was the nature of England's relationship with continental Europe in the fifteenth century?

2 Why was Richard II forced to abdicate?

3 How was Henry IV able to assume power in a bloodless coup in 1399?

4 Why did relations between England and Scotland deteriorate during this period?

5 Why did Henry IV face so many conspiracies and rebellions in England during his reign?

6 Why did the Percy family pose the greatest threat to Henry IV?

7 Why did relations between England and France deteriorate during this period?

8 How were the French able to invade England in 1405?

9 How much of a threat to Henry IV was the Glyndŵr rebellion?

10 How significant was the Long Parliament of 1406?

11 How successful was Henry IV's kingship?

12 How did Henry IV survive the challenges to his throne?

13 How secure was the Lancastrian dynasty by 1413?

Question practice

ESSAY QUESTIONS

1 How far do you agree that throughout the period 1399–1409 Henry IV was largely responsible for the problems confronting him?

2 Why was Henry IV able to defeat the challenges to his rule in the period between 1399 and 1413?

CHAPTER 2

Henry V and the war in France 1413–22

Henry V was a man who commanded both respect and fear in equal measure. Apart from the failed rebellion of the Earl of Cambridge in 1415, there was no serious challenge to his kingship. His inspirational leadership, dominant personality and success in war against the French earned the respect and loyalty of the nobility. His greatest claim to fame was his victory over the French at the Battle of Agincourt. He died on the verge of settling the war with France in England's favour. His kingship is explored through three themes:

★ Henry V: the warrior king

★ Henry V and the conquest of France

The key debate on *page 33* of this chapter asks the question: Was Henry V an 'able but short-sighted adventurer'?

Key dates

1413	Henry V succeeded to the throne	1417	Henry's successful campaign to capture Normandy
1415	Conspiracy against Henry V	1419	The sealing of the alliance with Burgundy
	Renewal of war against France	1420	Treaty of Troyes
		1421	Birth of son and heir, Henry
	English victory at the Battle of Agincourt	1422	Death of Henry V

1 Henry V: the warrior king

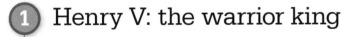

▶ *What challenges did the new king face?*

The accession of Henry V

Henry V succeeded to the throne on the death of his father, Henry IV, in 1413. Described as tall, clean-shaven, sinewy and agile, Henry was a healthy 26-year-old when he assumed power. Henry was a warrior king and to him the principal functions of kingship were twofold: to defend the kingdom and to rule with justice. Henry had learnt the art of war in Wales against the rebels under Glyndŵr. So impressed was he by Glyndŵr's leadership that on becoming king he offered the Welshman a pardon, but the rebel refused. Nevertheless, after

 **KEY TERM**

Lollards Followers of John Wycliffe who derived their name from the medieval Dutch word meaning 'to mutter' (probably reflecting their style of worship, which was based on reading the scriptures).

KEY FIGURE

John Wycliffe (1324–84)
A theologian, philosopher and religious reformer who taught at Oxford University. He was an influential dissident voice who criticised the wealth, power and corruption within the Church. He believed in the power of scripture and advocated the translation of the Bible into English. For this, he was declared a heretic.

Glyndŵr's death (thought to be in 1415) Henry recruited his only surviving son, Maredudd, into his household. Henry was determined to reconcile old adversaries and to bring peace to the kingdom. However, all was not well within England and Henry faced some serious challenges to his kingship. There were two main sources of opposition: the **Lollards** and dissident nobles.

The challenge of Lollardy

The Lollards, who were followers of **John Wycliffe**, were a minority religious reform movement who demanded an end to corruption in the Church and the translation of the scriptures into English. They were denounced by the Church as heretics but they were supported by a powerful group of knights at the court of Richard II. However, during Henry IV's reign, the Crown and Church had united against the Lollards and driven them underground. This persecution caused resentment and by the beginning of Henry V's reign some of the more radical Lollards planned to assassinate the king.

The leading Lollard knight and head of the conspiracy to murder the king was Sir John Oldcastle. Oldcastle had been among Henry V's most effective and loyal commanders in the war against the Welsh, but his support for Lollardy drove a wedge between the knight and his king. Under Henry's patronage Oldcastle had acquired wealth and power, and secured an advantageous marriage to an heiress, through whom he acquired the title of Lord Cobham. In 1413 some of Oldcastle's letters and manuscripts fell into the hands of his clerical critics, who used them to secure his arrest and trial for heresy. Oldcastle was found guilty and condemned to death, but the king spared his old comrade and imprisoned him in the Tower of London.

Oldcastle somehow escaped and fled to the Welsh border, where he began recruiting followers to join him in a rebellion against the Crown. He sent word to Lollard communities in the Midlands, the West Country and south-east England to join him in London in January 1414, where it was intended to capture and kill the king. However, only 250 Lollard rebels turned up rather than the 20,000 expected. The plan was discovered and the plotters were arrested before the rebellion could take place. Oldcastle went on the run for four years until his capture in 1418. He was hanged for treason and his body was burned on the gallows for heresy. According to Thomas Elmham, 'Lord Cobham, greatest and most beloved of the king's servants was the horn of Antichrist, arch-traitor to God and man'.

The Southampton Plot 1415

The Southampton Plot was hatched by a group of dissident nobles led by Richard, Earl of Cambridge, on the eve of Henry V's departure for France in 1415. The plotters were motivated by anger, frustration and greed. Cambridge was embittered by his lack of wealth and status, while his leading co-conspirators, Henry, Lord Scrope of Masham, and Sir Thomas Grey, felt aggrieved because Henry V appeared unwilling to reward them for their service.

The plot consisted of a plan to remove Henry V and replace him with his brother-in-law Edmund Mortimer, Earl of March (see page 20). Cambridge had originally planned to take Mortimer to Wales to start a rebellion there, but this changed and it was decided to murder the king and his brothers at Southampton (see Source A). The plan failed when Mortimer lost his nerve and told the king about the conspiracy to assassinate him. Cambridge and his two henchmen were arrested, tried for treason and executed, but Mortimer was spared and eventually pardoned by the king.

SOURCE A

Tito Livio Frulovisi, an Italian humanist scholar and author of the *Vita Henrici Quinti* (a biography of Henry V written in 1437), relates the events of the plot against the king at Southampton.

During an inspection of the army, a great conspiracy was discovered, led by three men. One of these was a kinsman of the king, an earl, the second was Thomas Grey, who held an important position among the king's councillors; the third was Henry Scrope, a knight who until this time, had ever been an ornament of chivalry. When they had been arrested and confessed their crimes they were punished according to the custom of the kingdom.

Study Source A and the attribution. Why might the reliability of this source be questioned? **?**

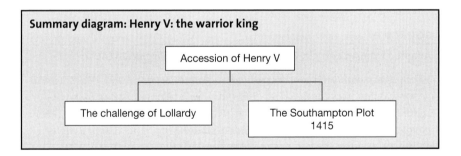

Summary diagram: Henry V: the warrior king

- Accession of Henry V
  - The challenge of Lollardy
  - The Southampton Plot 1415

(2) Henry V and the conquest of France

▶ *How successful was Henry V's French campaign?*

The French expedition

According to the chronicler Thomas Walsingham, Henry had set his sights on conquering France from the moment he succeeded to the throne. Henry was determined to renew England's war with France and thereby claim the French crown. Inspired by the warlike exploits of his great-grandfather, Edward III, Henry was infused with a sense of his own destiny, believing that glory on the battlefields of France awaited him. Henry believed that he had been chosen by God to humble the French and to bring them within the orbit of his power.

Henry summoned Parliament to meet in May 1414 and requested its support in his claim to the French crown. Parliament duly obliged and after some discussion it authorised an embassy to France to press Henry's claim to the throne. The embassy returned without a resolution to the claim, and a second Parliament met in November 1414 and authorised the sending of a second delegation of diplomats to the French court. This, too, failed because the French were hopelessly divided and could not come to a decision. In January 1415 Henry began to prepare for war (see Source B).

Henry V set sail for France in June 1415. He commanded an army estimated to have been 12,000 strong. The campaign began with the successful capture of the important port of Harfleur but the six-week siege had taken its toll on Henry's troops. Racked by dysentery – the bloody flux – and running short of supplies, Henry lost over 3000 men, a quarter of his force. Henry was advised to garrison Harfleur and return home to re-equip his army. Henry, however, decided to march the 130 miles (210 km) to the English-held port of Calais. Henry needed a quick victory that he hoped would tempt the French army into committing itself to a single decisive encounter. The French took the bait and marched to meet the English as they approached Calais, and the two sides drew up against each other at Agincourt.

SOURCE B

Adapted from an entry in Walsingham's _Historia Anglicana_ (1414).

When affairs had been properly settled in Ireland, Scotland and Wales, Henry decided to win back the kingdom of France which belonged to him by birth-right. First, however, he sought advice in all the schools and universities from men learned in divine and human law whether he might justly and without fear of wrongdoing, seek to regain the crown of France by force of arms. Without exception they all agreed he might pursue this plan. The king then sent an embassy to France with instructions to present his claim to a council of the French and, if by any chance the French should refuse him justice, to announce to them that King Henry would come with an army to claim his right.

? Study Source B. How did Henry justify his claim to the French crown?

The Battle of Agincourt, October 1415

It soon became clear that Henry had underestimated the strength of his French opponents. Henry's army of roughly 8000 men faced a French army of over 12,000. Henry commanded a force of mainly longbowmen (more than half of whom were Welshmen) supported by men-at-arms and a small troop of cavalry. The French force was more mobile, consisting of mainly heavy cavalry with a small contingent of archers. Henry positioned his army in a muddy field bounded on one side by thick woods and on the other by a marsh. By using the terrain to his advantage, Henry had ensured that his army could not easily be outflanked, while the muddy ground would slow the momentum of the cavalry attack.

The mass cavalry attack was met by a hail of English arrows that felled many French knights and panicked others. Unable to manoeuvre easily in the confines of the terrain, the French knights crashed into each other before withdrawing. Henry moved his cavalry up to capture hundreds of dismounted French knights unable to flee the battlefield. As the French regrouped, ready to mount a fresh attack, they were joined by reinforcements. On seeing this, Henry ordered that all the French captives should be put to death (see Source C). In the opinion of Tito Livio Frulovisi, Henry did this because 'The English were greatly outnumbered even by their French prisoners and were afraid lest they should have to fight again against their own captives as well as the new army.'

Henry's victory at Agincourt stunned the French. An anonymous Parisian writer recorded the shock of the defeat: 'Never since Christ was born has anyone done so much damage to France.' Unfortunately for Henry, he was unable to take advantage of the victory at Agincourt. His army was exhausted, desperately short of food and much reduced in size and strength. He was in no position to fight another battle. He returned home to prepare for another campaign.

SOURCE C

From Jean de Waurin, *Recueil des croniques d'Engleterre* (*English Chronicles*), 1399–1422. Waurin was the illegitimate son of a Flemish knight, Robert de Waurin, who fought with the French at the battle and was killed. Waurin witnessed the battle.

When the King of England perceived them coming thus he caused it to be published that every one that had a prisoner should immediately kill him, which those who had any were unwilling to do, for they expected to get great ransoms for them. But when the King was informed of this he appointed a gentleman with two hundred archers whom he commanded to go through the host and kill all the prisoners, whoever they might be. This esquire, without delay or objection, fulfilled the command of his sovereign lord, which was a most pitiable thing, for in cold blood all the nobility of France was beheaded and inhumanly cut to pieces, and all through this accursed company, a sorry set compared with the noble captive chivalry, who when they saw that the English were ready to receive them, all immediately turned and fled, each to save his own life. Many of the cavalry escaped; but of those on foot there were many among the dead.

> Study Source C. Why were some of the English troops reluctant to obey the king's order to kill their prisoners?

The Normandy campaign 1417–19

Having strained the kingdom's military and financial resources, Henry was unable to follow up his triumph at Agincourt for two years. During this period his uncle, Thomas Beaufort, Duke of Exeter, had successfully withstood a French attack on Harfleur in 1416. Keen to renew his campaign in France, Henry focused on the conquest of Normandy, which began in August 1417 with the landing of an English army of 12,000 men at the mouth of the River Touques. Henry's campaign was swift and successful, and in less than two years the strategically important city of Rouen had been captured and the duchy had been conquered. At its conclusion Henry was again forced to halt all military operations owing to dwindling supplies and lack of finance. Fortunately for Henry V, the bitter conflict between competing members of the French aristocracy left Paris undefended, enabling the English to take the city without a fight.

The French court was weak and divided because the king, Charles VI, was suffering from a mental illness, and was unable to control the ambitious French nobles. There were two rival groups vying for power at court:

- The Armagnac group was led by Bernard VII, Count of Armagnac, and included his son-in-law, Charles, Duke of Orléans, and the Dauphin, Charles, the son and heir of Charles VI.
- The Burgundian group was led by **John the Fearless**, Duke of Burgundy, and after his assassination in 1419 by his son, Philip the Good.

The rivalry between the two groups had erupted into civil war as far back as 1411. Henry V had planned to take advantage of this strife but in his first campaign he had found the French to be far stronger than he had anticipated. The army that confronted him at Agincourt and had fought him in the Normandy campaign had consisted of troops recruited and led by the Armagnacs. Thus far the Burgundians had remained neutral, but this changed with the assassination of John the Fearless in 1419.

The Burgundian alliance 1419–20

Henry realised that he was unlikely to win a war against the French by military means alone. He thus added a diplomatic string to his bow by negotiating an alliance with the Duke of Burgundy, Philip the Good. Henry was able to do this because Philip's father, John the Fearless, had been murdered by the heir to the French crown, the Dauphin, Charles (later King Charles VII). Prince Charles's regency of France had been challenged by his cousin, Duke John of Burgundy, who raised an army and captured Paris. On the fall of Paris an angry Dauphin ordered his cousin's assassination. This drove the Burgundians into the arms of the English, who took advantage of the civil strife to secure an alliance

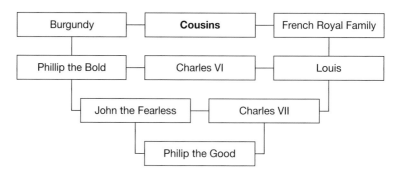

Figure 2.1 Family tree showing the relationship between the Burgundian and French royal families.

with Duke John the Fearless's successor, Duke Philip. Thus, Henry V was able to achieve his aim of taking Paris to successfully conclude his Normandy campaign.

The Burgundians now became the firm allies of the English and in May 1420 Duke Philip and Henry V sealed their alliance by signing the Treaty of Troyes. The treaty was highly significant because both sides agreed that:

- Henry V and his heirs would inherit the throne of France on the death of Charles VI.
- Charles VI's daughter, Catherine, would marry Henry V (see Source D).
- The Dauphin, Charles, was to be formally disinherited.
- Large tracts of land around Boulogne and Calais were given to Henry V, which he added to his gains in Normandy.

Following the capture by Henry V of Charles, Duke of Orléans, at Agincourt (he was to remain a prisoner in England until 1440), and the death of Bernard, Count of Armagnac, in 1418, the Armagnac group effectively disintegrated. Only the Dauphin remained but he was forced to flee south with a small band of followers. With the support of the Duke of Burgundy, allied to the detention of the insane French king, Charles VI, it seemed as if the whole of France now lay at Henry's feet.

SOURCE D

Study Source D. Why might viewers of this image conclude that the marriage was not universally popular with the French people?

Marriage of Henry V of England to Catherine of Valois. This is a fourteenth-century drawing made in France by an unknown artist.

The Dauphin strikes back

Most historians agree that the Treaty of Troyes was Henry's greatest triumph because it made him the regent and legal heir to Charles VI. The importance of the Burgundian alliance should not be underestimated because Henry's power in France depended heavily on his allies. Secure in his triumph, Henry returned with his bride to England. In Henry's absence, the Dauphin had been busy building up a power base in central and south-eastern France. Here he rallied his supporters and launched an offensive against the Anglo-Burgundian forces. The Dauphin's forces (known as Orleanists), supported by a force of Scots (traditional allies of the French), captured the fortified town of Bauge and killed its commander, Thomas, Duke of Clarence, Henry V's brother. Henry returned once more with an army to France and sought out the Dauphin but the latter evaded battle.

Henry now set his sights on wearing his opponent down by laying waste to vast tracts of land and by taking one fortified town after another. It was a slow, laborious task and one which took its toll on his troops. According to the chronicler Thomas Walsingham, Henry 'laid siege to the town of Meaux which was full of rebels. Because of the fighting and the lack of food, a great part of the king's army was exhausted and fell sick, and most returned to England.' Henry stubbornly refused to end the siege but as it wore on the shortage of food and clean water eventually struck him down too. After taking the town Henry contracted dysentery and died after a short, painful illness in August 1422.

Henry's legacy

Henry's most enduring legacy was war. He was a warrior by training and by inclination, and his ambition to secure the French crown set the tone for his reign. Although Henry spent the majority of his kingship focused on France, he ensured that England was well governed during his absences on campaign. Unfortunately for Henry, he never lived to secure the French crown; he died two months before Charles VI. The accession was disputed by the Dauphin, who continued the fight to succeed his father as king of France. The war would continue for another 30 years and end in defeat for the English.

Henry left a legacy of uncertainty over the kingship for although he and Catherine had a son, his heir, Henry, was only nine months old when he succeeded to the crown of England. The government of the kingdom was entrusted to a ruling council of nobles led by the infant king's uncles, John, Duke of Bedford, and Humphrey, Duke of Gloucester. Although they were effective in uniting the kingdom and successful in prosecuting the war against the French (at least until 1431), their achievements were to be undermined by the weak rule of Henry VI (see pages 38–50).

In the opinion of historian David Cook (writing in 1983):

> *[Even if Henry V] had lived, it is doubtful whether [he] could have ever have firmly established the Lancastrian dynasty in France. The spirit of resistance, albeit somewhat dimmed, still shone in many areas of France. In England, on the contrary, there were definite signs of war-weariness. Henry was hard pressed for both men and money in the last years of his reign. Parliament had readily granted taxation in a first flush of enthusiasm for the war, but by the early 1420s the Commons were growing increasingly reluctant. Loans postponed the inevitable crisis, but as debts mounted so creditors became ever more wary.*

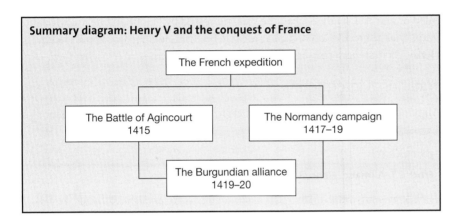

Summary diagram: Henry V and the conquest of France

- The French expedition
  - The Battle of Agincourt 1415
  - The Normandy campaign 1417–19
  - The Burgundian alliance 1419–20

3 Key debate

▶ *Was Henry V an 'able but short-sighted adventurer'?*

The personality of Henry V and the nature and achievements of his rule are hotly debated by historians. Henry has long been admired and lauded for his courageous exploits on the battlefield. The victory at Agincourt inspired poets and playwrights to praise Henry in verse and song. Even usually more sober chroniclers were apt to wax lyrical about Henry. The author of the *Gesta Henrici Quinti* (*Chronicle of Henry V*), Thomas Elmham (died in 1427), wrote:

> *Nor, indeed, is evidence to be found in the chronicles or annals of kings of which our long history makes mention, that any king of England ever achieved so much in so short a time and returned home with so great and so glorious a triumph.*

The man most responsible for immortalising Henry's greatness was William Shakespeare (died in 1616). His play *Henry V* and its depiction of Henry as a heroic figure did much to solidify the king's historical reputation for greatness. In the play, Henry is described as being 'full of valour as of kindness. Princely in both.' Elsewhere the king is quoted as saying 'But if it be a sin to covet honour,

I am the most offending soul alive.' The most inspiring speech was that allegedly given by Henry on the eve of Agincourt: 'We few. We happy few. We band of brothers, for he today that sheds his blood with me shall be my brother.' No king of England has ever come close to matching the reputation of Henry V, the victor at Agincourt.

Until comparatively recently most historians were willing to endorse this view of Henry as a patriotic icon. However, historical reputations are there to be scrutinised and challenged, and the debate began with the publication of K.B. McFarlane's book *Lancastrian Kings and Lollard Knights* (Oxford, 1972). He said of Henry, 'Take him all round and he was, I think, the greatest man that ever ruled England.' Clearly, McFarlane was impressed by Henry and he followed the traditional interpretation of him as an able English king. He was supported by Henry V's first modern biographer, Christopher Allmand.

Traditional interpretation

Allmand's biography of *Henry V* did little to challenge McFarlane's eulogistic assessments of the king.

EXTRACT 1

From C.T. Allmand, *Henry V*, Methuen, 1992, p. 443.

While we may think of Henry as a 'straightforward' enough character, he was much more complex a figure than may at first appear, driven less by personal ambition than by what he saw as right, seeking, even in making war in France, to set that kingdom in a harmonious relation with his English one, mainly through him as ruler of both. That part of his design was not to last; only in the short term can he be said to have been successful in France. But in most other enterprises which he undertook … he was successful to the advantage of his reputation and to that of the country. If, in the generations which followed, the estimation of him was to be based largely on the military success which he won against the French, later generations can see him as the king who strove to provide his people with good and wise government. A careful consideration of his whole achievement reveals much regarding Henry's stature both as a man and king. From it he emerges as a ruler whose already high reputation is not only maintained but enhanced.

The revisionist interpretation

The case put forward by McFarlane and refined by Allmand was compelling and influential until challenged in the 1980s. It was highly likely that a new generation of historians would seek to challenge and revise the theory of Henry V's greatness. Among the first to challenge the traditional interpretation was T.B. Pugh, who provided a more sober assessment of the king.

EXTRACT 2

From T.B. Pugh, *Henry V and the Southampton Plot*, Alan Sutton, 1988, pp. 138, 139–40, 145.

Henry V was an adventurer, not a statesman; the risks he took in the pursuit of his French ambitions were too great and the burdens involved for Englishmen were too heavy to be endured for long.

Henry's personal character was cold and singularly lacking in generosity, and in his treatment of his thrice-widowed cousin, Anne (d. 1438), countess of Stafford, he showed himself to be hard, grasping and unscrupulous.

Although he was more talented than any of his predecessors on the English throne since Henry II (whose prominence in English affairs he rivalled), Henry V was a man of limited vision and outlook and it is difficult to endorse K.B. McFarlane's dictum that he was 'the greatest man that ever ruled England'.

Post-revisionist interpretation

Ian Mortimer went further than Pugh by rejecting Henry's supposed 'greatness' and replacing it with a rather more jaundiced portrait of Shakespeare's hero-king. Mortimer's Henry V is a dour man who disliked frivolity and whose diplomacy was deceitful and his financial management imprudent. He was also a cruel king accused of the wilful murder of men and boys.

EXTRACT 3

From I. Mortimer, 'Henry V: The Cruel King', *BBC History Magazine*, 2009, pp. 24, 29.

'I am the scourge of God sent to punish the people of God for their sins.' For most English readers, this depiction of Henry V in action is difficult to accept. Surely Henry was a good man, and a great king? He was the Prince Hal in Shakespeare's Henry IV *plays, as well as the charming, wooing, gracious and triumphant monarch in* Henry V.

Contemporaries passed their awestruck enthusiasm for his kingship on to later generations, and they in turn saw in him a victorious leader who fought for England's sake, not his own or that of God.

But an objective view of the man should leave us in no doubt that he was hugely arrogant, lacked compassion, was distant from women, was ruthless and cruel on campaign. Golden boy Henry may have been to some – but cold steel would be a more suitable metaphor for most people who met him.

According to Extracts 1–3 was Henry V 'an able but short-sighted adventurer'?

Chapter summary

Henry V was a warrior king, a man who gloried in war and who had learnt the trade in war fighting against the Welsh. His accession to the throne was welcomed by the majority of people, mainly because they had grown weary of Henry IV. By the time he succeeded to the throne the Lancastrian dynasty was firmly established. This is evident by the confident way he dealt with the plot to assassinate him in 1415 and in the way he suppressed the Lollards. Henry is best remembered for his campaign in France to support his claim to the French throne. His stunning victory at Agincourt was a foretaste of his successful campaign to conquer Normandy. He proved that he was as much a diplomat as a soldier by negotiating an alliance with the powerful Burgundian faction in France. Their support helped him to gain a large swathe of territory in northern France, to contract an advantageous marriage with the daughter of Charles VI and to secure the French crown on the death of his father-in-law.

Historians have long debated the achievements of Henry V: whether he was simply an adventurer or one of the greatest kings ever to rule England.

 # Refresher questions

Use these questions to remind yourself of the key material covered in this chapter.

1 Why did Henry renew the war with France?

2 How strong a claim did Henry V have to the French crown?

3 What was the nature of England's relationship with France during Henry V's reign?

4 Why was the Burgundian alliance so important?

5 Why did Henry V marry Catherine, the daughter of Charles VI?

6 How significant was the Treaty of Troyes?

7 How serious a threat to Henry was the Southampton Plot?

8 How serious a threat to Henry were the Lollards?

9 Why is Agincourt regarded as a great English victory?

10 How great a king was Henry V?

Question practice

ESSAY QUESTIONS

1 'The French wars of 1415–25 were a disaster for England and Henry V was to blame.' How far do you agree with this statement?

2 'The period between 1413 and 1423 was characterised by royal incompetence and misrule.' How far do you agree with this statement?

3 How accurate is it to say that divisions within the French nobility were the main reason for Henry V's decision to invade France in 1415?

4 How accurate is it to say that strong support within England was the most important reason for Henry V's decision to invade France in 1415?

SOURCE ANALYSIS QUESTION

1 Study Source 1. Assess the value of the source for revealing the reasons for the peace negotiations between the English and the French in 1420. Explain your answer using the source, the information given about its origin and your own knowledge about the historical context.

SOURCE I

From *Historia Anglicana* by Thomas Walsingham. Walsingham was a monk at St Albans Abbey and was the author of several works, one of which, the *Chronicle of Normandy*, was dedicated to Henry V's campaigns and victories in the Hundred Years' War.

The duke of Burgundy was summoned to negotiate with the dauphin and his deceitful advisers at Montereaul and was there treacherously murdered by them. This was despite the fact that previously everyone had bound themselves by the same oath not to harm anyone of the other party who came to negotiate. The duke's son and heir, Philip the Good, sent representatives to the English king pledging through them an oath to support him in his war on the French king.

The most invincible king, Henry V, was giving thanks to God for his many victories when ambassadors came to him at Rouen from the so-called King Charles VI and from Philip, duke of Burgundy, with instructions to sue for peace. Henry received them graciously and sent the earl of Warwick, together with bishops, lawyers and a great many advisers to seek peace and negotiate a treaty.

Warwick made his way to the so-called King Charles VI and on the way he stormed and took by force several French fortresses. He then proceeded to Troyes where the most noble Charles VI, his wife and their virgin daughter, Princess Catherine, were staying. After many days of shrewd negotiation on both sides, peace and concord were achieved between Henry and Charles. A marriage was arranged between the most pure virgin, Princess Catherine, and the most invincible King Henry. When the matters had been decided, Warwick returned to the invincible king, and, in a private meeting, showed him the written documents. King Henry rejoiced in many victories and constant good fortune both in peace and in war and he agreed to the terms.

CHAPTER 3

'Under-mighty monarch': Henry VI 1422–53

A nation's government, security and well-being depend on the character and strength of its ruler. This was particularly evident during the fifteenth century, when kings had the power to pass laws, raise revenue and make war. However, when a weak-willed and indecisive monarch like Henry VI succeeded to the throne, some of the nobility began to grumble while others were stirred into action. Henry VI's weak and irresponsible rule led to noble disaffection, dynastic civil war and, ultimately, deposition. These events are examined as four themes:

★ Henry VI: politics, government and the king

★ Tension between Crown and nobility

★ Women and power at court: Margaret of Anjou and Eleanor Cobham

★ Failure in France

Key dates

1421	Birth of Henry VI	1447	Death of Humphrey, Duke of Gloucester
1422	Henry VI succeeded to the throne	1450	Normandy lost to the French
1431	Henry VI crowned king of France in Paris		Duke of Suffolk executed
1437	Henry VI took control of government	1451	Loss of Gascony
1444	Treaty of Tours	1453	Henry VI suffered a mental breakdown
1445	Marriage of Henry VI and Margaret of Anjou		Duke of York appointed Protector

1 Henry VI: politics, government and the king

▶ *What kind of king was Henry VI?*

Henry VI: character and personality

In the opinion of historian John Warren (writing in 1995), 'the king's personality touched and affected every facet of power and authority in the kingdom'. The king was expected to:

• defend the kingdom through force of arms
• ensure the stability and security of the kingdom
• provide peace, law and order within the kingdom

- rule wisely, fairly and effectively by means of what was called at the time 'good governance'.

To deliver on all these points was a tall order even for a talented or competent individual, but in Henry VI some or all of these elements were lacking. This was not through want of upbringing or education, for Henry received the best tuition available at that time. During Henry VI's minority he learnt the art of kingship and war from no less a personage than his late father's companion-in-arms, the well-travelled Richard Beauchamp, Earl of Warwick. For nine years (1428–37) Henry was schooled in the crafts of good governance, patronage and military leadership, but the lessons seemed not to have had the desired effect. Contemporary chroniclers are scathing in their assessment of Henry VI. For example:

- In 1446 John Capgrave reported that the naval and coastal security of the kingdom was neglected.
- By drawing attention to civil unrest and local injustice, John Hardyng criticised the king for failing to establish peace and effective law and order.
- One anonymous writer even noted Henry's 'habitual dilatoriness', that is, being indecisive, while another, writing in the mid-1460s, stated that 'the realm of England was out of all good governance'.

Nor did Henry 'cut a dash in war', being the first king of England never to command an army against a foreign enemy. As Henry VI's modern biographer, Ralph Griffiths, noted in 2004: 'He never visited France after 1432: the projected visit in 1445–7 to discuss peace with Charles VII never took place. He never fought in Scotland or crossed to Ireland, and he rarely set foot in Wales – perhaps only once, in August 1452, when he visited Monmouth.'

SOURCE A

Portrait of Henry VI, *c*.1540, by an unknown English artist.

Study Source A. What does this portrait reveal about Henry VI?

The weak rule of Henry VI

Henry's youth meant that the government of the kingdom was left to a council of nobles who ruled in his name until he came of age. This regency council consisted of the infant king's close family: his uncles, John, Duke of Bedford, and Humphrey, Duke of Gloucester, and his great uncles, Thomas Beaufort, Duke of Exeter, and Cardinal Henry Beaufort, Bishop of Winchester. Although these men wielded enormous political influence in the government of England they had to share power with the other noble members of the council. Of the four, only Gloucester made a bid to be **regent** on behalf of his infant nephew, but he failed to persuade the other members of the council to support him. As a concession, Gloucester was given the title of Lord **Protector**, but he was unable to make decisions without the approval of the council.

Even as he grew to adulthood and took a more active part in politics and government, Henry tended to employ courtiers to govern on his behalf. For example, he left the kingdom's military leadership in the hands of others, principally his uncle John, Duke of Bedford, and courtiers such as Edmund Beaufort, Duke of Somerset, William de la Pole, Duke of Suffolk, and Richard, Duke of York. Even Henry VI's wife, Margaret of Anjou (they married in 1445), showed a greater inclination to employ military means to achieve her aims of securing control of both the Crown and the government (see pages 45–6).

The weak leadership of Henry VI

It was Henry's failure to live up to the military reputation of his father, Henry V, on the battlefields of France that attracted most criticism. Kings were expected to lead their men in war, but the only occasion when his subjects saw Henry in battle array before the civil war, known as the Wars of the Roses, was in 1450 (and possibly again in 1452), when he rode through London with his nobles against his own people. This was the occasion of Cade's rebellion (see pages 65–6), an armed insurrection by the people of Kent who were intent on removing the king's closest advisers, whom they blamed for corruption and misgovernment in south-east England.

These are significant because they link in with what Abbot John Whethamstede of St Albans had to say about Henry VI in 1456, that he could 'not resist those who led him to unwise decisions'. This is key to understanding Henry VI, since he was a man of weak character who relied too much on the advice of those around him, the majority of whom he had personally chosen or appointed. He was clearly not a good judge of character and it is evident that those around him knew how to manipulate him. Their manipulation of Henry became decisive when the king began to suffer mental health problems that eventually led to his temporary lapse into insanity in 1453. According to the king's own chaplain and contemporary biographer, John Blacman, Henry VI was a good man but a bad king who became a '**fool of God**'.

KEY TERMS

Regent and protector
Interchangeable terms used to describe someone who governs the kingdom on behalf of a king.

Fool of God Contemporary term used to describe someone who is far too religious for his own good.

Contemporary assessments of Henry VI

We must remember that judgements on Henry VI in fifteenth-century chronicles may be distorted by the propaganda of civil war and later Yorkist or Tudor opinions of his reign (see Source B).

Henry was certainly a pious man who delighted in learning and religious patronage. Surprisingly, Henry VI's piety did not win him the respect of the Pope, Pius II, who described the king as 'a man more timorous than a woman, utterly devoid of wit or spirit, who left everything in his wife's hands'. Clearly, Henry's queen, Margaret of Anjou, cut more of a dash in politics and war than her husband! Writing in 1474, the chronicler John Warkworth believed that Henry was a disaster as king, though he himself was 'naive, innocent and well-meaning'.

It can be said that, at best, contemporary estimates of Henry VI hint at a monarch who, though possessed of worthy personal qualities, neglected some of his kingly duties. At worst, they depict Henry as tragically and spectacularly incompetent.

SOURCE B

From Polydore Vergil, *Anglia Historia* (*History of England*), *c*.1512. Vergil (see page 143) was a respected Italian scholar and author.

King Henry was a man of mild and plain-dealing disposition, who preferred peace before wars, quietness before troubles, honesty before utility, and leisure before business; and, to be short, there was not in this world a more pure, honest and more holy creature. He ruled his own affections, that he might more easily rule his own subjects; he gaped not after riches, nor thirsted for honour and worldly estimation but was careful only for his soul's health.

Study Source B. Why might this source be considered biased and inaccurate in its opinion of Henry VI?

Modern assessments of Henry VI

Modern historians have been even less flattering in their assessment of Henry VI. According to Bertram Wolffe (writing in 2001), it is a measure of Henry's personality that he should choose to mark his accession to the throne with a massive scheme of religious rather than military building. The castles and machines of war, such as siege engines and catapults, were set aside for churches, cathedrals and colleges such as those at Eton and Cambridge. J.R. Lander (writing in 1976) said of Henry that though he was an intelligent and precocious child, he 'developed or degenerated into a man who could hardly have been worse equipped to meet the stresses' of governing a kingdom. His mental breakdown suggests that there is some truth in this assessment. Perhaps the most devastating assessment of Henry VI is that by A.J. Pollard (writing in 2000): 'Henry VI proved to be improvident, malleable, vacillating, partisan, uninterested in the arts of government, and, above all, antipathetic [opposite]'.

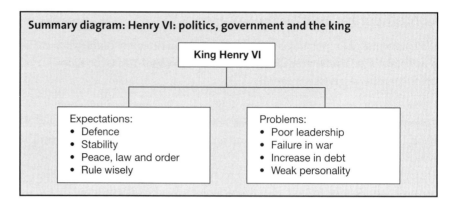

Summary diagram: Henry VI: politics, government and the king

King Henry VI

Expectations:
• Defence
• Stability
• Peace, law and order
• Rule wisely

Problems:
• Poor leadership
• Failure in war
• Increase in debt
• Weak personality

 # Tension between Crown and nobility

▶ *Why was there tension between the king and his nobility?*

A crucial relationship

It is important to remember that the king was not solely responsible for the tension that arose between him and his more ambitious nobility. The Duke of York and others of the nobility, both Yorkist and Lancastrian, must also shoulder some of the blame for the conflict. The 'good governance' of the kingdom depended as much upon the ruled as the ruler, so that the relationship between the monarch and his nobility was crucial if peace, prosperity and political stability were to be maintained. The king could not rule the kingdom alone. Lacking a civil service and police force, he needed the advice, co-operation, experience and local knowledge of the nobility to help him govern every corner of the realm. If the relationship between the ruler and his leading subjects broke down, then chaos and perhaps even civil war might ensue. Thus an '**under-mighty monarch**' was as much a cause of tension and conflict within a kingdom as the '**over-mighty subject**'.

 **KEY TERMS**

Under-mighty monarch
Used to describe a weak king.

Over-mighty subjects
Used to describe strong nobles who were very wealthy, powerful and often overly ambitious.

? Study Source C. How does this source suggest that Henry VI was controlled by those around him?

SOURCE C

Writing in the early 1440s, Henry VI's chaplain, Thomas Gascoigne, described the power the king's favourites exercised at the court.

Lord Saye, with other persons around Henry VI, would not permit anybody to preach before the king unless they had first seen the sermon in writing, or unless the preacher would swear and promise that he would not preach anything against those who were around the king, or against the actions of the king, or against the king, or against the actions of his privy – or more truly his evil – council.

'Under-mighty monarch'

It is perhaps fair to say that Henry VI comes closest to defining what it was to be an 'under-mighty monarch'. For the first sixteen years of his reign the king was a minor under the control of a select group of nobles tasked with the government of the kingdom and the prosecution of the war in France. Henry VI had no say on what must be done, when it ought be done and who should do it. When he reached his majority in 1437, Henry came under the influence of favourites such as Edmund Beaufort, Duke of Somerset, and William de la Pole, Duke of Suffolk. Henry may have been king but the effective running of government remained in the hands of noble ministers. This led to tension and rivalry at court between powerful and ambitious nobles, which the king seemed unable to manage or control.

Unchecked political rivalry could turn into personal animosity with fateful consequences. In 1447 Henry VI's uncle Humphrey, Duke of Gloucester, was brought down by his bitter rival at court, the Duke of Somerset's uncle, Cardinal Henry Beaufort. The king did nothing to help his uncle, who died in mysterious circumstances before he could be tried for treason. Henry VI seemed incapable of judging people or situations. It can be argued that:

- Henry VI mistook Cardinal Beaufort's offer to lend him substantial sums of money as friendship rather than as a means to control him. By 1444 Beaufort had lent the Crown various sums totalling in excess of £200,000, only part of which had been repaid.
- The king misunderstood the seriousness of the bitter rivalry that grew between and divided Richard, Duke of York, and Edmund Beaufort, Duke of Somerset. His failure to heal the rift and pacify the two warring dukes contributed to the outbreak of civil war.
- Henry mishandled the war in France by resuming the conflict in 1449 that resulted in the loss of Normandy and the fall of the Crown's chief adviser, William de la Pole, Duke of Suffolk, who shouldered the blame for the disaster.

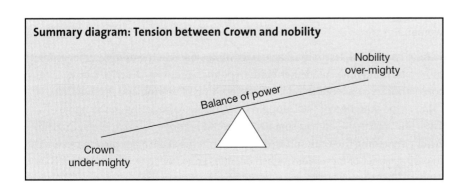

Summary diagram: Tension between Crown and nobility

Nobility over-mighty

Balance of power

Crown under-mighty

Women and power at court: Margaret of Anjou and Eleanor Cobham

▶ *How much power and influence did women exert at the English court?*

The fifteenth century witnessed the rise of remarkable women who came to play a significant role in the political, social and cultural life of England and Europe. Figures such as Christine de Pisan (died in 1430), Joan of Arc (died in 1431), Eleanor Cobham (died in 1452) and Margaret of Anjou (died in 1482) are just some of the many women who made their mark in history.

SOURCE D

From Piero da Monte, the papal tax collector in England, describing Henry VI's opinion of women in a letter written in 1437 to Pope Eugenius.

He [Henry] avoided the sight and conversation of women, affirming these to be the work of the devil and quoting from the Gospel, 'He who casts his eyes on a woman so as to lust after her has already committed adultery with her in his heart'. Those who knew him intimately said that he had preserved his virginity of mind and body to this present time, and that he was firmly resolved to have intercourse with no woman unless within the bonds of matrimony.

? What does Source D reveal about the teenage Henry VI's character and his attitude to women?

Christine de Pisan and Joan of Arc

The Venetian-born Christine de Pisan was an author and poet whose literary career spanned 50 years and whose works were lauded by her contemporaries. She attracted the patronage of powerful nobles such as Louis, Duke of Orléans, brother of King Charles VI of France, and of John the Fearless, Duke of Burgundy. She championed women's rights and was not afraid to criticise some men for their unfair treatment of women. One of her last works was entitled *The Tale of Joan of Arc*, in which she celebrated the exploits of another remarkable woman.

Joan of Arc was no less remarkable but unlike de Pisan the unlettered peasant girl from rural France made her mark in politics and war. Described by a contemporary as a 'poor maid knowing nothing of writing and fighting', she came to the attention of the Dauphin by claiming to be acting in the name of God. She said that God had sent her to defend France and to expel the English. After persuading the Dauphin to employ her in his army, Joan proved to be an inspiring leader of men. Her English enemies called her a witch and when they captured her she was tried and executed by burning for sorcery.

Eleanor Cobham

England, too, had its share of remarkable women. One of the first to make her mark at the court of Henry VI was Eleanor Cobham, the daughter of Sir Reginald Cobham and the wife of Humphrey, Duke of Gloucester. Her relationship with Gloucester caused a scandal because she bore him two children out of wedlock. Eleanor was Gloucester's mistress for several years before he obtained an annulment of his marriage to Jacqueline, Countess of Hainault. At court, the newly married Duchess of Gloucester exercised some influence over the young king and became obsessed with the possibility of her husband's succeeding the unmarried Henry VI. Gripped by her ambition, in 1441 she consulted astrologers to cast Henry VI's horoscope and to predict her personal fortunes. When they predicted that the king was likely to suffer a serious illness in the not-too-distant future, word soon spread that Henry VI's life was in danger. The king's advisers took steps to scotch the rumours and they arrested Eleanor's astrologers but she escaped detention and sought sanctuary at Westminster. Here, Eleanor was examined by a panel of ecclesiastical judges to answer a charge of treasonable **necromancy**. Eleanor pleaded not guilty to the charge but she did admit to procuring potions from Margery Jourdemayne, the Witch of Ebury, in order to conceive and bear Gloucester's child. She was found guilty of the crimes of which the Church accused her and evicted from her sanctuary. The Church annulled her marriage to Gloucester and she was sentenced to life imprisonment. She died eleven years later, in 1452, at Beaumaris Castle in north Wales. Eleanor's astrologers were convicted of treason and executed, followed by Margery the witch, who suffered death by burning.

Margaret of Anjou

The most powerful woman at the court of Henry VI was not English but a French noblewoman of impeccable pedigree. She was the daughter of René, Duke of Anjou, and the granddaughter of Louis II, King of Naples. She was also related to the French royal family and to half a dozen of the leading aristocratic families in France. Margaret's marriage to Henry VI in 1445 (see Source E, overleaf) was no love match but a political arrangement to help peace negotiations between the warring English and French: it secured a 21-month truce. Once they were married, Margaret supported and became involved in her husband's political affairs. Her letters show an awareness of her powerful position both as queen of England and as a patron of men and institutions. Margaret used her influence with the king to promote selected noblemen to high office, such as William de la Pole. Margaret was an intelligent, cultivated and strong-willed woman, and she proved to be far more politically astute than her husband the king.

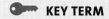 **KEY TERM**

Necromancy A form of magic involving communication with the dead – either by summoning their spirit as an apparition or raising them bodily – for the purpose of divination, foretelling future events or discovering hidden knowledge.

Margaret of Anjou and factionalism

Margaret's growing influence at court was a factor in promoting the impression of an 'under-mighty monarch'. She was a formidable woman and her strong will and domineering personality made the king appear even weaker and indecisive. As their marriage wore on, Margaret came to exercise a greater degree of influence over her husband. Some nobles like Richard, Duke of York, and John Mowbray, Duke of Norfolk, resented the queen's meddling in affairs of state. They were particularly unhappy with Margaret's close relationship with, and promotion of, William de la Pole, who was created Duke of Suffolk in 1448, partly as a reward for arranging the marriage between her and Henry VI. In consequence of Margaret's increasing influence at court, the king sought advice from an ever-decreasing circle of nobles. The excluded became ever more resentful but Margaret brushed them aside. Her political skill came to the fore during the period of her husband's mental incapacity, 1453–5.

SOURCE E

? Study Source E. How are the couple portrayed by the artist?

Wedding of Henry VI and Margaret of Anjou, an engraving made after the wedding in England by an unknown artist.

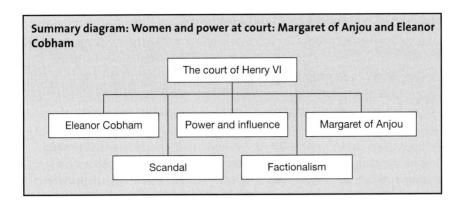

Summary diagram: Women and power at court: Margaret of Anjou and Eleanor Cobham

 # Failure in France

▶ *To what extent did Henry VI's failure in war in France affect his kingship?*

The French wars

War is an expensive business and the war in France, a continuation of the Hundred Years' War (see page 9), proved to be a massive drain on England's financial resources. The war proved costly in other ways also; not least in the damage it did to the image and prestige of the English crown. Kings were expected to be warriors, but Henry was no warrior and his failure to lead his subjects in war did much to harm his reputation and that of the English crown. Henry was unfortunate to be the son of a great man with a mighty reputation. The weight of expectation on Henry to be like his father was too much for him to bear. This may, in part, explain why Henry VI suffered a mental breakdown in the early 1450s. He recovered his physical health but his mental health remained impaired for the rest of his life. Not surprisingly perhaps, when contemporaries came to compare father and son there could only be one winner.

Henry's father, Henry V, had proven himself to be a strong character, a great soldier and an inspirational leader of men in war. His success in battle, at Agincourt in 1415, and in conquering large areas of northern France, brought the French king to the negotiating table. They agreed that Henry V should marry the French king's daughter and that their son, Henry VI, would succeed to the French crown. Unfortunately, Henry V died less than two years after making the agreement, leaving a nine-month-old son to succeed him. Taking advantage of the opportunity afforded by the king's death and his son's minority, the French resumed their war with the English.

The French war during Henry VI's minority

During Henry VI's minority the war was conducted with some success under the direction of his uncle John, Duke of Bedford. There was no repeat of the famous victory at Agincourt, but the English managed to hold the French at bay by denying them victory in a succession of decisive battles. To deny the enemy victory is not the same as winning it. The English were becoming adept at holding out against increasingly impossible odds. As a mark of English success in this respect, the ten-year-old king was able to travel to Paris to be crowned king of France in December 1431. However, even before the coronation the military situation had begun to turn against the English, partly as a result of the inspirational leadership displayed by the teenage Joan of Arc and partly as

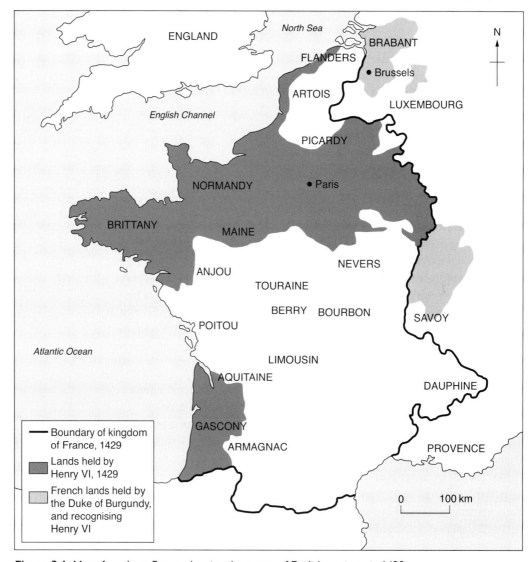

Figure 3.1 Map of northern France showing the extent of English territory in 1429.

a result of growing French military strength. Gradually the war turned into one of attrition; with vastly superior resources in men and money it would only be a matter of time before the French prevailed. What the English needed was a king of exceptional ability and the kind of decisive victory in battle that Agincourt had provided in 1415. Under Henry VI they were to get neither.

The French war during Henry VI's majority

Henry VI's greatest achievement was the Treaty of Tours in 1444, which established a fragile peace that lasted until 1449. The truce of Tours was opposed by the king's uncle, Humphrey, Duke of Gloucester, who argued that it favoured the French because it gave them time to regroup, re-equip and return to the field of battle stronger than before. Tours also marked the marriage between Henry VI and Margaret of Anjou, the daughter of the French queen's sister. The marriage was not popular in England because Margaret was dowerless (the promised **dowry** of 20,000 francs was never paid) and, as part of the truce, Henry agreed to hand the French the strategically vital territory of Maine. When war resumed in 1449 it was not the fault of the French but the English. Foolishly, following the advice of the Duke of Suffolk, Henry VI backed the attack on and capture of the Breton town of Fougères. This error in renewing the conflict in France would ultimately lead to a French victory.

SOURCE F

A contemporary French chronicler, the monk Jean Chartier (died in 1464), described the French victory in taking Normandy from the English in the summer of 1450.

Never had so great a country been conquered in so short a space of time, with such small loss to the populace and soldiery, and with so little killing of people or destruction and damage to the countryside. To do this within the space only of a year and six days was a great miracle and an extraordinary marvel.

The rising cost of the war

The longer the war went on, the greater the burden of taxes at home. The noble and gentry taxpayers of England may not have minded paying for success but they were reluctant to fund failure. Nor could the king win them over by persuasion and example when it was clear to all that his heart was not in the fight. Defeat and failure in France – principally the loss of Normandy in 1450 and Gascony in 1451 – affected not only morale at home but the incomes of a large number of noble families. A war of conquest enables the victor to reward his followers with grants of land, and under Henry V the English nobility had been well provided for. However, under the faltering kingship of Henry VI England lost its right to rule those French territories that had been granted to, and settled by, those same English nobles. A disillusioned nobility were not about to pledge their loyalty to a king who, in their eyes, had failed in his primary duty to ensure stability, security and victory in war.

KEY TERM

Dowry Law by which a father provided his daughter with a sum of money or property to give to her husband on marriage.

Study Source F. Apart from military might, what other reason does the chronicler hint at to explain the success of the French?

Mounting debts

Equally unsettling for a king, denied the opportunity to reward loyalty with grants of land in France, was the fact the Crown was in serious debt. The royal debt spiralled out of control and it has been calculated that, by 1450, the Crown owed in the region of £370,000 (over £168 million in today's money). One of those to whom the king owed money, in excess of £38,000 (£17 million today), was Richard, Duke of York. To make matters worse, the regular annual income enjoyed by the Crown had fallen from a high of £120,000 (£55 million today) in the reign of Henry IV to as little as £45,000 (£21 million today) in that of Henry VI. This sharp drop in income and rising level of debt was due to a number of factors:

- a reduction in income from customs and taxes resulting from a general trade depression
- a reduction in income from Crown lands due to inflation and rising arrears in payments of rent
- an increase in spending on the war in France
- an increase in loans, and interest payments, from Italian bankers and merchants.

Henry was unable to offer the kind of cash incentives that his nobility might have accepted in lieu of land in France. Not that this deterred Henry from spending money he did not have or from granting away Crown lands in England he could ill afford to lose. This led to a collapse in royal finances, which handicapped the Crown because it increased its dependence on the nobility and the growing financial potential of Parliament. By 1455 the Lancastrian dynasty was virtually bankrupt.

Anger and resentment

With so little wealth to go around, anger and jealousy increased against those who seemed to be unaffected by the reduction in **royal patronage**. Indeed, some, the king's favourites – principally Edmund Beaufort, Duke of Somerset, Cardinal Henry Beaufort and William de la Pole, Duke of Suffolk – appeared to be doing rather well as a result of the king's generosity. Consequently, these royal favourites bore the brunt of the hatred and resentment that were increasingly being directed towards the Crown. Opposition to the king's favourites or '**evil councillors**', as critics came to describe them, soon turned into a demand for their removal. People were more willing to join an opposition group if it could be shown that the aim was not to attack the king but simply to remove those who would damage both him and the country.

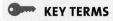 **KEY TERMS**

Royal patronage Rewards given by the Crown for faithful service. The rewards were often given in the form of property, money, title or office.

Evil councillors A useful and often-used contemporary label to brand those around the king as the enemies of sound advice and good government.

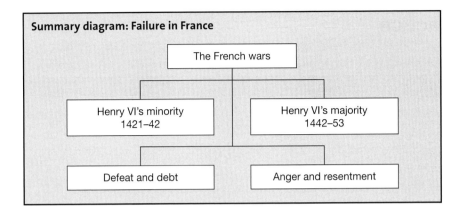

Summary diagram: Failure in France

The French wars

Henry VI's minority
1421–42

Henry VI's majority
1442–53

Defeat and debt

Anger and resentment

Chapter summary

Henry VI was a weak-willed and indecisive monarch who failed to rule the kingdom effectively. As his reign wore on, some of the nobility began to grumble while others plotted either to control or to replace him. Henry's inept government enabled powerful nobles to build power blocks in the kingdom which led to faction fighting at court. The strong leadership of Richard, Duke of York, contrasted with the weakness of a king who descended into madness. The king's reliance on and enrichment of favourites was greatly resented. This tension between the Crown and the nobility was exacerbated by the scheming of Queen Margaret and by the losses in the war in France. Under the leadership of the unwarrior-like Henry VI the Hundred Years' War came to an end with the French as the victors. At home, Henry VI's irresponsible rule led to dynastic civil war, the Wars of the Roses, and, ultimately, his deposition.

Refresher questions

Use these questions to remind yourself of the key material covered in this chapter.

1 Why has Henry VI been described as an 'under-mighty monarch'?

2 Why were contemporary estimates of Henry VI so unflattering?

3 How effective was royal government during Henry VI's reign?

4 Why did Henry's marriage with Margaret of Anjou cause tension with some of the nobility?

5 Who ruled England: Henry VI or his wife, Margaret of Anjou?

6 Why did faction become a particular problem under Henry VI?

7 Why was the Parliament of 1449 less compliant than had been the case previously?

8 Why did Richard, Duke of York, challenge the power and authority of the king?

9 Why did the English lose the war in France?

10 How far was the defeat in France the fault of Henry VI?

 Question practice

ESSAY QUESTIONS

1 How far do you agree that throughout the period 1422–47 the nobility were essential props to royal power and authority?

2 'The responsibility for the outbreak of civil war in the period between 1445 and 1455 must lie firmly with Margaret of Anjou.' How far do you agree with this statement?

3 'Henry VI's failure to consolidate his position as king in the years 1445–53 was due to his own mistakes.' To what extent do you agree with this statement?

4 'The most important reason why Henry VI lost the throne in 1461 was the poor leadership and advice of Margaret of Anjou.' How far do you agree with this statement?

SOURCE ANALYSIS QUESTIONS

1 Using Sources 1–4 in their historical context, assess how far they support the view that Margaret of Anjou was responsible for Henry VI's downfall.

2 With reference to Sources 3 and 5 (page 53), and your understanding of the historical context, which of these two sources is more valuable in explaining why Henry VI lost his grip on the throne?

3 With reference to Sources 1, 3 and 5 (page 53), and your understanding of the historical context, assess the value of these three sources to a historian studying the role played by Queen Margaret in the decline in the authority of Henry VI.

SOURCE I

Polydore Vergil offers his opinion on Margaret of Anjou in *Anglica Historia*, 1513.

This woman saw that the king, her husband, would do nothing without first seeking the advice of Humphrey, duke of Gloucester. She took it upon herself to become her husband's adviser and, little by little, she sought to deprive the duke of his great authority. She feared that she might be thought weak if she allowed her husband, now of mature years, to remain under another man's power.

SOURCE 2

From John Stodeley's letter to the Duke of Norfolk, 1454. Stodeley sends the latest news from the court in London to his master, the Duke of Norfolk.

The queen has made a bill of five articles the first of which expresses her desire to rule the kingdom; the second is that she may appoint the chancellor, treasurer and other officers of state; the third is that she may have the power to appoint all the bishoprics of this land, and all other Church offices belonging to the king's gift; the fourth is that she may have sufficient funds granted to the king, the prince and herself. As for the fifth article, I cannot yet find out what it is.

SOURCE 3

From *Whethamstead's Register*, 1453. A chronicler comments on Henry VI.

A disease and disorder of some sort overcame the king in 1453 so that he lost his wits and his memory for a time, and nearly all his body was uncoordinated and out of control that he could neither walk, nor hold his head upright, nor easily move from where he sat. Henry VI was his mother's stupid offspring, not his father's, a son greatly degenerated from his father, who did not cultivate the art of war. He was a mild-spoken, pious king, but half-witted in affairs of state. It was left to Queen Margaret to order her husband's affairs.

SOURCE 4

From *A Chronicle of the Reigns of Richard II, Henry IV, Henry V and Henry VI*, c.1465. A chronicler comments on Margaret of Anjou.

In 1459 the queen ruled the realm as she liked, gathering innumerable riches. The officers of the realm, especially the earl of Wiltshire, treasurer of England, was allowed to enrich himself by fleecing the poor people, disinheriting rightful heirs and by doing many wrongs. The queen was denounced that he who was called prince was not her son but a bastard conceived in adultery.

SOURCE 5

From the *Brut Chronicle*, written in London in c.1459 by an anonymous chronicler.

As a result of Henry VI's breaking his promises, and because of his marriage to Queen Margaret, the realm of England has suffered grave losses. By losing Normandy and Guienne, by the division of the realm, and by the rebelling of the commons against their princes and lords, the king has lost his power. The division among the lords will lead to the murder and slaying of them. And, in the end, the king will be deposed and the queen with her son forced to flee.

CHAPTER 4

Henry VI and the challenges to the crown 1453–61

If the primary, long-term cause of the Wars of the Roses was the dangerous precedent set by Henry IV's usurpation of the throne in 1399, the more immediate or short-term cause almost inevitably centres on Henry VI. The character and personality of Henry VI have been contrasted with the charismatic and strong leadership of Richard, Duke of York. Henry VI's failure to manage the royal debt and prosecute the war in France led to challenges to his throne and eventually to his death during the civil conflict that he had helped to create. The fall of the House of Lancaster was mirrored by the rise of the House of York. These events are examined as three themes:

★ Origins of the Wars of the Roses

★ The rise of York

★ The fall of Lancaster

Key dates

1453	Henry VI descended into insanity	**1459**	'Parliament of Devils'
	War in France was lost	**1460**	Death of Richard, Duke of York
1455	The Wars of the Roses began	**1461**	Edward IV usurped the throne by removing
1458	The 'Loveday'		Henry VI

 # Origins of the Wars of the Roses

▶ *How has historical opinion of the Wars of the Roses changed?*

Defining the Wars of the Roses

The Wars of the Roses were a dynastic struggle between the noble families (and their supporters) of Lancaster and York. Both sides believed that the crown of England rightfully belonged to them. The result of this rivalry was war; between 1455 and 1487 Lancastrians and Yorkists fought a series of pitched battles to secure control of the crown. In seeking to explain why major historical events such as the Wars of the Roses happen, historians tend to classify and categorise their conclusions into long- and short-term causes. One key area of debate concerning the origins of the Wars of the Roses is how far back historians should look for explanations. The majority of historians believe that the root cause of the later dynastic struggle between Lancaster and York can be found in the reign of Richard II (1377–99). For more immediate or short-term causes of the Wars of the Roses, historians focus on the period from the early to mid-1440s or, more specifically, when Henry VI came of age and became responsible for the war in France and the government of his kingdom.

The long-term causes of the Wars of the Roses

The origins of the dynastic struggle between Lancaster and York can be traced back to the usurpation of the Plantagenet king Richard II:

- The Plantagenets had ruled England more or less unchallenged for around 200 years until 1399, when some members of the aristocracy became unhappy with the arbitrary and authoritarian rule of Richard II.
- By promoting some noble favourites at the expense of others, some of whom were stripped of their titles and exiled, Richard contributed to a growing sense of discontent and resentment.
- Chief among the exiled nobility was Richard's cousin, Henry Bolingbroke, who had a distant claim to the throne. Denied his inheritance, the Dukedom of Lancaster, Bolingbroke returned from exile and gathered enough support to win the crown for himself.
- Richard was **deposed** and imprisoned in Pontefract Castle, where he later died. The usurpation set a dangerous precedent which would be copied later in the century by Richard, Duke of York.

 **KEY TERM**

Depose To rid the kingdom of its reigning monarch by forcing him to abdicate or resign.

The short-term causes of the Wars of the Roses

In view of Henry VI's weak will and indecision, the majority of historians would agree that, to find the most significant short-term cause of the Wars of the Roses, it is unnecessary to look back further than the personal rule of Henry VI:

- Historian B.P. Wolffe (writing in 1983) believes that Henry's incompetence alone explains the dynastic conflict that led to his usurpation. By promoting the rise of a few noble favourites, Henry VI alienated some of the most powerful nobles in England. Foremost among them was his cousin, Richard, Duke of York, a man who could also claim descent from Edward III.
- However, some historians, such as John Watts and Alison Weir, believe that Richard, rather than Henry VI, should be blamed for the conflict. Others disagree, most notably A.J. Pollard (writing in 1995), who countered by stating that York had been driven to rebel by the king's mismanagement of him.
- Equally serious in the minds of the politically powerful was the king's failure to prosecute the war in France. As the military losses mounted, so the Crown's popularity declined. Henry's failure to cure lawlessness and disorder, curb corruption and misgovernment, and reduce the burden of taxation added to the monarchy's woes.

- The result was the popular uprising known as Cade's rebellion (1450), which some historians see as the opening salvo in what was becoming a more volatile and violent period in England's history.
- The Crown's failure to prevent the keeping of armed retainers maintained by the nobility helped to exacerbate the political instability because these private armies were used to defy the law and perpetuate the conflict.
- Apart from those few who opted to remain neutral (if they could), the majority of the nobility were faced with the dilemma of who to support should the political struggle turn to military confrontation. Taking sides was no easy choice for the nobility because they had so much to lose. The simmering resentment of the 1440s boiled over into armed conflict in the 1450s and the scene was set for civil war.

The term 'Wars of the Roses'

The term 'Wars of the Roses' was first used in the first half of the nineteenth century to describe the sequence of dynastic plots, rebellions and battles that took place in England between 1455 and 1487. Historians, especially those in the eighteenth and nineteenth centuries, are fond of attaching labels to historical events in order to give them shape and form, and to make them easier to study. Historical events can be defined by date, personality or, as in this case, emblem. It seemed sensible to see the conflict in terms of the badges that each side wore because flags, emblems and uniforms are a distinguishing feature of war even in our own time. However, there is a problem. The warring parties did not use the red and white roses as their badge or emblem. The idea of 'warring roses' was inspired by Tudor propaganda created by Henry VII after he had secured the throne in 1485. The reason why Henry adopted the emblems was to make it easier for people:

- to identify with a colourful image or symbol
- to understand his claim to be the heir to the Lancastrian crown
- to represent his marriage with Elizabeth of York as the union of the red and white roses bringing peace, order and prosperity after decades of anarchy and war.

The popularity and longevity of the symbolism associated with the white rose of York and red rose of Lancaster are due largely to the effective use made of them by William Shakespeare in his history plays *Henry VI (Part II)* and *Richard III*. Written in the 1590s, Shakespeare's plays did much to promote what Henry VII had begun a century before – to mythologise and legitimise the Tudors' claim to power.

The view of modern historians

In the twentieth century, historians questioned the use of the term 'Wars of the Roses' because it was unknown in the fifteenth and sixteenth centuries. Some historians prefer to call this turbulent period in English history a 'civil war', but it really involved only the nobility, gentry and a minority of peasantry, who had been pressed into war service by their masters. This is why other historians champion the use of the term 'dynastic struggle' because it better describes the conflict for control of the crown by the landowning noble elite. A minority of **revisionist historians** go further by claiming that the use of the term 'Wars of the Roses' makes no sense because, in the words of John Warren, 'they were not wars at all, but scrappy, short-lived and insignificant conflicts that scarcely merit even the name of battles'. The fact that there still exists some disagreement over the use of the term 'Wars of the Roses' means we are stuck with it because it has become such a familiar and convenient label.

Conflict and confrontation: the battles in context 1455–87

Ties of kinship, friendship and clientship made it almost inevitable that many of England's noble families would be drawn into the conflict between Lancaster and York. In a society dominated by thoughts and images of **chivalry**, heroism and dynasticism, confrontation between nobles was often settled by force of arms. These conflicts might take the form of individual trials of strength, personal duels between one nobleman and another, or larger groupings where the nobleman would lead his retainers in combat against his foes.

The scale of the combat is important because some historians have called into question the use of the term 'battle' to describe the character of the fighting that took place during the Wars of the Roses. To some, like Warren, they were, with the exception of Towton, no more than skirmishes. Others challenge this view by arguing that whether they are called battles or skirmishes does not matter because the fact remains that some were so decisive that they paved the way for a change of kingship and dynasty. What can be said with confidence is that some battles were bigger, bloodier and more significant than others.

J.R. Lander's research in the 1960s concluded that some 35 nobles either sided with or fought for the Lancastrians, while around twenty supported the Yorkists. However, this has been challenged by Pollard (in the 1990s), who believes that 'one cannot describe the combatants as being irrevocably divided into two parties called Lancastrians and Yorkists; allegiances and alliances were considerably too fluid to enable one to allocate individual lords and gentlemen to one or other side throughout the period'.

 **KEY TERMS**

Revisionist historians Those who revisit historical events and revise earlier historical interpretations.

Chivalry Relating to the medieval institution of knighthood. It is usually associated with ideals of knightly virtues, honour and fair play.

Chronology of the Wars of the Roses

There were three distinct phases of civil war, involving some eighteen battles or skirmishes.

The first phase 1455–64

What began as a political struggle for control of royal government eventually led to outright war for possession of the crown. Between 1455 and 1464 eleven battles or skirmishes were fought between Lancastrian and Yorkist armies.

1455

In 1455 the aim of Richard of York and his supporters had been to control the king and his government. York achieved his aim after the First Battle of St Albans and the civil war might have ended there had the warring parties agreed to resolve their differences. However, the antagonism and distrust between York and the king's advisers and allies, principally the queen, Margaret of Anjou, ran too deeply to be healed. When, four years later, the Lancastrians felt strong enough, they tried again to rid the kingdom of York and so, war flared up again.

- *The Battle of St Albans, May 1455*. This skirmish marks the beginning of the civil or dynastic war. By confronting the king, Henry VI, with an armed force the Duke of York had set in motion the means by which the nobility of England would settle their quarrels by fighting.

1459–61

York responded by challenging the king directly for possession of the crown. The battles fought between 1459 and 1461 were aimed at overthrowing Henry VI. York was killed at the Battle of Wakefield and was succeeded by his son and heir, Duke Edward of York. The most decisive battle of the period was that fought at Towton, after which Edward deposed Henry VI and took the crown for himself. This period of the civil war was the most intense, bloody and decisive, and resulted in a change of dynasty (see page 10).

- *The Battle of Blore Heath, September 1459*. This was a victory for the Yorkists, who killed the Lancastrian commander Lord Audley.
- *The 'Rout' of Ludford, October 1459*. This marked a defeat for the Yorkists, who fled Ludford when Henry VI turned up to confront them.
- *The Battle of Northampton, July 1460*. The Lancastrians were heavily defeated by the Yorkists. Henry VI was captured and Buckingham, the Lancastrian commander, was executed. Queen Margaret and her son Edward escaped.
- *The Battle of Wakefield, December 1460*. The Yorkists were crushed by a much larger Lancastrian force. York was killed and his severed head was stuck on the walls of York with a paper crown on it.
- *The Second Battle of St Albans, February 1461*. The Yorkists under Warwick suffered another decisive defeat at the Second Battle of St Albans.

- *The Battle of Mortimer's Cross, February 1461.* The Lancastrians were routed in a significant Yorkist victory that had been planned and led by the teenage Edward, son and heir of the Duke of York.
- *The Battle of Ferrybridge, March 1461.* Ferrybridge was a skirmish that took place a day before the much larger and bloodier Battle of Towton.
- *The Battle of Towton, March 1461.* Towton was the largest and bloodiest battle of the war, with more than 50,000 men involved. The Lancastrians were routed by the victorious Yorkists.

SOURCE A

The French chronicler Jean de Waurin reported the deposition of Henry VI in 1461.

The changes that took place in the kingdom were due to the simple-mindedness of the king who was neither intelligent enough nor experienced enough to manage a kingdom such as England. It is a true proverb which says, 'Very afflicted is the land whose prince is a child or rules like one'.

King Henry himself and his wife Queen Margaret were overthrown and lost that crown which his grandfather Henry IV had violently usurped and taken from King Richard II, his first cousin, whom he caused to be shamelessly murdered. Men say that ill-gotten gains cannot last.

Study Source A. Why might the chronicler be unsympathetic in his opinion of Henry VI?

1464–5

The battles fought in 1464 represent a last-ditch attempt by the Lancastrians to restore Henry VI. They failed and Edward IV remained king until 1469. In 1465 Henry VI was captured and imprisoned by Edward IV. This period, and the later one between 1469 and 1471, witnessed an upsurge in local rivalries where the great magnates such as Percy and Neville in the north and Bonville and Courteney in the south-west took advantage of the chaos of war to strike at each other.

- *The Battle of Hedgeley Moor, April 1464.* The Lancastrians were soundly beaten by a tactically better Yorkist army.
- *The Battle of Hexham, May 1464.* The Lancastrians were cut to pieces by a ruthless and victorious Yorkist force.

The second phase 1469–71

The period between 1469 and 1471 marks the bitter rivalry between two competing Yorkist factions that led to a civil war within a civil war. The Yorkists were turning on each other rather than fighting the Lancastrians. Edward IV's close friend and ally, Richard Neville, was not satisfied with the position and power the king had given him. Warwick was a rich and powerful nobleman who had used his power to help make Edward king in 1461. He is a good example of what historians have called an 'over-mighty subject' – a nobleman with too much power who was a threat to the king. His power was such that Richard Neville earned the nickname 'Warwick the Kingmaker'.

1469–70

Warwick's rebellion succeeded in toppling Edward IV and restoring Henry VI. Exiled Lancastrians returned to England in the belief that their cause had triumphed. Henry VI was king in name only, for the real power lay in Warwick's hands. Warwick's triumph was short lived: Edward IV returned from exile in France to challenge for the throne a second time.

- *The Battle of Edgecote, July 1469*. Edgecote marks the beginning of the Yorkist feud in which one Yorkist faction turned on another. Warwick and Clarence turned against Edward IV and his chief ally, the Earl of Pembroke. Pembroke and his largely Welsh army were heavily defeated at Edgecote. Pembroke was captured and executed. Edward IV was captured by Warwick.
- *The Battle of Losecoat Field, March 1470*. Edward IV succeeded in defeating a rebel force under the command of Sir Robert Welles, an ally of Warwick.
- *The Battle of Nibley Green, March 1470*. Nibley Green was caused by a private quarrel between the Berkeleys and Talbots which resulted in armed conflict.

1471

With the support of Burgundy and in spite of the interference of France, Edward IV launched his bid for the throne. Victory at Barnet secured the crown while Tewkesbury put paid to the remnants of the Lancastrian party, many of whom fled again into exile.

- *The Battle of Barnet, April 1471*. This was a Yorkist victory which enabled Edward IV to secure the throne and re-establish himself as king. Warwick was killed.
- *The Battle of Tewkesbury, May 1471*. This was a Yorkist victory which resulted in the death of the Lancastrian Prince Edward, the capture of his mother, Margaret of Anjou, and the eventual murder of Henry VI.

The third phase 1483–7

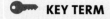 **KEY TERM**

Coup d'état French term used to describe the overthrow of a monarch or government.

This period began with a *coup d'état* when Richard, Duke of Gloucester, usurped the rightful heir to the throne, his young nephew Edward V. The fact that the king was the son of his brother, Edward IV, whom he had pledged to protect, did not deter Richard or his chief ally, the Duke of Buckingham, in ruthlessly killing off enemies. Buckingham's rebellion in late 1483 was a sign that all was not well with the regime, but Richard III held the crown until 1485. Challenged by a Lancastrian with a distant claim to the throne, Henry Tudor, Earl of Richmond, Richard brought his enemies to battle at Bosworth (see family tree diagram on page 17).

- *The Battle of Bosworth, August 1485*. This battle settled the question of who would be king of England. Richard III was defeated and killed; Richmond took the throne and was crowned King Henry VII.
- *The Battle of Stoke, June 1487*. Henry VII's tenure of the throne was perilously weak in the first few years and he, like Richard III, was forced to fight for

Figure 4.1 Map of England and Wales marking the locations of the main battles of the Wars of the Roses.

the survival of his regime. Unlike Richard, Henry succeeded and thereby established the Tudor dynasty. Stoke is regarded by many historians as the final battle of the Wars of the Roses.

The impact of the Wars of the Roses

The death and destruction caused by the Wars of the Roses has been exaggerated by historians. In reality, most of the battles (Towton excepted) were nothing more than skirmishes affecting only a small percentage of the population. The most intense period of fighting was between July 1460 and

March 1461, but, as a whole, there was barely more than two years' military activity throughout the 30-year conflict. Civilian casualties and physical destruction to towns and private property were light. Even at its worst, most people were able to go about their everyday affairs.

On the other hand, as historian John Warren (writing in 1995) has pointed out, 'this is not to claim that the country was a "merrie England" of peaceful peasants and bustling towns with the occasional and rather picturesque battle to enliven the dull routine of the workaday world'. Warren claims that 'English society was marked by an undercurrent of violence and disorder' which, in the short term, the wars made worse. This violence was independent of the wars and it often involved personal quarrels between powerful noble families.

There was considerable political upheaval and instability (especially in the years 1459–61 and 1469–71) as the Houses of Lancaster and York competed for the throne. There was also a strong element of nobles' feuding and rivalry for local dominance, especially in northern and south-western England. The nobles had seized their opportunity to take control of the provinces, so that it was their orders that were obeyed rather than those of the king. If Edward IV, Richard III and Henry VII were to prove themselves to be strong kings, they would have to subdue these over-mighty subjects.

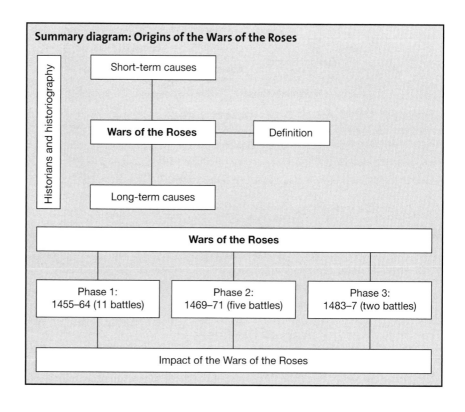

2 The rise of York

▶ *How and why was York able to rise to become an 'over-mighty subject'?*

'Over-mighty subjects'

If Henry VI comes closest to defining what it was to be an 'under-mighty monarch', then it can be argued that Richard, Duke of York, comes equally close to defining what it was to be an 'over-mighty subject'. York was a blood relation of the royal family, a descendant of King Edward III and the owner of a vast, landed estate that stretched across England as well as English-controlled northern France. He seemed to be everything that Henry VI was not: a capable politician, a warrior of distinction and a father of healthy sons. His strength of personality matched his ambition, which, by the 1450s, had come to embrace the crown of England.

York was not alone, however, in aspiring to even greater land, wealth and power; these aims were shared by almost all his noble compatriots. Where he and they differed was in his overreaching ambition, which included the kingship itself. In the opinion of some historians, this is what marks out the 'over-mighty subject', but this may be too narrow a definition because it would exclude men like Edmund Beaufort, Duke of Somerset, William de la Pole, Duke of Suffolk, and Humphrey, Duke of Gloucester. They too may be described as 'over-mighty subjects' but unlike York they did not covet the crown; they only sought to control it.

That this period saw the rise of the 'over-mighty subject' says as much about the king and his relationship with his nobles as it does about the nobility itself. In his relations with the nobles, the monarch had numerous advantages over them, not the least of which was the power of patronage and reward. The distribution of royal favour stood at the heart of the relationship between the Crown and the nobility and took the form of titles, estates, offices and **wardships**. Even marriage was within the power of the Crown to control; no nobleman or woman could normally be wed without the king's knowledge and approval.

Competition for royal patronage

The competition for royal patronage should have worked to the advantage of the monarch, who was in a unique position either to bestow or to withhold rewards. This policy is traditionally referred to as 'divide and rule' since a divided nobility would be too preoccupied with their own quarrels and rivalries to trouble, let alone challenge, the king. The monarch was able to act as a referee with the power to arbitrate in disputes between competing nobles. The key to success lay in not allowing these rivalries and quarrels get out of hand. Under a strong and decisive king, this policy worked well, but Henry was weak and indecisive,

 **KEY TERM**

Wardship The practice whereby the king took control of the estates of minors (those who were too young to be legally responsible for their inheritance) and received most of the profits from their estates.

Richard Plantagenet, Duke of York

1411	Born
1438	Married Cicely, daughter of Ralph Neville, first Earl of Westmorland
1452	Failed to remove king's chief adviser, Duke of Somerset
1453–4	Returned and took up post of Lord Protector during Henry VI's first bout of mental illness
1455	Removed from position when king recovered and forced out of power. Responded with armed rising to defeat royal forces at St Albans
1456	Took up post of Lord Protector during king's second bout of mental illness
1457	Removed again when king recovered
1460	Killed in battle at Wakefield

Richard of York was the only son of Richard, Earl of Cambridge. He had a fine pedigree, being the paternal grandson of Edmund, fifth son of King Edward III. In 1415 he succeeded his uncle, Edward Plantagenet, as third Duke of York and ten years later he inherited the possessions of his uncle, Edmund de Mortimer, fifth Earl of March. By the age of sixteen he was one of the richest noblemen in England (see family tree diagram on page 17).

York was an ambitious soldier and politician. He served with distinction in France in 1436–7 and again in 1440–5. He rose to become the king's lieutenant in France, which gave him the power to direct the war against the French. In 1447 he was appointed Henry VI's lieutenant in Ireland. By the early 1450s York was pushing for even greater power but his attempt to remove the king's chief adviser, the Duke of Somerset, failed. The king's mental illness gave him the opportunity to bid again for power but he was eventually driven out of government, which led to the Wars of the Roses.

Richard of York did much to influence politics and the way in which the Wars of the Roses began. He was ambitious and after first trying, and failing, to control and rule through the king, he turned eventually to claim the crown for himself. York was a good soldier but he lacked political judgement. Queen Margaret of Anjou did not trust York and she became his most implacable enemy. On his death his cause was taken up by his son and heir, Edward of York.

which enabled some of the more ambitious nobles to become too powerful. The outbreak of the Wars of the Roses showed that Henry was no longer in control of his nobility and that they, in turn, had allowed their political rivalry to spill over into armed conflict. This suggests that the Wars of the Roses may be regarded as much as a war between nobles as between the nobility and the monarchy.

The exclusion of Richard, Duke of York

As the king's closest living male relative, Richard, Duke of York, expected to be one of the power brokers at court. The fact that he was excluded from the centre of power became a burning source of resentment for him. His exclusion was due to three factors:

- The opposition of the king's chief advisers, William de la Pole, Duke of Suffolk, and **Edmund Beaufort**, Duke of Somerset. These men created and led a household or court faction that enabled them to monopolise royal patronage. They were not prepared to share power by admitting York into this 'charmed circle', nor were they prepared to tolerate his leadership.
- The queen, Margaret of Anjou, did not like or trust York because of his forcefulness, his blood relationship with the king and his claim to the throne.

 **KEY FIGURE**

Edmund Beaufort, Duke of Somerset (1406–55)

Somerset had a distinguished military career. He was appointed commander of English forces in France in 1431 and was praised for lifting the siege of Calais in 1436. He became a favourite of Henry VI, who rewarded him with land and titles. Somerset led the king's government between 1451 and 1453.

Her suspicions of York deepened when, with the death of Henry VI's uncle, the Duke of Gloucester, in 1447, he became heir-presumptive. This meant that, if Henry VI should die childless, York and his heirs would succeed to the throne. Margaret succeeded in keeping York at arm's length from both the king and court.

- York was his own worst enemy in that he was too arrogant, stubborn and demanding. Instead of exercising patience and cultivating friendships, he preferred confrontation and challenge. He had little time or respect for those whom he considered his inferiors in title, intellect and military skill.

York's feud with Somerset

Having served twice (1436–7 and 1440–5) with some distinction as the king's military commander in France, York was mortified when he was removed and replaced by Somerset. Thus began a bitter feud with Somerset, whom York suspected of having 'kingly ambitions' on account of his being a grandson of John of Gaunt, son of King Edward III. York's suspicion intensified the longer that Henry VI remained childless. York's complaints to the king and Suffolk that Somerset was ill equipped to command English armies in France fell on deaf ears. Angry at being owed over £38,000 by the Crown for his service in France, York pressed the king to settle at least part of the debt or employ him in some meaningful role. In an effort to silence him and remove him from England, York was appointed to the lieutenancy of Ireland. This was not what York had in mind, but he reluctantly accepted the post. His debts remained unpaid and it was only with the financial assistance of his friends and the sale of some his properties that York was able to survive.

The fall and execution of Suffolk, and the Act of Resumption

York's complaint about Somerset and the conduct of the war in France was proved valid when, after the resumption of hostilities in 1449, English forces suffered catastrophic defeats, resulting in the loss of Normandy and Gascony. In an effort to restore England's declining military fortunes in France, Henry VI twice called on Parliament, in February and November 1449, to provide funds for the war. However, after reluctantly granting only half of what the king had expected, Parliament was dissolved. The fact that Suffolk had been instrumental in renewing the war meant that he, too, alongside Somerset, was blamed for the defeats. When Henry VI again called on Parliament to raise money to finance the war, the **Commons** not only refused but charged Suffolk with treason. Suffolk was accused of misgovernment, mismanaging the war and financial corruption. Imprisoned in the Tower of London, he was saved by the intervention of Henry VI, who banished him for five years. To ensure his safety, the king provided Suffolk with a ship to take him to France. Unfortunately for Suffolk, his ship was intercepted in the Channel and he was captured by his enemies. In a public snub to the king's authority, Suffolk was executed by the crew of the *Nicholas of the Tower* on behalf of the 'community of the realm'.

 **KEY TERM**

Commons One of the two Houses of Parliament staffed by elected representatives, mainly gentry landowners, to assist in the business of government.

KEY TERMS

Act of Resumption Act of Parliament intended to recover Crown lands given away as reward for service.

Commonweal The common good or common wealth of the people and the nation.

As the price of any further grants of taxation, the Commons demanded that the king approve the passing of an **Act of Resumption**. The passing of this act made it possible to recover most, if not all, of the grants of land with which the king had rewarded his favourites over the last decade. This was a humiliation for the king since it undermined his authority and his ability to offer rewards for faithful service. The discontent expressed by the Commons in Parliament was matched by the social class who usually played little part in matters of state – the peasants. Cade's rebellion, with its epicentre in Kent, was a serious blow to the Crown's authority and prestige.

Cade's rebellion 1450

Cade's rebellion simply made matters worse for the king and his principal adviser, Somerset. Described by historian John Warren as 'a kind of armed petition to the king', the Kentishmen did not regard themselves as rebels but as members of the wider '**commonweal**' supporting the demands of Parliament. In the opinion of historian David Cook (writing in 1984), 'Political reform was their desire, not revolution'. To the Crown, of course, they were rebels, led by a man, Jack Cade, whom the government claimed was nothing more than a murderous criminal. The rebels pledged their loyalty to the king but demanded:

- the removal and punishment of royal officials found guilty of corruption and misgovernment in Kent
- fair and impartial justice, and the restoration of law and order
- the removal of the king's 'evil councillors'
- the appointment of the Dukes of York, Buckingham and Exeter to the royal council.

The rebellion eventually collapsed, but not before it had taken London and captured a number of courtiers, some of whom, including Lord Saye, the king's treasurer, were executed. The rebellion was crushed after a battle on London Bridge between Cade's followers and a militia of Londoners angered by the drunkenness and looting of the rebels.

Cade fled the capital but was captured near Lewes. During the skirmish, Cade was mortally wounded and died a few days later. Unable to put him on trial, the government publicly beheaded Cade's corpse at Newgate and then dragged his body through the streets of London.

SOURCE B

What does Source B reveal about the social and economic condition of England in 1450?

A London lawyer and chronicler, Robert Bale, recorded instances of unrest in south-east England during 1450.

In January 1450 an individual calling himself Queen of the Fairies rode into Kent and Essex but did no harm to anyone. In February a man calling himself William Bluebeard, who had laboured to raise a great fellowship aspiring to have had rule among the lords, was drawn through the city and hanged. Then all Englishmen driven out of France, Normandy and Anjou came home in great misery and poverty rode into the several parts of the land giving themselves over to theft and misrule. In June the men of Kent arose and chose themselves a captain, a rogue, an Irishman, called Jack Cade who came into the city.

The return of York

In spite of rumours to the contrary, there is no evidence to suggest that York had anything to do with the rebellion. Taking advantage of the growing dissatisfaction with the Crown, he left Ireland without permission and, in September 1450, returned to London. His return was greeted with enormous public support. Emboldened by the popular reaction to his return from Ireland, York presented the king with a list of grievances which were contained in two bills of complaint:

- First bill: a list of personal grievances concerned with York's position as heir, his debts and the fact that his advice had been ignored.
- Second bill: a list of general grievances that echoed what Cade's rebels had drawn up; namely, the increase in lawlessness and disorder, the corruption of royal officials and the king's 'evil councillors', and the demise of 'good governance'.

Backed by a force of 3000 armed retainers, York succeeded in persuading the king to meet some of his demands. He was appointed to the royal council, a more effective Act of Resumption was passed, and the king promised to re-establish law and order throughout the kingdom. However, Somerset still dominated the king's council, monies owed to York were not paid and his position as heir-presumptive was not legally recognised. In fact, when Thomas Yonge, one of York's councillors, proposed a bill in Parliament recognising the duke as heir of the king, the MP for Bristol was arrested and put in the Tower of London. To make matters worse, Somerset was made captain of Calais, giving him command of the largest army at the Crown's disposal.

York miscalculates

A frustrated attempt was made by York to impeach Somerset in Parliament, but when this failed he decided that force of arms was the only alternative left to him. In February 1452 York's army met the king's forces at Dartford, but the duke had miscalculated. Apart from the Earl of Devon and Lord Cobham, the most powerful nobles in the kingdom, including the Duke of Buckingham and the Neville Earls of Salisbury and Warwick, remained loyal to the king. York was outnumbered and forced to submit. The tide was turning against York, for not long after being compelled to make a public apology in St Paul's Cathedral and take a solemn oath to remain faithful to the king, it was announced that the queen was pregnant, a serious blow to York's position as heir-presumptive.

York's protectorate

In August 1453, on hearing the news of devastating defeats in France that all but ended English hopes of victory in the Hundred Years' War, Henry VI suffered a mental breakdown. His pregnant wife, Margaret of Anjou, assumed a more active role in politics. Working closely with Somerset, she hoped to exclude York from power and set herself up as regent until such time as her husband recovered. This appalled the nobility, who promptly rejected the idea. The noble elite turned on Somerset and switched to supporting York. In an effort to conciliate her enemies, Margaret ruthlessly abandoned Somerset and imprisoned him in the Tower. Dissatisfied by the turn of events, one of the most powerful noble families in England, the Nevilles, threw in their lot with York. One reason for this change of allegiance was the Neville feud with the Percy Earls of Northumberland, whom the king had favoured and Margaret continued to support. Margaret could not prevent York, made more powerful by the support of the Nevilles, from assuming the powers and authority of Protector and Defender of the Realm in March 1454. In effect, York had become king in all but name.

York's protectorate was short lived, but in the twelve months he was in power he did succeed in reducing the size and expenditure of the royal household and in restoring greater law and order, particularly in the north. On the other hand, he failed to have Somerset put on trial for treason and fell short of enlisting all but a handful of nobles to serve in his government. In spite of York's attempts to present himself as the champion of justice and enemy of corruption, the majority of England's noble families stopped short of openly supporting him, preferring instead to remain aloof and cautious.

Margaret of Anjou seizes power

When Margaret gave birth to a healthy son, Edward, in October 1453, she became convinced that York posed a threat to his inheritance. After the return to health of her husband in December 1454, Margaret retained her political power and tightened her grip on the court. Margaret was determined to destroy York but apart from having him stripped of his powers as Protector, she failed at first to have him banished from the court. In fact, after the king had shown that he had recovered sufficiently to rule again he publicly recognised York's importance by declaring him to be his principal royal adviser.

This act of conciliation was short lived. Margaret persuaded Henry VI to exclude York from the decision-making process on important matters of state. In addition, Somerset was released from the Tower and reappointed to the king's council and to the post of captain of Calais. It can be argued that, thereafter, Henry VI became little more than a puppet in the hands of his more politically astute wife. This was all too much for York, who fled north to raise an army. With the support of the Nevilles, York intended to rid the kingdom of Queen Margaret and to impose his will on the king and his council.

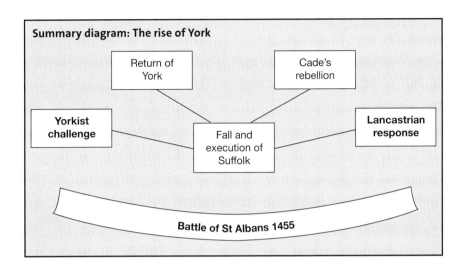

Summary diagram: The rise of York

The fighting begins: St Albans

The fall of Lancaster

▶ How and why was Henry VI overthrown?

The fighting begins: St Albans

What began as a political struggle for control of the king and royal government eventually led to outright war for possession of the crown. In 1455 Richard, Duke of York, led his supporters, principally the Neville Earls of Salisbury and Warwick, into rebellion against Henry VI. Their aim was the destruction of Somerset, the elimination of Margaret's influence and the control of the king. At this point, York had no intention of taking the crown for himself. Aware that the birth of Prince Edward had rendered his position as heir-presumptive redundant, York was determined to carve out a new career as the king's chief councillor; to become the power behind the throne. Somerset and the queen had other ideas and they convinced the king that York was plotting treason.

Henry VI summoned York to Leicester to explain himself. York surprised the king by attending the meeting backed by a force of over 3000 men. The king had less than 2000 troops so he was forced to negotiate; the failure of these talks led to the so-called Battle of St Albans. Although the 'battle' was little more than a skirmish in which some 60 or 70 men were killed, Henry VI was wounded by an arrow and among the dead lay the king's principal adviser, Somerset, and Henry Percy, Earl of Northumberland.

York had prevailed but he lacked the noble support necessary to control the king and his government. A compromise was reached whereby York was reappointed to the council and became the king's principal adviser. In addition, York had his ally Warwick appointed captain of Calais. The strain proved too much for the king, who again lapsed into insanity. Between November 1455 and February 1456 York served a second term as Protector. In the opinion of historian David Cook, 'the remarkable aspect of the years 1456–9 is that civil war did not break out again before 1459'.

The 'Loveday'

Peace between the warring parties was fragile and, ultimately, short lived. In spite of Henry VI's attempts at reconciliation in March 1458, the so-called 'Loveday', distrust and suspicion lingered and eventually turned into bloody conflict. The 'Loveday' was the name given to the elaborately staged ritual reconciliation that saw members of the rival factions march arm-in-arm into St Paul's Cathedral and which sought to heal the divisions between the victims and victors at the Battle of St Albans. It was a superficial act of unity that fooled no one. While York was away dealing with problems in Ireland, a bitter feud developed between Margaret and Warwick. The queen tried to have Warwick arrested on charges of piracy and riot but failed owing to a lack of support.

The fighting resumes: Blore Heath and the 'Rout' of Ludford

Convinced that York was plotting to take the throne, Queen Margaret and her principal ally, Humphrey Stafford, Duke of Buckingham, raised an army to destroy the Yorkists. To defend themselves, York and his supporters, Salisbury and Warwick, each raised an army. To prevent the three Yorkist armies joining together, the Lancastrians under Lord Audley intercepted Salisbury at Blore Heath. Audley was defeated and killed. The Yorkists merged their armies and awaited the Lancastrians at Ludford. When Henry VI himself turned up to lead the royal forces a substantial part of the Yorkist forces defected to the Lancastrians. After a brief but bloody skirmish, York, Salisbury and Warwick fled, leaving their troops to surrender. Not long afterwards, the Yorkist leaders left England; York took refuge in Ireland while Salisbury, Warwick and York's heir, Edward, took shelter in Calais.

The 'Parliament of Devils'

Having removed the Yorkists, Margaret persuaded the king to call a Parliament in Coventry in order to disgrace publicly York and his adherents. Meeting in November 1459, Parliament branded York, Salisbury and Warwick as traitors, sentenced them to death and ordered their lands and goods to be seized. In a gross violation of long-held custom that protected the rights of innocent offspring, Parliament also disinherited the Yorkist leaders' heirs. This last act shocked the nobility, turning some against the Crown. This Parliament became notorious and earned the nickname 'Parliament of Devils'. The harsh treatment meted out to the Yorkists backfired since it only stiffened their resolve to seek revenge.

Northampton and Wakefield: the death of York

The opportunity for revenge presented itself in June 1460 in the so-called '**Yorkist Invasion**', when Warwick, Salisbury and York's heir Edward, Earl of March, returned to England, landing on the south coast with an army of 2000 Calais veterans. Having returned from exile, the Yorkists set about taking London, which they did with ease, and recruiting more troops to take on the Lancastrians. A Yorkist army under Warwick encountered Henry VI's army near Northampton. Led by the Duke of Buckingham, the Lancastrians were heavily defeated owing to the treachery of Lord Grey of Ruthin, who changed sides and joined the Yorkists. Henry VI and Buckingham were captured and the latter was executed. Margaret and her son Edward escaped.

Control of the government was no longer enough for York and, three months after the Yorkist victory at Northampton, he all but claimed the throne for himself by forcing Henry VI to agree to the **Act of Accord**. According to the terms of the act:

- Henry VI was to remain king for the rest of his life.
- Henry VI's son, Prince Edward, was disinherited.
- Henry VI's wife, Queen Margaret, was banished for life.
- The succession was entrusted to Richard of York, and his offspring, who was recognised in law as heir-proper.

Queen Margaret refused to accept this and raised troops in the north. York, his son Edmund, Earl of Rutland, and Salisbury marched to Yorkshire to meet her in battle. However, at Wakefield the Yorkists were crushed by a much larger Lancastrian force. York and Rutland were killed, and Salisbury was captured and later executed. York's severed head, with a paper crown on it, was stuck on the walls of York. He was succeeded by his eldest son and heir, the nineteen-year-old Edward, Earl of March.

Yorkists triumphant: Henry deposed, Edward proclaimed

To exploit her victory at Wakefield, Margaret hurried south to rescue her husband, who was in Warwick's custody. The Yorkists, under Warwick, suffered another decisive defeat, at the Second Battle of St Albans. Henry VI was released from captivity and reunited with his wife. Margaret failed to follow up her victory by not taking London. Warwick fled to the Welsh border to join up with York's son and heir, Edward.

Edward, Duke of York and Earl of March, was determined to avenge the defeat and death of his father at Wakefield. He marched north from Gloucester to intercept a Lancastrian army under James Butler, Earl of Wiltshire and Lieutenant of Ireland, and Jasper Tudor, Earl of Pembroke. The Lancastrians were routed in a significant victory at Mortimer's Cross that had been planned and led by the teenage Edward. Within a month of his victory, Edward was in

KEY TERMS

Yorkist Invasion Used by historians to describe the return of armed Yorkists to England from exile abroad.

Act of Accord Act of Parliament responsible for determining the line of succession to the throne.

London, where he was proclaimed King Edward IV on 4 March 1461. However, before he could be crowned he had to march north to confront the Lancastrians.

Ferrybridge was a skirmish that took place a day before the much larger and bloodier Battle of Towton. A small force of Lancastrians under Lord Clifford attempted to stop Yorkist troops under Warwick from using a river crossing at Ferrybridge. In the ensuing fight Clifford was killed, Warwick was wounded and the Lancastrians fled.

Fought in a snowstorm the following day, the Battle of Towton witnessed the largest armies ever assembled in the kingdom, with more than 50,000 men involved. The slaughter was great and the Lancastrians were routed. Towton was the decisive engagement that both sides had been seeking since the renewal of war in 1459. Henry VI, Queen Margaret and their young son Edward fled to Scotland while Edward returned to London to be crowned. The Yorkists had triumphed.

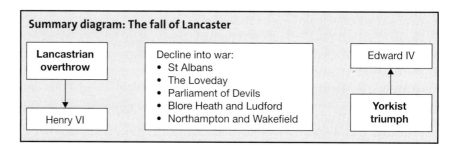

Summary diagram: The fall of Lancaster

Lancastrian overthrow	Decline into war:	**Edward IV**
↓	• St Albans • The Loveday • Parliament of Devils • Blore Heath and Ludford • Northampton and Wakefield	↑
Henry VI		**Yorkist triumph**

Chapter summary

The fifteenth century witnessed the breakdown of royal authority and an increase in lawlessness and disorder. The frequent breaks in the kingships of Henry VI and Edward IV illustrate the disturbed condition of England during this period. England was a nation seemingly at war with itself, a civil war in which nobles fought each other either for possession or control of the crown. The century began with Henry IV's usurpation of the throne when Richard II was forcibly removed and imprisoned. This period witnessed the rise of ambitious nobles like Richard, Duke of York, laying claim to the crown. War with France was an added complication that dominated English history for the first half of the century. Failure in the war against the French between 1429 and 1453 did much to cause civil war in England in 1455. For some 30 years thereafter, until 1487, nobles fought each other intermittently in a series of dynastic wars known to history as the Wars of the Roses. In stark contrast to the beginning, the century ended in peace and prosperity due in large part to the leadership, security and stability provided by Henry VII, the first of the Tudor monarchs.

Refresher questions

Use these questions to remind yourself of the key material covered in this chapter.

1 What were the Wars of the Roses?

2 What were the principal causes of the civil war?

3 How far can Henry VI be blamed for the civil war?

4 What impact did the French wars have on politics and power in England?

5 What was the significance of Cade's rebellion?

6 What impact did Henry VI's madness have on English politics?

7 Why did Richard of York challenge Henry VI for the crown?

8 How powerful an influence at court was Margaret of Anjou?

9 What was the 'Loveday' and how significant was it?

10 What was the 'Parliament of Devils' and how significant was it?

11 What impact did Richard of York's death have on the Yorkist cause?

12 How was Edward of York able to seize the crown from Henry VI?

 Question practice

ESSAY QUESTION

1 'Civil war broke out not because of 'over-mighty subjects' but because of an 'under-mighty monarch.' How far do you agree with this statement?

SOURCE ANALYSIS QUESTIONS

1 Using Sources 1–4 (page 74) in their historical context, assess how far they support the view that Henry VI was responsible for his own downfall.

2 With reference to Sources 4 and 5 (pages 74 and 75), and your understanding of the historical context, which of these two sources is more valuable in explaining why Henry VI was deposed?

3 With reference to Sources 4–6 (pages 74 and 75), and your understanding of the historical context, assess the value of these three sources to a historian studying the reasons for Richard III being able to usurp the crown.

4 Study Source 7 (page 75). Assess the value of the source for revealing the reasons for the removal of Henry VI. Explain your answer, using the source, the information given about its origin and your own knowledge about the historical context.

SOURCE 1

From Jack Cade, *The Complaint of the Poor Commons of Kent*, 1450. Here, Cade gives his views about the government of England in an appeal to the people.

The king should have as his advisers men of high rank from his royal realm, that is to say, the high and mighty prince, the Duke of York, exiled from the service of the King by the suggestions of that traitor the Duke of Suffolk. He should also take advice from those mighty princes the Dukes of Buckingham and Norfolk, together with the earls and barons of this land.

SOURCE 2

From *The Annals of the Kings of England* (*Annales rerum anglicarum*), May 1451. A chronicler reports on the debate in Parliament regarding the succession.

In Parliament Thomas Yonge, a lawyer from Bristol, stated that because the king had no offspring, it would be necessary for the security of the kingdom that it should be openly known who should be his heir. He named the Duke of York as the fittest man in the kingdom to be heir. For daring to do this, Thomas was afterwards imprisoned in to the Tower of London.

SOURCE 3

From *The Anonymous London Chronicle*, 1455. A chronicler describes the dispute between York and Somerset.

Soon after Easter 1455, another dispute arose between the noble Duke of York and the evil Duke of Somerset. Somerset was plotting the destruction of the noble Duke of York. He offered advice to the king, saying that the Duke of York wished to depose the king and rule England himself – which was false.

Because of this, around the middle of May, the Duke of York and the Earls of Shrewsbury and Warwick approached London with seven thousand armed men. When the Duke of Somerset heard this, he suggested to the king that York had come to take the throne by force. For this reason Henry VI sided with the Duke of Somerset.

SOURCE 4

From *A Chronicle of the Reigns of Richard II, Henry IV, Henry V and Henry VI*, c.1465. A chronicler comments on the government of England in 1459.

The realm of England was not well governed for King Henry VI was child-like and influenced by greedy advisors. His debts increased daily, but he made no payments; all the possessions and lordships that belonged to the crown the king had given away, some to lords and some to other lesser persons, so that he had almost nothing left of his own. And the money taken from the people was wasted, as all the taxes that came from them were spent in vain. The king did not have a proper household as a king should, nor was he able to maintain any wars.

SOURCE 5

From William Hardy, editor, *Recueil des Croniques et Anchiennes Istories de la Grant Bretaigne* (*Account of the Chronicles and Old Histories of Great Britain*), Longman, Green & Co., 1864. The chronicle was written by the Burgundian soldier and diplomat Jean de Waurin (1415–71).

In 1461 King Henry himself and his Queen, Margaret of Anjou, were overthrown and lost that crown which his grandfather, Henry IV, had violently usurped and taken from King Richard II, his first cousin, whom he caused to be shamelessly murdered. Men say that ill-gotten gains cannot last. Henry has been replaced by one of his noblemen, a young man named Edward of York.

SOURCE 6

From 'Gregory's Chronicle' of 1461. William Gregory was mayor of London.

The King was removed from London against his will and the Duke of York declared himself king. The Queen fled to Wales but was attacked and robbed by her own servant showing how lawless times had become. From then on she travelled about in secret, fearing for her own life and for that of her son the prince. The Lords sent forged orders, supposedly from the King, demanding that she hand herself over, for they claimed that she was the reason for the opposition to their plans and that she was more intelligent than the King. The Queen, having knowledge of this, sent for help from the Earl of Somerset and the Earl of Devon urging them to come as quickly as they could with their armies. Some of the lords that came to her aid did so more out of expectation of reward than loyalty to her position.

SOURCE 7

From 'Gregory's Chronicle' of 1461. William Gregory was mayor of London and favoured the Yorkists.

On 17 February 1461 King Harry rode to St Albans, accompanied by the Duke of Norfolk, the Earls of Warwick and Arundel, Lords Bourchier and Bonville, many great lords and knights and esquires and commons numbering 100,000 men. There they had a great battle with the queen, who had come from Wakefield to St Albans with her lords. I believe that less than 5000 men fought in the queen's party, for most of the northern men fled away, some being taken prisoner. In the midst of the battle King Harry went to his queen and abandoned his lords, trusting better to her party rather than his own lords. King Harry's lords fled, or were killed in battle or were captured and beheaded like Lord Bonville. The number of men slain was 3500.

On 29 March 1462 King Harry was removed from London against his will and the Duke of York declared himself king. The Queen fled to Wales but was attacked and robbed by her own servant showing how lawless times had become. From then on she travelled about in secret, fearing for her own life and for that of her son the prince. The Lords sent forged orders, supposedly from the King, her husband, demanding that she hand herself over, for they claimed that she was the reason for the opposition to their plans and that she was more intelligent than the King. The Queen, having knowledge of this, sent for help from the Earl of Somerset and the Earl of Devon urging them to come as quickly as they could with their armies. Some of the lords that came to her aid did so more out of expectation of reward than loyalty to her position.

CHAPTER 5

The first reign of Edward IV 1461–70

The accession of Edward IV seemed to have brought stability and security to England but this was not so in reality. In spite of efforts to consolidate his power, Edward IV struggled to impose his authority on the kingdom. Noble disaffection, laced with jealousy over Edward's promotion, combined to threaten his throne. Nor could he look to those closest to him for support, for his once steadfast allies turned into vengeful enemies. These developments are examined as four themes:

★ Edward IV: consolidation of Yorkist power and the restoration of order

★ Edward IV and the nobility

★ The king and the 'Kingmaker': Edward IV and the Earl of Warwick

★ Warwick's rebellion and the restoration of Henry VI, 1469–71

Key dates

1461	Reign of Edward IV began
1464	Edward IV married Elizabeth Woodville
1465	Henry VI captured and imprisoned
1468	Edward IV's sister Margaret married Duke Charles of Burgundy
1469	Warwick and Clarence rebelled against Edward IV
	The Battle of Edgecote

1470	Henry VI restored to the throne by Warwick
	Edward IV and his brother Richard forced into exile in Burgundy
1471	Edward IV restored to the throne after victory at the Battle of Barnet, in which Warwick was killed
	Henry VI murdered, his son Edward, Prince of Wales, killed in Battle of Tewkesbury

1 Edward IV: consolidation of Yorkist power and the restoration of order

▶ *How successful was Edward in consolidating his power and restoring law and order?*

The civil war continues: 1461–5

If Edward thought his coronation in June 1461 as Edward IV would bring an end to the civil wars he was sadly mistaken. It took him over three years to eliminate his Lancastrian enemies, who concentrated their power in Northumberland and were sustained by Scottish and French help. A number of Lancastrian plots were unearthed, there were invasion scares on the south coast and disturbances occurred in several parts of the kingdom:

- In Wales, the Lancastrians lost a skirmish in the Tywi valley near Dryslwyn but they had better success in the north, where Harlech Castle was besieged but held by them for nearly seven years until it finally fell in 1468.
- In Northumberland, the castles of Alnwick, Bamburgh and Dunstanburgh became the focal point of Lancastrian resistance in the north. These castles were besieged and taken twice by the Yorkists and twice they were recaptured by the Lancastrians.

Early in 1464 Henry VI and Margaret returned to England to rally the substantial support they still enjoyed in the north. Their principal support came from the Percy Earls of Northumberland. It was to Sir Ralph Percy that Henry VI and Margaret marched with a largely French-financed army consisting mainly of Scottish and French mercenaries. They were joined by troops raised by Henry Beaufort, Duke of Somerset (son and heir of the king's principal adviser, killed at St Albans in 1455). Edward IV responded by sending a Yorkist army north under the command of Warwick's younger brother, John Neville, Lord Montagu. At Hedgeley Moor, in April 1464, the Lancastrians were soundly beaten with Percy among the casualties. Somerset escaped and offered battle three weeks later at Hexham. This time Montagu made no mistake when he cut the Lancastrians to pieces, captured Somerset and executed him. Margaret and her son escaped and sought refuge in France while her husband went on the run. Henry VI was eventually captured in Lancashire in 1465.

SOURCE A

Study Source A. Why might Mancini be biased?

Adapted from Dominic Mancini, *The Usurpation of Richard the Third*. Mancini was an Italian visitor living in England in 1482–3. He provided one of the earliest descriptions of the new king, Edward IV.

Edward was of a gentle nature and cheerful aspect: nevertheless should he assume an angry countenance he could appear very terrible to beholders. He was of easy access to his friends and others, even the least notable. Frequently he called to his side complete strangers, when he thought that they had come with the intention of addressing him more closely. He was wont to show himself to those who wished to watch him, and he seized any opportunity that the occasion offered of revealing his fine stature to onlookers. He was so genial in his greeting, that if he saw a newcomer bewildered at his appearance and royal magnificence, he would give him courage to speak by laying a kindly hand upon his shoulder.

He was more favourable than other princes to foreigners, who visited his realm for trade or for some other reason. He very seldom showed munificence, and then only in moderation, still he was very grateful to those from whom he had received a favour. Though not rapacious of other men's goods, he was yet eager for money, and in pursuing it he acquired a reputation for avarice. He adopted this artifice for piling up wealth.

Security and consolidation

In order to secure his crown and consolidate his power, Edward IV realised that he had to deal with threats and problems both external and internal.

External

Concerned by the scale of support the Lancastrians had obtained from both Scotland and France, Edward was determined to establish better foreign relations. He successfully negotiated truces with James III of Scotland and Louis XI of France. Edward hoped this would be enough to deny the Lancastrians any aid abroad, be it political, financial or military. The king also opened negotiations with the powerful Duke of Burgundy to exploit trading opportunities and to secure an ally should the French renege on their truce. In an effort to turn the truce with France into something more lasting, Warwick tried to persuade Edward IV to marry the French king's daughter. However, his attempt to cement an Anglo–French alliance through marriage failed when Edward ignored his advice and secretly married Elizabeth Woodville instead. This was a serious miscalculation on Edward's part for it alienated the French. Equally significant was Edward's failure to persuade the influential Hanseatic League (see page 14), an organisation of German merchants, to agree to his request for trading concessions. These concessions had the potential to increase trade and customs revenue for the king.

Internal

Fearful of further fighting, Edward adopted a policy of conciliation. Lancastrians were offered pardons and encouraged to serve the Crown. Henry VI was imprisoned in the Tower of London but was well treated. Lawlessness and disorder were tackled alongside the national debt and the economy. Edward tried to improve the efficiency and authority of the departments of government, particularly in the farthest reaches of the kingdom. Unfortunately, Edward's successes were few. Law and order were restored in some regions, government was improved, mainly by the professionalism of its personnel, but its effectiveness remained questionable. The Crown's finances were well on the way to recovery but the **national debt** remained high. Perhaps the most glaring failure was Edward's tendency to over-reward close family and a small circle of noble supporters. This bred resentment, not just among Lancastrians but among some Yorkists, too.

In the final analysis, the fact that Edward was deposed with what appeared to be relative ease in 1469 shows that he had failed not only to restore law and order but also to secure and consolidate his power.

KEY TERM

National debt Money owed by the Crown to members of the English nobility and continental bankers/financiers. The Crown borrowed the money to help pay for the costs of the court, the royal household and the government.

SOURCE B

Portrait of Edward IV, c.1470s by an unknown artist.

Study Source B. Why do you think Edward IV commissioned an artist to paint this portrait?

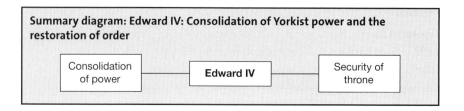

Summary diagram: Edward IV: Consolidation of Yorkist power and the restoration of order

```
┌──────────────┐        ┌──────────────┐        ┌──────────────┐
│ Consolidation │────────│  Edward IV   │────────│  Security of │
│   of power    │        │              │        │    throne    │
└──────────────┘        └──────────────┘        └──────────────┘
```

 ## Edward IV and the nobility

▶ *How successful was Edward's relationship with the nobility?*

Managing the nobility

Edward was well aware that the success of his kingship depended largely on his relationship with the nobility. He wished to avoid the problems encountered by Henry VI by widening the circle of patronage, but, as a result of the war, the nobility were more bitterly divided than ever. Thus, the task of managing and satisfying them would be a difficult one. His policy was based on two general principles:

- Pardon and reconciliation for Lancastrians.
- Employment, patronage and reward for nobles of both factions.

Edward thus began his reign with the best of intentions but his laudable aims fell well short of their target. Almost from the beginning, he encountered difficulties, not the least of which being that some Lancastrians were reluctant to accept his offers of reconciliation and employment in the service of the Crown. Indeed, Edward did not have the financial or material resources to reward them if they had sought it. Owing in part to his inexperience of kingship, he had badly miscalculated the resources available to him. In fact, he was hard pressed to recompense his own Yorkist supporters, many of whom waited impatiently for their rewards in land and office. Then there were the demands made on him by his closest allies and family, such as Warwick and the Woodvilles.

In order to meet the demands of his Yorkist supporters, Edward turned to exploiting his defeated Lancastrian enemies. He set in motion a large-scale redistribution of titles, offices and estates that he confiscated from at least thirteen Lancastrian peers and from almost 100 well-off gentry (see Source C, opposite). **Attainted** for **treason** in the Parliament of 1461, the dispossessed Lancastrians had no choice but to accept their fate. The fact that some of them had been killed in battle meant that their families bore the brunt of the confiscations. Naturally, this bred resentment and it was not long before some of them began to plot Edward's downfall.

 **KEY TERMS**

Attainder The process by which nobles who broke the law were condemned and then punished. This law enabled the king to seize the law-breaker's estates so that he could benefit from the profits.

Treason Betrayal of one's country and its ruler.

SOURCE C

Adapted from Clement Paston's letter to his brother Sir John Paston written in 1461. Sir John was advised not to ignore the king's orders.

Brother I recommend me to you.

Sir, it was told to me by a right worshipful man that loves you right well, and you him, and you shall know his name hereafter, but put all things out of doubt he is such a man as will not lie: on the eleventh day of October the king said, 'We have sent two sealed letters to Paston by two yeomen of our chamber, and he has disobeyed them; but we will send him another tomorrow, and by God's mercy and if he come not then he shall die for it. We will make all other men beware by him how they shall disobey our writings'.

> How does Source C reveal Edward IV's determination to demonstrate his power?

Royal patronage and the nobility

In 22 years of Edward IV's reign he created or revived at least 37 noble titles, 22 of which were bestowed during his first reign, 1461–9. This apparent generosity was intended to bolster a depleted peerage, many peers having been killed in the wars, and provide him with a wide circle of grateful supporters. The policy failed because the bestowal of a title did not necessarily bring with it any land. For all his promises, many of the confiscated estates ended up in the hands of a privileged few. The principal beneficiaries were:

- Edward's brothers: George and Richard were created Dukes of Clarence and Gloucester, respectively. Clarence was endowed with lands to the value of some £3660 (£1.78 million in today's money) annually and offices with a combined annual salary of just over £650 (£305,000 today).
- The Nevilles: William, Lord Fauconberg, was made Earl of Kent; John, Lord Montagu, was given the Earldom of Northumberland, while George was appointed Archbishop of York. The most favoured of the family was Richard Neville, the **Earl of Warwick**. The gifts in land and money bestowed on him were on a scale that dwarfed that given to any other courtier. Even more significantly, he was given unparalleled power in the north of England, ruling it virtually as king's **viceroy**.
- The Woodvilles: Edward IV's wife, Elizabeth (see Source D), was keen to see her family benefit from her marriage. Her father Richard was created Earl Rivers and her brother, Anthony, Lord Scales, was entrusted with considerable influence at court.
- Favoured individuals: men such as Sir William Herbert and William Lord Hastings benefited from Edward's largesse. Hastings became the king's closest friend and was appointed chamberlain of the royal household. Herbert was advanced to the peerage as Earl of Pembroke. He was virtually given Wales to rule as viceroy of the king, a position of power comparable to Warwick's authority in the north of England.

🔑 KEY FIGURE

Earl of Warwick (Richard Neville) (1428–71)

Known as the 'Kingmaker', Neville was among the wealthiest and most powerful noblemen in England. He was instrumental in helping Edward IV to seize the throne but he became disillusioned with the young king. He changed sides in 1470 and helped in the restoration of Henry VI. Neville was killed at the Battle of Barnet.

🔑 KEY TERM

Viceroy Title given to a nobleman entrusted with royal authority to rule as the king's deputy in some part of the realm.

The favoured clique

In practice, Edward IV relied on a comparatively small group of nobles to help him exercise his royal authority. They are estimated to have been no more than a dozen strong and were created by the king. This favoured clique bears comparison with the inner ring of noble councillors on whom Henry VI relied to govern his kingdom. Very little, it seems, had changed. The resentment that led to civil war in 1455 was as much a contributing factor in the subsequent civil war in 1469.

SOURCE D

? Study Source D. When Elizabeth Woodville married Edward IV she was not pregnant but the artist has shown her to be so. Why do you think this was done?

The wedding of Edward IV and Elizabeth Woodville. The centre panel of a three-part painting thought to be from the fifteenth century but now suspected to be a nineteenth-century fake produced in France.

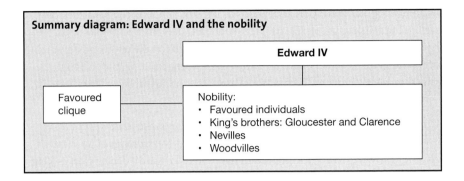

Summary diagram: Edward IV and the nobility

Edward IV

Favoured clique

Nobility:
- Favoured individuals
- King's brothers: Gloucester and Clarence
- Nevilles
- Woodvilles

3 The king and the 'Kingmaker': Edward IV and the Earl of Warwick

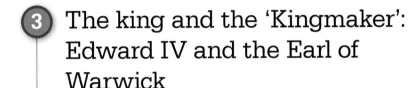

▶ *Why did Edward IV and the Earl of Warwick quarrel?*

Warwick the man

The life, character and career of Richard Neville, Earl of Warwick, have long fascinated historians. Known as the 'Kingmaker', a nickname first applied in the sixteenth century, Warwick was, in the opinion of modern historian A.J. Pollard (writing in 2000), 'the mightiest of over-mighty subjects', who was instrumental in putting Edward IV on the throne in 1461. Equally significant is the fact that he played a pivotal role in deposing Edward IV in 1469 and restoring Henry VI in 1470. Warwick was certainly mightier than Richard, Duke of York, but he, too, fell from power. As far as the man is concerned, we know comparatively little about him. No effigy or painting survives, nor do we have a contemporary description of him. He seems not to have been a patron of the arts but devoted himself to politics and war.

Warwick's career

Warwick's career began in 1449 when, aged 21, he succeeded to the wealthy Earldom of Warwick in right of his wife, the heiress Anne Beauchamp. Anne's father, Richard Beauchamp, Earl of Warwick, was among the richest nobles in England and when he died without sons to succeed him all his wealth and possessions passed to his daughter. Through her, and with the king's approval, Richard Neville successfully claimed the title and earldom of his deceased father-in-law. When Richard, Duke of York, claimed the regency in 1453, Warwick offered his support and took up arms with him at the Battle of St Albans in 1455. His reward was the prestigious and powerful post of captain of Calais. He took part in the 'Loveday' procession of 1458 (see page 70) and became a popular hero soon afterwards as a result of his successful attack on a fleet of Spanish ships off Calais. He defended Calais from Somerset who, on being appointed captain by Margaret of Anjou, tried to take up his post but found the gates closed against him. Warwick returned to England in 1460, gained an easy victory at Northampton and brought the captive Henry VI to London (see page 59).

After the death of York, Warwick transferred his allegiance to Edward, Earl of March, son and heir of Richard, Duke of York. After the victories at Mortimer's Cross and Towton, Warwick smoothed the path to Edward's declaration as king and assisted in organising the coronation. Warwick's power owed much to the fact that he possessed vast estates that stretched across the length and breadth of England and Wales. He held the title to four earldoms, to which were added offices of state, many of which were bestowed on him by a grateful Edward IV. It is this, his position as Edward IV's right-hand man, his most trusted adviser and most generously rewarded favourite, that marks Warwick out as a figure of enormous interest to contemporaries and modern historians alike. However, his favoured position is also the source of much debate regarding the extent of his influence and power.

Kingmaker or Kingserver?

The key issue is the extent to which Warwick deserves the title of 'Kingmaker': did he make and unmake kings or did he merely serve them? It is accepted that Warwick was a rich and powerful man and there is general agreement that by putting his vast resources at the disposal of the Yorkist cause he contributed to Edward's triumph in 1461. More debatable is the extent to which Edward relied on Warwick and his wealth and whether without them he could have become king and maintained his hold on the crown. Equally debatable is the nature of the relationship between Warwick and the king and the extent to which one was subject to the authority of the other. In short, who actually ruled England? There are two schools of thought:

- Warwick not only 'made' King Edward (and unmade him) but also ruled England in his name.
- Warwick's influence has been exaggerated and he was merely a servant of the king, albeit a powerful and favoured one.

Contemporary opinions of Warwick

In the opinion of one contemporary, James Kennedy, Bishop of St Andrews, Warwick was 'governor of the realm of England beneath King Edward'. This statement, from a man who was himself the most influential politician in Scotland, has been taken to imply the Scotsman's contempt for the authority of the young King Edward. Kennedy's sympathies lay with the Lancastrians, as shown by the protection he offered Henry VI and Margaret when they fled to Scotland.

More damning is the witty remark of the governor of Abbeville, who reported to his king, Louis XI of France, in May 1464, that in England 'they have but two rulers – M. de Warwick and another, whose name I have forgotten'. From across the English Channel, Warwick may well have appeared to be all powerful, especially as he was better known to the French because he was entrusted with conducting the king's foreign policy. This miscalculation of Edward's position and power by the French would come back to haunt King Louis.

Even as far afield as Italy, the perception appeared to be that Warwick was the real power behind the throne. In a letter to the Duke of Milan, written in April 1461, the papal legate, Francesco Coppini, wrote, 'My lord of Warwick … has made a new king of the son of the duke of York'.

Historians' opinion of Warwick

Some modern historians agree with this image of an all-powerful Warwick. In 1901 the *Dictionary of National Biography* stated with confidence that Warwick 'was the real ruler of England during the first three years of Edward's reign'. In 1955 historian P.M. Kendall had no doubt that Edward's usurpation of the throne in 1461 was the first true example of Warwick's 'kingmaking', after which 'Warwick governed in the saddle from the periphery of the realm'. Another popular pithy turn of phrase is that coined by the Victorian historian J.A. Froude, 'Warwick ruled while Edward reigned'.

More recently, however, historians have been inclined to play down the extent of Warwick's kingmaking. In the opinion of Edward IV's modern biographer, Charles Ross (writing in 1983), 'the whole pattern of Edward's activities in these years [1461–9] suggests that he was very much king in fact as well as in name'. Andrew Pickering (writing in 2000) stated emphatically that 'Edward was neither "made" by Warwick nor controlled by him'. David Cook (writing in 1984) expressed his view that the relationship between Warwick and Edward IV was 'an alliance of mutual interests which triumphed in 1461, not a puppet and puppeteer'. According to A.J. Pollard (writing in 2000): 'It was largely to foreign observers that Warwick appeared all powerful. In reality the relationship between the two was more a partnership between mighty subject and insecure king, and it would be entirely wrong to suppose that Warwick was the sole author of royal policy during these early years.'

The alienation of Warwick

It may have come as something of a shock to Edward IV to discover that his close friend and ally was not satisfied with the position and power he had been given. Nor was Warwick sufficiently grateful for the freedom accorded him in the conduct of national affairs. Among the most important offices showered on Warwick were the following:

- captainship of Calais
- constableship of Dover Castle

- wardenship of the Cinque Ports
- admiralship of England and Ireland
- wardenship of the eastern and western marches on the Scottish border.

Short of monopolising royal patronage and alienating the other Yorkist nobility, there was not much more that Edward could do or give the earl. Warwick was evidently greedy and grasping, and it was his desire to add the whole of Wales and the March (see page 108) to his portfolio of authority that brought him into conflict with William Herbert, Earl of Pembroke. Pembroke believed that his contribution to putting Edward on the throne was equally deserving of reward. The two men, Pembroke and Warwick, would quarrel and eventually become the deadliest of enemies.

Edward's inexperience of kingship added to Warwick's ambition was a recipe for disaster. For the first three years of Edward IV's reign all seemed well between them, probably because they still faced a common and very real threat in the Lancastrians. However, this changed after 1465 with the defeat in battle and subsequent exile of the Lancastrian leaders, and the capture of Henry VI. The first sign that all was not well occurred in May 1464 when Edward IV secretly married Elizabeth Woodville. The fact that Warwick neither knew of nor was consulted about the union is telling. In fact, Edward shocked and angered members of his own family with his decision to marry a widow with children whose family had, until recently, been staunch Lancastrians. In the opinion of historian Charles Ross (1983), this was 'the first major blunder of his political career'.

SOURCE E

Sforza de Bettini of Florence, Milan's ambassador in France, wrote to Galeazzo Maria Sforza, Duke of Milan, in 1470.

The Queen [Margaret of Anjou] and the Prince of Wales, her son, arrived here the day before yesterday, and on the same day the Earl of Warwick also arrived. The same evening the king [Henry VI] presented him to the queen. With great reverence Warwick went on his knees and asked her pardon for the injuries and wrongs done to her in the past. She graciously forgave him and he afterwards did homage and fealty there, swearing to be a faithful and loyal subject of the king, queen and prince as his liege lords unto his death.

The marriage of Warwick's daughter to the Prince Edward is announced. His Majesty has sent for the lady to Amboise where the marriage will be consummated. In two days Warwick will leave for his fleet.

Study Source E. Why did Margaret of Anjou and Richard Neville, Earl of Warwick, settle their differences and enter into an alliance?

Warwick's anger and frustration

Warwick was left embarrassed by this marriage because he had been working hard to cement an alliance with the French by proposing a match between Edward IV and Louis XI's sister-in-law. It was, in part, their disagreement over the conduct of foreign policy that led to a rift between Warwick and Edward.

Warwick favoured an alliance with France but Edward preferred a treaty with the Duchy of Burgundy. Burgundy had been England's ally during the Hundred Years' War and, although that war had ended in 1453 (see pages 48–9), the Duchy had remained an enemy of France. Louis XI feared an Anglo-Burgundian alliance as he thought it might persuade the English to renew the war for control of France. While Louis XI was keen to destroy Burgundy's trade and end its commercial power, Edward IV was equally keen to exploit it. Since Burgundy's rulers, Phillip and his successor Charles the Bold, wished to maintain their independence of the French Crown, an alliance with England suited their purpose.

Unhappy with having to negotiate with foreign powers according to the dictates of the increasingly influential Woodvilles, Warwick withdrew from the court in 1467. The final straw came in 1468, when Edward arranged the marriage of his sister, Margaret, to Duke Charles of Burgundy. This ended any hope of a French alliance and turned Louis XI into a dangerous enemy. As the Woodvilles' influence increased, Warwick's declined. Over time, the earl's advice either was not sought or was ignored. Warwick's role as the king's chief councillor appeared to be all but over. Whether Warwick's young protégé, the king, had, in the words of David Cook (1984), 'hurt his grossly inflated ego', we have no way of knowing, but it may have occurred to the 'Kingmaker' that in order to retain his power and influence he might have to contemplate removing Edward from the throne.

The alienation of Clarence

Warwick was not the only one with grievances, real or imagined, against Edward IV. The king's unstable and overambitious brother, George, Duke of Clarence, had opposed Edward's marriage and he resented the Woodville influence at court. Clarence shared Warwick's irritation at the way the Woodvilles were cornering the marriage market. By the beginning of 1467, the Queen's siblings had contracted marriages with the Duke of Buckingham and the heirs of the Earls of Arundel, Essex, Kent and Pembroke. In addition, the queen's eldest son from her first marriage, Thomas Grey, took as his wife the heiress to the Duke of Exeter, while her twenty-year-old brother, John Woodville, married the 65-year-old Duchess of Norfolk. Described by a contemporary chronicler as a *maritagium diabolicum* (a diabolical marriage!), this union is taken as evidence of Woodville greed and ambition.

Fearful of losing his privileged status at court, Clarence turned to Warwick for support. It was agreed that Clarence should marry Warwick's eldest daughter, Isabel, but the king refused to sanction the match. This was a serious blow to Clarence and Warwick, who blamed the queen and her brother Anthony, Lord Scales, for influencing the king against the marriage. Neither Clarence nor Warwick was prepared to tolerate this public humiliation, so together they plotted the destruction of the Woodvilles and the downfall of the king. They were sustained in their plotting by the knowledge that while Warwick was generally popular in the kingdom the Woodvilles were not. Warwick was a politician with a talent for propaganda and the cultivation of friendships. Unfortunately for him, it became clear that his 'popularity' was not as widespread as he had thought for while the Commons supported him, the majority of the nobility did not.

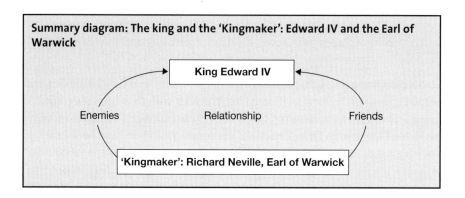

Summary diagram: The king and the 'Kingmaker': Edward IV and the Earl of Warwick

4 Warwick's rebellion and the restoration of Henry VI, 1469–71

▶ *Why did Warwick rebel in 1469 and why was Henry VI restored?*

Political upheaval and instability

Jealousy, bitterness and greed lay at the root of the renewal of civil war in 1469. Unlike in previous conflicts, this was not a war between two sides – the Lancastrians and Yorkists – but between two halves of the same side. Warwick's rebellion split the Yorkists and forced Edward on to the defensive. Trouble began in April 1469 in the north of England when two separate Warwick-inspired risings led by **'Robin of Redesdale'** and **'Robin of Holderness'** broke out. Taking advantage of the growing economic crisis due to a series of bad harvests, general discontent and a slide into disorder that was gripping the country from mid-1468, Warwick hoped to keep Edward busy in the north while he and Clarence slipped over to Calais to plot the king's usurpation.

 KEY TERM

'Robin of Redesdale' and 'Robin of Holderness'
Pseudonyms used to mask the true identities of the rebel leaders.

Warwick and Clarence's rebellion

In Calais, Warwick and Clarence took command of the garrison of veteran troops and issued a manifesto outlining their grievances and stating their intention to rid the kingdom of the Crown's 'evil councillors'. To seal their alliance, Clarence was married to Warwick's daughter. Warwick and Clarence's public joint declaration and return to England in July 1469 alarmed Edward, who called on his principal supporters, the Earls of Pembroke and Devon, to bring their forces to join his. However, Warwick and Clarence managed to intercept Pembroke, and his largely Welsh army was heavily defeated at Edgecote. Pembroke was captured and executed. On hearing the news, Edward IV's troops deserted him and he fled but was soon captured by Warwick.

Warwick's attempt to govern the kingdom failed. The economic crisis and increased disorder that had served his purpose earlier in the year now threatened to topple him. The nobility remained cautious and aloof, to the extent that they did not support him in the face of a Lancastrian rising in the north-west. To help put down this rising and to quell other significant pockets of unrest, Warwick released Edward IV from custody. The relationship between the two men was strained and it soon became clear to Warwick that he would never again regain his former position as the king's principal adviser. With peace restored in much of the kingdom, Warwick began a new plot to oust the king. In an effort to dispose of Edward, in March 1470 Warwick secretly encouraged a rebellion under Sir Robert Welles in Lincolnshire. At the Battle of Losecoat Field the rebels were defeated by Edward, who pursued them as they tore off their incriminating coats and badges. Welles was captured and executed.

Private quarrels

As events nationally spiralled out of control, some members of the nobility took advantage of the chaos and confusion to pursue bitter family feuds. The battle at Nibley Green in March 1470 was one such private quarrel – between the Berkeleys and Talbots. There were numerous other private quarrels settled by combat, although most did not result in pitched battles. For example, in the autumn of 1470 Lord Stanley besieged the Harringtons in Hornby Castle.

SOURCE F

Adapted from the *Warkworth Chronicle*. The contemporary chronicler, John Warkworth, revealed Edward's harsh treatment of rebels in 1470.

King Edward then came to Southampton and commanded the earl of Worcester to sit in judgement of the men who had been captured. Twenty gentlemen and yeomen were hanged, drawn and quartered, and then beheaded, after which they were hung up by their legs and a stake was sharpened at both ends; one end of the stake was pushed in between their buttocks, and their heads were stuck on the other. This angered the people of the land and forever afterwards, the earl of Worcester was greatly hated by them, for the unlawful manner of execution he had inflicted upon his captives.

Study Source F. Why might Edward IV have approved of Worcester's harsh treatment of the rebels?

France and Burgundy

As England descended into civil war, the rulers of France and Burgundy looked on with great interest. They hoped to use the situation to their advantage by backing one side against the other. In fact, France and Burgundy were to play a crucial role in this phase of the Wars of the Roses.

France

As relations between the king and Warwick deteriorated, the latter, in the company of Clarence, fled to France. Louis XI intended to use them as a diplomatic tool in his conflict with Burgundy. In an often tense and hostile round of negotiations, Louis managed to persuade Warwick, Clarence and Margaret of Anjou to set aside their differences and join forces. The French king had long hoped to arrange a Neville–Lancastrian alliance in order to restore Henry VI to the English throne. In return, Louis expected the English to break their treaty with Burgundy and help him in his conflict with Duke Charles. To seal this alliance it was agreed that Margaret's son, Prince Edward, should marry Warwick's youngest daughter, Anne.

In September 1470 Warwick returned to England. With French financial assistance and a core of **mercenaries** at his disposal, Warwick set about recruiting an army. He was able to do this almost unmolested because Edward IV was in the north putting down a rebellion led by Lord FitzHugh, Warwick's brother-in-law. At about the same time, in what may have been part of a co-ordinated plan, Warwick's brother John, Lord Montagu, betrayed the king by switching his allegiance. To avoid being caught in a pincer movement, King Edward, together with his brother, Richard, Duke of Gloucester, Lord Hastings and Earl Rivers, was forced to flee and seek shelter in Burgundy. Charles the Bold now played host to a group of exiled English nobles and, like Louis of France, he intended to use them in his conflict with the French.

Burgundy

As part of Warwick's agreement with Queen Margaret, Henry VI was released from prison and restored to the throne. The **readeption** of Henry VI brought England into conflict with Burgundy. True to their word, Warwick and Margaret of Anjou supported Louis XI when he attacked Burgundy. This proved disastrous for Warwick because he lost the support of Parliament, which had not been consulted about the declaration of war, and the powerful merchant community, who feared the damage this conflict would do to the kingdom's chief export, wool. Duke Charles responded by gifting Edward IV 50,000 crowns (£11,000 in contemporary English currency or £5 million today), helping him plan his return to England and putting at his disposal a bodyguard of Burgundian troops.

It may be argued that in providing a safe haven for exiles, together with financial, military and diplomatic assistance, France and Burgundy had done much to determine the course of English political history in the latter half of the fifteenth century. Of course, they did so not because it mattered to them what happened in England but because it kept the English weak and distracted by civil war. The bargains the French and Burgundians struck with individuals such as Edward IV, Margaret of Anjou and Warwick, and later with Jasper and Henry Tudor, were only ever intended to be advantageous in the short term.

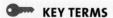 **KEY TERMS**

Mercenaries Professional soldiers who fight for hire and profit.

Readeption The restoration of Henry VI as king.

The defection of Clarence and the murder of Henry VI

Edward returned from Burgundy in March 1470 and hastily set about recruiting an army. On his march to London, Edward was joined by his brother, Clarence, whom he forgave for betraying him. Clarence's defection was caused by his disappointment at Warwick's failure to consider, let alone support, his candidature for the crown. His opposition to the restoration of Henry VI inevitably brought him into conflict with Warwick. Warwick condemned Clarence's duplicity and resolved either to kill him in battle or to execute him should he be captured. Warwick never got that chance, for in April the earl was defeated and killed at the Battle of Barnet. 'False, fleeting, perjur'd Clarence', as Shakespeare referred to him in his play *Henry VI*, survived to betray another day.

Within weeks of his crushing victory at Barnet, Edward IV scored another success at the Battle of Tewkesbury. A number of Lancastrian magnates were killed, including the Duke of Somerset and, crucially, Margaret of Anjou's son, Prince Edward. The queen herself made good her escape, only to be captured a few days later. It is widely believed that, in an effort to end the wars once and for all, Edward IV ordered the execution of Henry VI. The constable of the Tower, where Henry VI was incarcerated, was Edward's brother, Richard, Duke of York, and it is thought that he may have been responsible for carrying out the deed.

The destruction of the Lancastrians

Following the destruction of the Lancastrians at Tewkesbury (see Source G, overleaf), Henry VI's half-brother, Jasper Tudor, fled to France, taking his fourteen-year-old nephew, Henry, Earl of Richmond, with him. Created Earl of Pembroke by Henry VI in 1452, Jasper Tudor was one of the few die-hard Lancastrians who refused to come to terms with Edward IV. After the death in 1456 of his elder brother Edmund, Earl of Richmond, Jasper Tudor had been entrusted with the government of Wales. Under him, the Principality of Wales was well governed and it remained solidly behind Henry VI. Although Henry VI trusted his half-brother, he never promoted him to the ministerial front bench. This may have saved Jasper Tudor's life since he never became a major figure at court and, therefore, never became a target for his Yorkist enemies. This was to change after 1471.

The devastating losses suffered by the Lancastrian nobility, together with the murder of Henry VI and death of his son Prince Edward, meant that the Tudors were one of the few families who could reasonably lay claim to the throne. This elevated their status from renegade exiles to serious political opponents. However, Edward IV's triumph in 1471 meant that the futures of Jasper and Henry Tudor looked bleak. Edward IV seemed secure on the throne and the Wars of the Roses appeared to be over. Nevertheless, in time, these Lancastrian exiles in France would become a convenient rallying-point for dissidents in England.

SOURCE G

Study Source G. Why might the artist have focused his attention on the death of Prince Edward, son of Henry VI?

Battle of Tewkesbury 1471 illustrated in a near-contemporary manuscript.

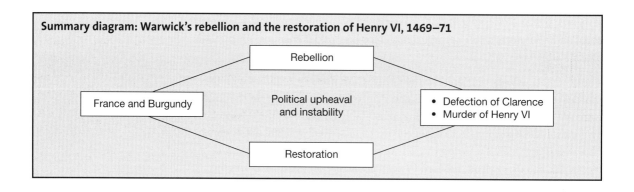

Summary diagram: Warwick's rebellion and the restoration of Henry VI, 1469–71

Rebellion

France and Burgundy

Political upheaval and instability

- Defection of Clarence
- Murder of Henry VI

Restoration

Chapter summary

In 1461 Edward, Duke of York, seized power and was crowned king. He spent the next eight years consolidating Yorkist power, the success of which rested on his ability to restore order after the chaos of the civil wars. An important element in his search for stability and continuity was his relationship with the nobility. Edward knew that some were opposed to him while others were lukewarm in their support. He had either to win them over or to impose restrictions on their political freedom.

In an effort to improve England's foreign relations, Edward's sister, Margaret, married Duke Charles of Burgundy. Edward's position was considerably strengthened when Henry VI was captured and imprisoned. To strengthen his dynasty, Edward married Elizabeth Woodville in order to have a son and heir. This marriage upset Edward IV's relations with his mentor and key adviser Richard, Earl of Warwick. Relations between Edward and Warwick steadily declined until the latter rebelled in 1469. Warwick, in concert with Edward's brother, the Duke of Clarence, defeated Edward, who fled into exile. Henry VI was restored to the throne.

 ## Refresher questions

Use these questions to remind yourself of the key material covered in this chapter.

1 How did Edward seize the throne?

2 What steps did Edward IV take to consolidate his power?

3 Why and with what results did Edward IV restore law and order in England?

4 What was the nature of Edward IV's relationship with the nobility?

5 Why was Edward's marriage with Elizabeth Woodville unpopular?

6 Why did Edward's relationship with the Earl of Warwick break down?

7 Why did Warwick rebel against Edward IV?

8 Why did Warwick restore Henry VI to the throne?

9 Why did Clarence join Warwick in opposition to his brother, the king?

10 What was the nature of Edward IV's relationship with continental Europe?

 ## Question practice

ESSAY QUESTIONS

1 'It was the weakness of Henry VI as king that explains the successful usurpation of the throne by Edward IV in 1461.' Explain why you agree or disagree with this view.

2 To what extent was Edward IV's failure to consolidate his position as king in the years 1461–9 due to his own mistakes?

3 To what extent was the ambition of Richard Neville, Earl of Warwick, the main reason for instability in England in the years 1461–71?

4 'The most important reason for Edward IV's failure to establish royal authority in the period 1461–70 was the power of the Earl of Warwick'. How far do you agree?

SOURCE ANALYSIS QUESTIONS

1 With reference to Sources 1 and 2, and your understanding of the historical context, which of these two sources is more valuable in explaining why there was a change of monarchy in 1461?

2 With reference to Sources 1–3, and your understanding of the historical context, assess the value of these three sources to a historian studying the Yorkist seizure of the throne in 1461.

SOURCE 1

From 'Whethamstead's Register' of 1459, recorded by John Whethamstead, abbot of St Albans Abbey.

When Richard of York returned from Ireland there were varied and contrary rumours amongst the people about his return. Some said that his arrival was peaceful and that he intended nothing else but the restoration of harmony among the quarrelling lords of the realm, bringing peace to the kingdom, and reforming it, by his authority. Yet others, including those who were older and wiser, suspected that he meant to act against the king for the royal crown and claim it for himself by title of hereditary right.

SOURCE 2

From 'Gregory's Chronicle' of 1461. William Gregory was mayor of London.

The King was removed from London against his will and the Duke of York declared himself king. The Queen fled to Wales but was attacked and robbed by her own servant showing how lawless times had become. From then on she travelled about in secret, fearing for her own life and for that of her son the prince. The Lords sent forged orders, supposedly from the King, demanding that she hand herself over, for they claimed that she was the reason for the opposition to their plans and that she was more intelligent than the King. The Queen, having knowledge of this, sent for help from the Earl of Somerset and the Earl of Devon urging them to come as quickly as they could with their armies. Some of the lords that came to her aid did so more out of expectation of reward than loyalty to her position.

SOURCE 3

From the 'London Chronicle' written by Matthew Gough, 1461.

On Thursday 26 February 1461 the earl of March and the earl of Warwick came to London with a great army and, on the Sunday afterwards, they gathered their army in St John's field and there were read certain articles and points in which King Harry VI had offended against the realm. Then it was demanded of the people whether Harry was worthy to reign still and the people cried 'Nay'. Then they were asked if they would have the earl of March as king and they cried 'Yea'.

CHAPTER 6

The second reign of Edward IV 1471–83

During his first reign Edward was never fully secure on the throne. He began his second reign determined to establish his dynasty and revive the power of the Crown. In a period spanning twelve years, Edward largely succeeded in restoring peace and prosperity to England. He strengthened royal government, restored the kingdom's finances and managed Parliament. He made war on France and ruthlessly cut down his enemies at home. The Wars of the Roses seemed to be at an end. These developments are examined as four themes:

★ Edward IV restored: establishing the Yorkist dynasty, 1471–83

★ The politics of rivalry: Clarence and Gloucester

★ Government and administration

★ Parliament and finance

Key dates

1471	Edward IV restored to the throne	**1475**	Edward IV invaded France. Signed the Treaty of Picquigny
1472	Edward's brother, Richard, made Duke of Gloucester		
1473	Edward signed a treaty with King James of Scotland	**1478**	Edward's brother, the Duke of Clarence, executed after being found guilty of treason
	Parliament passed an Act of Resumption	**1483**	Death of Edward IV

1 Edward IV restored: establishing the Yorkist dynasty, 1471–83

▶ *How was Edward able to restore the Yorkist dynasty?*

Edward had learnt his lesson (see Source A). There were to be no more 'over-mighty' subjects and no alternative kings, either free or in prison. The Battle of Barnet had destroyed the Nevilles as Tewkesbury had ruined the Lancastrians. Henry VI was murdered, his son was slain and Margaret of Anjou was imprisoned. To hide the truth of what he had done, Edward made it known that Henry VI had died of 'melancholy' (sadness) on hearing the news of his son's death. Edward had come to realise how powerful **propaganda** could be when

KEY TERM

Propaganda Method by which ideas are spread to support a particular point of view.

Proclamations Official or public announcements that had the power of law. These were used by the Crown as an alternative to acts of Parliament.

managed effectively. One method Edward used to ensure his message was heard and understood was by the issuing of royal **proclamations**. Proclamations were royal commands that had the force of law and they had to be obeyed. Edward's second reign would be cast in a different light, where his successes would be magnified, his failures buried and rumours scotched.

SOURCE A

Adapted from the *Warkworth Chronicle*. The contemporary chronicler John Warkworth had no doubt why Edward's first reign as king had ended so disastrously in 1469.

The [Yorkists] had expected prosperity and peace from Edward IV, but it was not to be. One battle followed another, and there was widespread disorder, and the common people lost much of their money and goods [mainly through heavy taxation]. England had been reduced to the direst poverty. Many people thought that King Edward was to blame for harming the reputation and esteem of the merchants, for, at that time, both in England and abroad, these were not as great as they had been in times past.

? Why, according to Source A, was Edward IV so unpopular after less than a decade in power?

The restoration of law and order

The personal activity and support of the king was a vital element in the process of restoring law and order. Edward was determined that he should be obeyed and for those who were slow to bend to his will there was only one outcome: punishment. When Sir John Paston, a troublesome knight from Norfolk, failed to answer two royal summons to appear before the royal council, Edward angrily announced that 'if he come not then he shall die for it'.

When Paston finally did appear before the king's council, he was flung in prison alongside the county sheriff, Sir John Howard, for his inability to execute efficiently the king's command. Royal agents were keen to cultivate an image of a well-informed king who took a personal interest in all matters connected with law and order within his realm.

Thomas Neville (c.1429–71)

Son of William Neville (c.1410–63), Earl of Kent and Baron Fauconberg, an English nobleman and soldier who helped put Edward IV on the throne in 1461. Thomas served Richard, Earl of Warwick, as captain of his navy and took part in the attempt to reinstate Henry VI. He was beheaded at Middleham in Yorkshire. His severed head was set on London Bridge.

Opposition was crushed and rebellion, where it broke out, was ruthlessly put down. The first victim of this policy was **Thomas Neville**, the Bastard of Fauconberg, who stirred up rebellion in Kent. In an echo of Cade's rebellion (see pages 65–6), Fauconberg issued a call to arms to the people of Kent to resist the usurper Edward IV and demand reform of the government. The rebellion failed and a little later Fauconberg was executed. The fact that Fauconberg had been supported by the pro-Neville governor of Calais meant that Edward would need to stamp his authority on this important English outpost.

Trouble in Wales

The most serious threat to the new Yorkist regime came from Wales. Here, the Lancastrians continued to defy Edward and they scored a notable success when they captured and executed a die-hard Yorkist, Roger Vaughan of Tretower. However, by October 1471 the final Lancastrian strongholds in Wales, Pembroke and Tenby, had surrendered. Edward used Parliament to issue acts of attainder (see page 80) against those who had dared defy him. As the representative body of the king's subjects (the landowners and the politically active, at least), Parliament offered the Crown a means of claiming that it had the support and consent of the people.

Pardon and reconciliation

For those Lancastrians who submitted, such as the lawyer **Sir John Fortescue**, the cleric John Morton and former diehards like Sir Richard Tunstall (see box on page 98), Edward offered pardon and the possibility of future reward so long as they remained loyal. For the remainder, those Lancastrians considered too dangerous to negotiate with, such as Jasper Tudor, Earl of Pembroke, and John de Vere, Earl of Oxford, there was no pardon, only persecution and exile. So, by these means, a combination of reward and punishment, Edward secured his throne, established his dynasty and restored law and order. There were to be no more serious plots or rebellions during his reign.

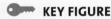

KEY FIGURE

Sir John Fortescue (c.1394–c.1480)

An English lawyer recommended for his wisdom, gravity and uprightness. He is said to have been favoured by Henry VI, who appointed him chief justice of the king's bench. He held office during the reign of Henry VI but was attainted of treason in the first Parliament of Edward IV. He was later pardoned.

John Morton

1420	Born in Dorset, the son of a minor landowner
1473	Appointed to government office as master of the rolls (responsible for government records)
1475	Appointed to negotiate the Treaty of Picquigny with France
1479	Promoted and appointed Bishop of Ely
1485	Appointed to Henry VII's ruling council
1486	Promoted to Archbishop of Canterbury
1493	Promoted to Cardinal by Pope Alexander VI of Rome
1500	Died

John was born in Dorset, the son of Richard Morton, a minor landowner of Milborne St Andrew. He was educated at Balliol College, Oxford, where he graduated with a doctorate in canon (Church) law.

Morton began his career in the late 1440s as an ecclesiastical lawyer practising in the Church. In 1461 he declared his support for the Lancastrians and was forced to flee abroad after defeat at the Battle of Towton. In 1470 he returned to England where he made his peace with Edward IV. His government career began under Edward IV, who promoted him to high office. In 1474 Morton was appointed by Edward IV to go on an embassy to Hungary. His diplomatic career continued in 1475 when he was sent to negotiate the Treaty of Picquigny with France. The king's trust in Morton was such that in 1479 he chose him to tutor Prince Edward. Richard did not trust Morton and when he seized the throne in 1483 the cleric was arrested and imprisoned. He escaped to join Henry Tudor in exile. On Henry VII's accession, Morton joined his council and two years later, in 1487, he was appointed lord chancellor and took charge of the government.

Morton had served Edward IV loyally but he was especially trusted by Henry VII and, as a result, was able to exert a great deal of influence over the Crown and shape government policy. He was an experienced administrator and possessed the leadership qualities Henry VII needed to run his government. Morton's control and management of the Church ensured that it and its senior clerics remained loyal to the Crown.

Richard Tunstall

1427	Born into the Lancastrian gentry
1452	Knighted by King Henry VI
1460	Fought at Battle of Wakefield
1461	Fought at Battles of St Albans and Towton. Escaped to Scotland and continued to fight for Lancastrian cause
1468	Surrendered and sent to Tower of London
1470–1	Returned to royal service under restored Henry VI
1472	After Edward IV's return to throne, arrested and pardoned again, thereafter served the Yorkist kings
1485	Pardoned by Henry VII and became sheriff of Yorkshire
1492	Died

Sir Richard fought with distinction for Henry VI in the Wars of the Roses. He fought at Wakefield, St Albans and Towton.

After Towton he escaped with Margaret of Anjou to Scotland. He led an army of Scots across the border and was with the Lancastrians at Hedgeley Moor. He went on the run with Henry VI, but when the king was captured Tunstall fled to Harlech and continued the fight from there. He eventually surrendered in 1468 and was sent to the Tower of London. After a year in custody he was pardoned.

When Henry VI returned to the throne in 1470–1 Tunstall was taken back into royal service. Following Henry VI's deposition and murder, Tunstall was again arrested and imprisoned. In 1472 he was pardoned for a second time and taken into Edward IV's service. He served the Yorkist kings, Edward IV and Richard III, loyally thereafter. He was pardoned in 1485 and employed by Henry VII as sheriff of Yorkshire until his death.

KEY TERMS

Retaining Employing or maintaining armed servants and/or private armies.

Livery The giving of a uniform or badge to a follower.

Maintenance The protection of a follower's interests.

Indenture of retainder Agreement or contract between a master and his servant where the latter is retained in service.

Livery and maintenance

One of the most serious problems that Edward IV had to contend with was that of illegal **retaining**, often referred to as **livery** and **maintenance**. This was a common practice whereby great lords recruited those of lesser status as their servants or followers to help advance their ambitions (by force of arms if necessary) and to increase their own prestige. They were given a uniform on which was emblazoned their master's crest or coat of arms showing whom they served.

Kings had permitted this practice to exist because it could help the magnate to control his particular locality and provided a quick and efficient way of raising an army, both of which were important to the king. Apart from these obvious uses, it was felt to be only natural that a nobleman should be attended by a retinue of men of respectable social status. However, the Wars of the Roses had shown that these retainers could also create lawlessness at both local and national levels, and could be used as an effective force against the king.

Retainers could also be used as armed forces to threaten those who opposed their master. Such behaviour occurred to settle not just the lord's disputes but also those of his servants. This was because the lords had obligations to their followers, the **indenture of retainder** requiring them to be good lords to their men. However, it was originally meant to be based on principles of honour and mutual respect, with a lord accepting the responsibility of advancing and protecting the interests of his servants, but not where they clashed with the law. Thus, maintenance was now all too often abused, with nobles frequently going beyond the bounds of 'good lordship'.

Controlling the nobility

In order to control the nobles and restrict their ability to raise and employ armed servants, Edward attempted to pass legislation to deal with this practice. The Parliament of 1468 had passed a statute prohibiting retaining except for domestic servants, estate officials and legal advisers. However, this law was largely ineffectual because it allowed the continuance of retaining for 'lawful service'. Therefore, during Edward's reign, nobles continued to maintain their retinues, using the excuse that they were doing so within the existing framework of the law. Indeed, as many as 64 new indentures of retainder for one nobleman alone were recorded for the years 1469–82 alone. Historians now believe that Edward intended this statute merely as a public relations exercise and passed it to soothe the fears of the House of Commons but with no intention of strictly adhering to it.

Foreign policy

Foreign policy was a major concern for Edward. The intervention of both France and Burgundy, and to a lesser extent Scotland, in the Wars of the Roses convinced the king that a coherent policy was necessary, if only to prevent future foreign interference in English affairs.

Relations with France

Edward sought to revenge himself on Louis XI because the French king had supported both Warwick and Margaret of Anjou. This would be neither forgotten nor forgiven by Edward. Indeed, Edward had cause to complain to Louis over more recent events, when the French king had given refuge to Jasper and Henry Tudor in 1471. However, Edward's more immediate concern was the defence of England's last continental possession, Calais. In Edward's military mind, the best form of defence was attack and for the next four years, 1471–5, he planned his invasion of France and prepared his armed forces for war.

Relations with Scotland

Before he could go to war, Edward had to ensure that England was free from the threat of a Scottish invasion. So, in October 1473, he negotiated a treaty with James III of Scotland. Under its terms Edward agreed to offer his four-year-old daughter, Cecily, in marriage to James's six-month-old son. To sweeten the deal, Edward also offered a cash sum of 20,000 crowns (just over £4000, which is about £2 million in today's money) to the cash-strapped Scottish king. The betrothal would last until both parties were of marriageable age – fourteen – so that Edward could be reasonably assured of peace for at least a decade.

In the event, the truce lasted until 1481, when Edward determined to invade Scotland after the Scots had broken the terms of the truce by raiding the border towns of northern England. The honour of leading the English army into Scotland was given to Edward's brother Gloucester. The invasion was a spectacular success. Edinburgh was captured and the Scottish army retreated rather than fight. Having made his point, and to avoid a costly occupation, Gloucester withdrew his army and the Scottish king came to terms with Edward.

Relations with Burgundy and Brittany

Prior to his invasion, Edward also tried hard to make alliances with Burgundy and Brittany. He hoped to exploit their fear and hatred of the French and persuade them to join him as allies in a war against France. He met with only limited success. The Dukes of Burgundy and Brittany were reluctant to stir up the French against them. They were well aware of how wealthy and mighty the French had become since their defeat of England in the Hundred Years' War. Only when the French threatened them did they turn to Edward IV for support. For example, in 1472, Edward sent 3000 archers to aid Brittany when the French invaded. When the French invasion failed, a grateful Francis II, Duke of Brittany, signed a treaty with Edward promising 8000 troops if the English should invade France. Duke Charles of Burgundy, Edward's brother-in-law, proved less willing to support the English but he did all he could to avoid confrontation with the French. The result was the Treaty of London, which was ratified in 1474, in which it was agreed that, if either nation was attacked by the French, the other would go to its aid.

Edward IV invades France

By 1475 Edward IV was ready to invade. Leading an army of over 12,000 well-trained and well-armed men, Edward made his way from Calais into the heart of northern France. However, it was not long before Edward's triumphal invasion began to go wrong. The troops promised by Duke Francis of Brittany did not turn up and the French army kept its distance, hoping to draw the English further away from their supply lines. Frustrated by his failure to force the French into a decisive battle, Edward sued for peace. Louis XI was relieved since he wanted to avoid a prolonged war, and so the two kings met at Picquigny on the Somme, where they signed a treaty in August 1475. Edward did rather well out of the treaty. Besides agreeing a seven-year truce, Louis paid Edward £15,000 immediately, to be followed by an annual pension of £10,000. Thereafter, until the end of his reign in 1483, Edward had little to fear from the French or any other of his continental neighbours.

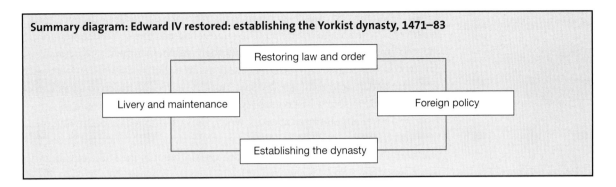

Summary diagram: Edward IV restored: establishing the Yorkist dynasty, 1471–83

 # The politics of rivalry: Clarence and Gloucester

▶ *Why did Clarence and Gloucester quarrel?*

Background

The most serious problem Edward faced during his second period as king was the political rivalry that flared up between his brothers. After his restoration, Edward was determined to control royal patronage. The main beneficiaries were members of his own family, especially Richard, Duke of Gloucester (see Figure 1.6 on page 17). Gloucester was given all of Warwick's confiscated properties in northern England and was entrusted with the government and defence of that region. His wealth and power were thereby considerably enhanced by the generosity of the king.

Clarence

Clarence, too, was treated generously by the king and, in spite of his earlier betrayal, he was restored to all of his properties (including Warwick's estates in southern England) and was even given substantial additional lands confiscated from the Courtenay Earls of Devon. All Edward asked of his brother in return was that he give up the Percy properties, which he had been granted during the first reign, so that they could be restored to the family. However, rather than being grateful for his good fortune, Clarence resented the favour shown to his younger brother, Richard. Aware of Clarence's resentment, Edward hoped to satisfy him by granting him the lands of the Earldom of Richmond (the earl, Henry Tudor, was in exile), which he had originally given to Gloucester.

Gloucester

With Clarence satisfied, Edward now had the task of compensating Gloucester. When Gloucester requested the king's permission to marry Anne Neville, Warwick's daughter, Edward agreed. This angered Clarence, who feared that the couple, once married, might lay claim to his Warwick properties. Clarence tried to prevent the marriage but failed. The quarrel had become so bitter and public that the king summoned the dukes to put their case before the king's council. The matter was settled when Clarence was assured that his Neville properties were safe and, as if to reinforce this fact, the king agreed to his creation as Earl of Warwick and Salisbury. Not content with his victory, Clarence also pressed the king for a royal appointment at court, which Edward granted by bestowing on him the office of great chamberlain of England in May 1472. The man forced to part with this office and make way for the appointment of the Duke of Clarence was none other than Gloucester.

SOURCE B

Adapted from the *Crowland Chronicle*, which reported the quarrel between Clarence and Gloucester in 1472.

Richard, Duke of Gloucester, sought Anne in marriage. This proposal did not suit the views of his brother, the Duke of Clarence, who had previously married the elder daughter of the earl of Warwick. Such being the case, he caused the damsel to be concealed, in order that it might not be known by his brother where she was; as he was afraid of a division of the earl's property, which he wished to come to himself alone in right of his wife, and not to be obliged to share it with any other person. However, the astuteness of Gloucester so far prevailed that he discovered the young lady in the city of London disguised in the habit of a cookmaid; upon which he had her removed. In consequence of this, such violent dissensions arose between the brothers and so many arguments were put forward on either side, in the king's presence, who sat in judgement in the Council chamber, that all present, and the lawyers even, were quite surprised that these princes should find arguments in such abundance to support their respective causes. At last their most loving brother, King Edward, agreed to act as a mediator between them.

> **?** Why might Source B suggest that Clarence and Gloucester were equally responsible for the quarrel between them?

The row rumbled on and Edward was forced to intervene in November 1473 when Parliament passed an Act of Resumption, under whose terms both Clarence and Gloucester were deprived of all the estates they held by royal grant. This was clearly designed to remind the feuding dukes of the power and authority of the Crown. The estates were not restored until a further act of Parliament was passed in May 1474.

Clarence's conflict with the Woodvilles

Clarence failed to heed the lesson. He temporarily set aside his feud with Gloucester and turned his attention to the Woodvilles. He made known his resentment at the growing power of Anthony, Earl Rivers, in Wales and the queen's increasing influence at court. Clarence's feud with the queen surfaced when his wife died in 1476 and he looked to secure a foreign bride. Clarence's choice was Mary, daughter of Charles the Bold, Duke of Burgundy, but Edward refused to agree to the match. The king feared becoming drawn into Burgundy's continental problems if the marriage went ahead. Edward also felt that the marriage of an English nobleman with the daughter of a foreign ruler might set a dangerous precedent. Clarence's ambition knew no bounds. Thwarted in his Burgundian adventure, for which he blamed the queen, he now looked to the daughter of the king of Scotland. Edward again refused to sanction the marriage.

It was becoming clear to Edward that Clarence's aspirations were verging on the over-mighty and he had to be stopped. It has been claimed that Gloucester was mainly to blame for persuading his brother, the king, to arrest and convict Clarence of treason, but the queen, Elizabeth Woodville, also bears some responsibility. She was convinced that Clarence was conspiring against the succession of her son, Prince Edward. In February 1478 Clarence was tried for high treason, found guilty and executed. The ultimate responsibility for his death rested with Edward IV.

After Clarence's death, Edward drew ever closer to his brother, Gloucester. Over the next five years (1478–83) Gloucester's power grew and he was entrusted with the government of the north of England.

SOURCE C

Adapted from Dominic Mancini, *The Usurpation of Richard the Third*, 1483. Mancini was an Italian visitor living in England in 1482–3. He described the events leading to the death of Clarence in 1478.

The Queen remembered the insults to her family and that it was said she was not the legitimate wife of the king. Thus she concluded that her offspring by the king would never come to the throne, unless the Duke of Clarence was removed; and of this she easily persuaded the king. The queen's alarm was intensified by the character of Clarence which would make him appear worthy of the crown: besides he possessed such mastery of popular eloquence that nothing upon which he set his heart seemed difficult for him to achieve. Accordingly whether the charge was fabricated, or a real plot revealed, Clarence was accused of conspiring the king's death by means of spells and magicians. When the charge had been considered before the court, he was condemned and put to death. The mode of execution preferred in this case was, that he should die by being plunged into a jar of sweet wine.

How does Source C suggest that Clarence was framed for a crime he might not have committed?

Summary diagram: The politics of rivalry: Clarence and Gloucester

Politics

Clarence vs Gloucester

Rivalry

Government and administration

▶ *How effective was Edward IV's government of the kingdom?*

Governing the kingdom

Edward IV had found that governing the kingdom was no easy task. War, lawlessness and disorder had combined to make the task of government that much harder. Edward was determined to re-establish the rule of law and 'good governance' after the dislocation and strife caused by the Wars of the Roses. Fortunately for Edward, he had one huge advantage in that the Crown continued to command respect. This reverence for the institution of monarchy had survived the war but, in order to ensure its continuance, Edward enlisted the aid of the Church. In an age without a police force, the Church was the only organisation with the means and the authority to reach every community in the realm. England and Wales were divided into parishes and every parish had a church and every church a priest. The Church and the majority of its clergy were respected and it preached peace and obedience. To disobey the king was the same as disobeying God. By careful use of Parliament, proclamation and pulpit Edward strove to make the Crown's authority felt in all parts of his kingdom.

The Church as an instrument of control

Rulers were seen as God's deputies on earth, acting as guardians of His people. Therefore, any threat to the ruler or to the internal peace and security of the nation was interpreted as a challenge to God. By the same reasoning, when a ruler like Richard III lost his life in battle it was thought to be an indication of God's displeasure with His deputy whose authority had rightly been challenged. Rebellion or any type of civil unrest was abhorrent to most people from nobleman to peasant because, as Sir Thomas Elyot wrote, 'Where there is any lack of order needs must be perpetual conflict'. This meant that the worst fear for most people was an outbreak of general anarchy.

The late Middle Ages were littered with examples of this type of unrest: the Peasants' Revolt in 1381 against the poll tax, the conflict over the crown in the middle of the fifteenth century, and Cade's rebellion in 1450 (see pages 65–6), stemming mainly from the ill-feeling caused by what was regarded to be an unfair or unjust rule. On all these occasions, resentment built up slowly and people took up arms only as a last resort. There was little violence for the sake of violence.

The fates of Richard II and Henry VI (see pages 15–16 and 71–2) acted as a warning to Edward IV of how an unscrupulous or incompetent monarch could be overthrown. The Wars of the Roses showed him that, with the support of the Church, his subjects would quickly return to obedience if he and his bishops proved capable of asserting the right degree of authority. In the absence of a police force and standing army, Edward recognised the Church's important role in maintaining social stability and in ensuring people's loyalty.

Council and councillors

Unlike Henry VI, Edward was an energetic king determined to establish strong government at the heart of his kingdom. The structure and machinery of central government did not change, but Edward brought a new dynamism to its operation.

The centre of medieval English government was the king himself and the men he chose to sit on his council. Therefore, the king's council remained the key co-ordinating body and was staffed by the monarch's most trusted advisers. The primary functions of the council were the same under Edward IV as they had been under Henry VI:

- to advise the king on matters of state
- to administer law and order
- to dispense justice
- to draw up and issue letters, warrants and proclamations.

The composition of the council was not fixed and, in times of crisis, might include upwards of 125 members but, in practice, Edward relied on a core group of between ten and fifteen men.

These royal councillors consisted of a mix of Yorkists and former Lancastrians, the latter including men like John Morton and Sir Richard Tunstall. In fact, Morton, promoted to Bishop of Ely by the king, came to earn Edward's 'secret trust and special favour'. In the opinion of Richard III's modern biographer, the historian Charles Ross (writing in 1983), Morton's 'rapid rise in the royal service is a good example of Edward's political realism in making use of talent wherever he found it'. Edward was not afraid to promote men of humble backgrounds so long as they had the administrative and bureaucratic talent to serve him. Some of the most prominent members of the king's government, and household, were loyal Yorkists such as John Fogge, John Scott, William Parr and Thomas Vaughan.

Noble councillors

Edward did not neglect the nobility and higher clergy, many of whom filled the chief offices of state such as chancellor, treasurer and keeper of the **privy seal**. For example, when the king was absent he appointed his treasurer, Henry Bourchier, Earl of Essex, to chair meetings of the royal council. The key difference between Edward IV and previous kings was that he was not prepared to appoint members of the nobility to serve him on his council simply because of their status and title. Unless they possessed some skill or particular talent, they were unlikely to be summoned to serve on the king's council. For example, Edward's cousin, the Duke of Norfolk, and his brother-in-law, the Duke of Suffolk, were never appointed to the council.

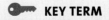 **KEY TERM**

Privy seal The king's personal seal was a substitute for his signature and was used to authenticate documents.

Besides offering the king advice and helping to shape and direct policy, the councillors were responsible for law and order, finance, trade and a host of other duties that occurred on a daily basis. While the king could concentrate on making decisions, his councillors could focus on carrying them out.

Regional or provincial councils

There was no radical difference between Edward's two reigns in the way he governed the outlying regions of the kingdom. The policies that had served him reasonably well in his first reign were pursued in the second. In the 1460s Edward entrusted the government of the regions to powerful men, like Neville in the north and Herbert in Wales. Edward still relied on a core group of powerful men but they were more closely tied to him through blood rather than by title. The regional councils are a good example of how Edward extended the authority of central government into the provinces. By relying on trusted servants and members of his own family to enforce his will in the outlying areas, Edward was ensuring that personal government was felt in even the remotest parts of his realm.

The North

The Council of the North was based in the city of York. Its primary function was to ensure the good governance of a lawless and undisciplined region that was too remote from London to be effectively controlled from there. In addition, it was given responsibility to oversee the defence of the northern counties of England, which were vulnerable to attack from a potentially hostile Scotland. This northern council was closely linked to the king's council, enjoying similar administrative and judicial power to enable the law to be enforced swiftly and efficiently, and it was ultimately subordinate to the king. Control of the north and the council that governed it was given over to Edward's trusted younger brother, Richard, Duke of Gloucester.

SOURCE D

Adapted from the *Crowland Chronicle*, reporting on Richard, Duke of Gloucester's successful campaign against the Scots in 1483.

The Duke of Gloucester, being Warden of the West Marches, by his diligent labours has subdued a great part of the west borders of Scotland to the great surety and ease of the north parts of England. The King grants that the Duke shall have to him and his heirs male the Wardenship of the West Marches of England and also the making and ordaining of the sheriff of the county of Cumberland.

? What does Source D reveal about the relationship between Edward and his brother Richard?

SOURCE E

Study Source E. Why was the seat of the Welsh government located in an English border town?

An engraving of Ludlow Castle, seat of the Council of Wales (nineteenth century, unknown artist).

Wales and the March

Wales consisted of the Principality (made up of what later became the counties of Anglesey, Caernarfon, Merioneth, Cardigan and Carmarthen) and the Marcher Lordships (made up of some 50 semi-independent lordships located either side of the modern boundary between England and Wales). Ruled since 1301 by the king's eldest son, the Principality was acknowledged to be separate from England, in consequence of which, its shires did not return members to Parliament. The lordships of the March were relics of the piecemeal Norman/English conquest of Wales in the two centuries between 1066 and 1282. These had their own systems of government, different from each other and from that of England. Both the Principality and the lordships owed allegiance to the king of England and he had ultimate control over them, but the absence of continuous effective rule from London (see page 2) had resulted in frequent outbreaks of disorder caused by criminals. This disorder was particularly marked during the Wars of the Roses, when it was famously said that, 'the king's writ [written orders] did not run' in the March.

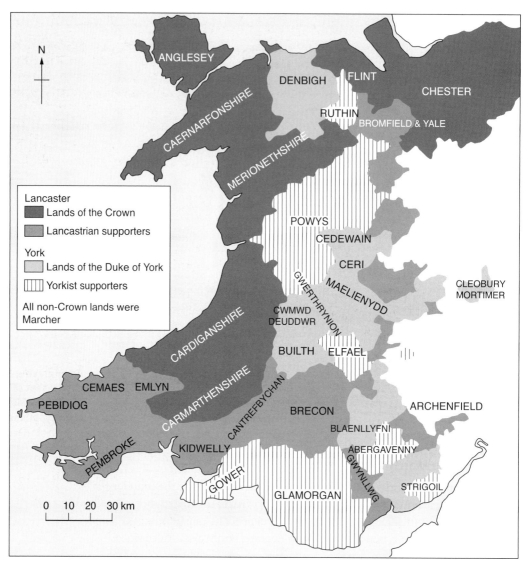

Figure 6.1 The complex division of Wales into Marcher and Crown Lordships, and the Counties of the Principality. Why did English kings find Wales so difficult to govern?

With the freedom to raise troops for war, the Marcher lords were drawn into the dynastic conflict on the side of both Yorkists and Lancastrians. Until Edward IV established a council to govern Wales in 1471, no attempt had been made to weld together into a single system the counties and lordships of the Principality and the March, or to abolish the privileges of the individual Marcher lords. Although Edward never succeeded in either respect, his council had improved the situation in Wales by restraining what one contemporary called 'the wild Welshmen and the evil disposed persons from their accustomed murders and outrages'.

Wales and the Woodvilles

In 1471 Edward entrusted the government of Wales and the March to his wife's family, the Woodvilles, with Anthony, Earl Rivers, at their head. This angered William Herbert's son and heir, the second Earl of Pembroke, who expected to succeed his father (killed in 1469) as ruler of Wales. In fact, Edward went further for he also forced the younger Herbert to give up his lands in Wales and exchange the Earldom of Pembroke for the less significant (and less wealthy) Earldom of Huntingdon. Apart from Ireland, it seems that the king was determined not to allow any magnate to establish a hereditary title to any office or region of his realm.

Ireland

As king of England, Edward was also lord of Ireland. However, the island was not ruled in a conciliar way like Wales and the north. The king appointed a **lord lieutenant** – George, Duke of Clarence, held the post between 1472 and 1478 – but this was an honorary position. The actual work of governing Ireland was carried out by a **lord deputy**.

Ireland presented a far more difficult problem to Edward than any of the other outlying areas of the kingdom (apart from the period of peace between 1472 and 1478). Only in the English Pale (see page 2), a narrow band of territory about 50 miles (80 km) long to the north and west of Dublin, was the king's authority really felt. In the rest of the island, the effective rulers were the Anglo-Irish lords (descendants of English settlers who had come over earlier in the Middle Ages) and Irish chieftains, who held power by exploiting and controlling family loyalties. Of these, the most important families were the Geraldines, Earls of Desmond and Kildare, and Butlers, Earls of Ormond.

No English king had been able to dominate these lords, not even Richard, Duke of York, in the 1450s, and so Ireland remained very much a law unto itself. At the beginning of Edward's reign, the Geraldine family held the most important offices, those of lord deputy and chancellor of Ireland. Edward found that in order to avoid conflict it was easier to bestow these positions on the Irish leaders. Thus, Gerald FitzGerald, eighth Earl of Kildare succeeded his father, a prominent Yorkist, as lord deputy of Ireland in 1477, a post he held until 1513.

The Midlands and the south-west of England

William Lord Hastings was given charge of the Midlands, and the queen's son from her first marriage, Thomas Grey, Marquis of Dorset, was entrusted with the care of the south-west of England. There was room for local magnates like the Percy Earls of Northumberland and the Stanleys of Cheshire to exercise royal authority, but not everyone was included in Edward's attempt to share out power in the localities. The second Earl of Pembroke, the Duke of Buckingham and the king's brother, Clarence, were left largely on the sidelines.

The most frequent problems in the regions that Edward had to face were the disputes between members of the nobility. His favoured method of dealing with

KEY TERMS

Lord lieutenant In times of peace the office had no function beyond the ceremonial, such as the state opening of the Irish Parliament, but in times of war it was responsible for raising and leading the Crown's forces in Ireland.

Lord deputy The effective ruler of Ireland invested with the power and authority to govern the Irish on behalf of the Crown.

this was to travel around the country intervening in disputes and personally hearing cases in the common law courts. Because of his energy and efficiency, this system proved quite successful until his death in 1483.

Local government

While great magnates dominated regional government at local or county level, the gentry ran the local administration. During the Wars of the Roses the system of local government had almost completely collapsed and Edward IV had no choice but to attempt to rebuild this structure almost from scratch. He tried to do this in three ways:

- He appointed Crown commissioners to travel the country to support local law enforcement.
- He appointed only the most trusted gentry to serve as justices of the peace (JPs) and sheriffs.
- He appointed powerful local magnates to control particular regions or areas.

In order to increase his authority throughout his kingdom, Edward increased the size of his household. This enabled him to draw on a larger pool of servants, from whom he appointed Crown commissioners, JPs and sheriffs. In effect, he created a two-tier system whereby his household was divided into those servants who attended him at court on a daily basis and those who could do so only on an occasional basis. The fact that the latter could not attend the king on a regular basis at court did not matter to Edward. His aim was to mark out publicly these men as servants of the Crown and thereby extend the reach and influence of the royal household into the localities.

The sheriffs

Local government was carried out in each of the 50 or so counties of England by a complex network of local officials who were directly responsible to the king. He communicated with them through written orders known as writs, and their work was checked by senior judges or **justices of assize** and **commissioners of 'oyer et terminer'** at regular intervals. The two most important royal officials in each county were the sheriff and the JP. The sheriff was appointed annually from among the local landowners in each county and was the closest thing fifteenth-century England had to a police officer. He kept the king's peace and was responsible for the arrest, detention and prosecution of criminals.

The sheriff was as much a judge as a law officer and he had his own court where he administered the king's laws. He also organised and supervised elections to Parliament and MPs could only take their seats if they had the sheriff's writ to confirm their election. The sheriff also had a military role, being responsible for supervising the **muster of the militia**. Although sheriffs continued to play an important role in local justice and administration they gradually gave way to the JPs. For example, as early as 1461 Edward IV had transferred the criminal jurisdiction of the sheriff to the JP.

 **KEY TERMS**

Justices of assize Senior judges who dealt with serious crimes and dispensed justice in the king's courts, which were held twice a year in each county.

Commissioners of 'oyer et terminer' Literally meaning to 'hear and determine' (also to summon and to dissolve), these commissions were given the power to investigate any crime or disturbance thought serious enough for the Crown to become involved.

Muster of the militia The muster was a method by which local representatives of the Crown called up fit and able men to serve in the army. The militia was an army of conscripts raised to serve the king for a set period of time.

The justices of the peace

The JPs were appointed annually from among the local landowners, the average number commissioned for a county being about eighteen. The local bishop would usually head the list of those appointed, with the lay landowners following in strict order of social precedence (see below). Although some of the largest landowners were sometimes chosen to be JPs, it was the knights and squires who carried out the majority of the commission's duties on a daily basis. JPs were responsible for the maintenance of public order and for implementing the various statutes of a social and economic nature, such as those concerned with the regulation of wages and the guilds. They also acted as judges, ready to dispense justice to deal with the criminals brought before them by the sheriffs. Four times a year they were required to meet in Quarter Sessions so that they could try those accused of the more serious crimes – except treason, which was left to the council to investigate.

Although JPs had the authority to pass judgment on all other crimes, more difficult cases were traditionally passed to the Assize Courts. The assizes were sessions held twice a year in each county in England by professional judges acting under special commission from the Crown. The position of JP did not carry with it any form of payment, because, as property owners, it was in their own interests to carry out this role. In fact, it had always been felt that to offer rewards for such work would be inappropriate as it was thought to be a natural part of the landowning classes' responsibility to ensure an effective system of law enforcement.

Th., Lord Audley of Walden, Chancellor; D. of Norfolk, Treasurer; D. of Suffolk, President of Council;

J. Russell, kt., Keeper of Privy Seal; B. of Coventry & Lichfield, President of Council in the Marches of Wales;

B. of St. Davids; Walter, Lord Ferrers; Nich. Hare, Ed. Croft, Rice Mansel, J. Vernon, kts; J. Pakington; Th. Holte;

David Brooke; J. ap Rice; Rich. Hassall; p. Rich. Devereux; Th. Jones; J. Phillip; W. Morgan of Kidwelly;

Jenkin Lloyd of Kidwelly; Jas. Williams; Walter Vaughan; Griffith Dwnn; J. Lloyd senior; W. Morgan of Llangathen;

Th. Bryne; Howel ap Rither; Th. Hancock; David Vaughan.

Figure 6.2 Example of a royal commission with a list of those appointed by the Crown. This example is for Carmarthenshire and is dated 12 March 1543.

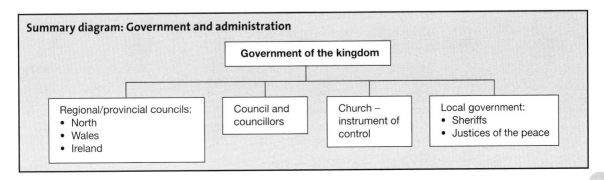

Summary diagram: Government and administration

Government of the kingdom

Regional/provincial councils:
- North
- Wales
- Ireland

Council and councillors

Church – instrument of control

Local government:
- Sheriffs
- Justices of the peace

Parliament and finance

▶ *How successfully did Edward IV manage Parliament and the kingdom's finances?*

King, Lords and Commons

In the fifteenth century the government of England was clearly the responsibility of the king and his council. Parliament played no regular part in the maintenance of law and order. It met only to grant taxes and to pass laws, and it was in this latter role that it was of use to the king in controlling his subjects. Parliament was the meeting of the two Houses of Lords and Commons. The importance of the Lords can be gauged by where they met: the Lords were invited to meet in a room in the royal palace of Westminster, while the Commons were denied access to the palace and were instead summoned to meet in the nearby, and more humble, chapter house of Westminster Abbey.

The Lords was made up of two groups: the **Lords spiritual** (the archbishops, bishops and abbots, the heads of the more important monasteries) and the **Lords temporal** (the peers).

Tradition gave the Lords greater authority than the Commons, which is why important legislation had first to be introduced in the House of Lords.

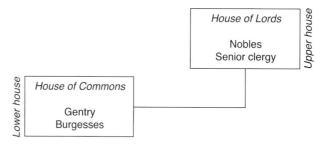

Figure 6.3 Diagram showing the working relationship between the Houses of Parliament.

The Commons was composed of MPs chosen by a very limited electorate made up of those who possessed considerable property. Two members were elected to represent each **county** and **borough**. The men sitting in the lower house were typically drawn from the local gentry representing the counties, while merchants and lawyers represented the boroughs. In practice, Parliament was the meeting of the king, his councillors and the Lords. The Commons met while the king discussed issues with the Lords, but he only spoke to them, and they with him, through the Speaker. Although the Speaker was elected from among

 **KEY TERMS**

Lords spiritual Senior clergy such as bishops, abbots and the two archbishops who sat in the House of Lords.

Lords temporal Nobility – barons, viscounts, earls, marquises and dukes – who sat in the House of Lords by hereditary right.

County The key unit of administration in England. The kingdom was divided into counties, very much like today, to make the government of England easier. Each county elected representatives to sit in Parliament.

Borough A town with a royal charter granting privileges for services rendered, usually dating well back into the Middle Ages.

the membership of the Commons, in reality he was almost always a royal nominee. Parliament was summoned only when there was a special need, and when it met the meeting normally lasted only a few weeks.

Edward's pliant Parliament

The Parliaments of Edward IV's reign were both pliant and compliant to the king's wishes. They were summoned on only six occasions during his reign, meeting for little more than 84 weeks in total. In order to enact legislation dealing with lawlessness and disorder, Parliament was summoned to help unify the kingdom by crushing those who challenged the authority of the Crown. For example, the Parliament of 1478 was summoned to secure the attainder of the king's brother Clarence (see page 101). In all, Parliament issued 113 attainders on the king's enemies. However, the majority of the statutes passed by Edward's Parliaments were concerned mainly with finance and the economy. In fact, one of the key features of Edward's use of Parliament was the passing of Acts of Resumption. Four such acts were passed, bringing back into the hands of the Crown estates that had been granted out to favourites by previous monarchs. The accumulation of estates added greatly to the regular income of the king.

Finance

A major limitation facing Edward in the management of his financial affairs was that throughout the Middle Ages English kings had been expected to **'live of their own'**. They formally swore to do so at their coronation. This meant that they had to manage on the regular income that came to them annually as monarchs and as landowners. It has been calculated that in order to govern the kingdom effectively the Crown had to spend in the region of £50,000 per annum (£25 million in today's money). The income Edward IV inherited from his predecessors did not match this expenditure. To make up the difference, Henry VI had borrowed money but Edward now had to pay off these debts, settle the interest, and raise enough money to help pay for the cost of governing the realm.

The king knew that any proposal to raise money from new sources would arouse suspicion and probably provoke opposition. The king could not ask Parliament for a grant (additional taxation) except in unusual circumstances, such as war. There was always the fear that, if additional direct taxes were demanded frequently, rebellion might follow. This might explain why, in 1467, Edward told the Commons that 'I purpose to live upon my own, and not to charge my subjects but in great and urgent causes concerning … the defence of them, and of this my realm.' He was determined to prove that the existing sources of income available to the Crown could be expanded sufficiently to give him the financial strength he needed.

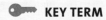

KEY TERM

'Live of their own'
A contemporary term meaning monarchs should pay their own way, using money from their own pockets, rather than burden the state with taxes.

Study Source F. Why was the chronicler impressed by Edward IV's financial policies?

SOURCE F

Adapted from the *Crowland Chronicle*, praising Edward IV's financial management of the kingdom's finances.

The king turned all his thoughts to the question, how he might in future collect an amount of treasure worthy of his royal station out of his own substance, and by the exercise of his own energies. Throughout all ports of the kingdom he appointed inspectors of the customs, men of remarkable shrewdness, but too hard, according to general report, upon merchants. The king himself also having procured merchant ships put on board the finest wools, cloth, tin and other goods, and like a private individual living by trade, exchanged merchandise for merchandise. He also examined the registers and rolls of Chancery, and exacted heavy fines from those whom he found to have intruded and taken possession of estates without prosecuting their rights in form required by law. Added to this there was the yearly tribute of ten thousand pounds due from France. All these particulars, in the course of a very few years, rendered him an extremely wealthy prince.

Sources of income

It is possible to make a distinction between two separate types of revenue that rulers received at this time. These were 'ordinary' and 'extraordinary' revenue. It is important to clarify what is meant by both these terms:

- Ordinary revenue came in every year, in different amounts, from Crown lands and custom duties. It also included the profits of justice (fines) and feudal dues on lands held in return for military service. It was largely on the income from ordinary revenue that kings were expected to 'live of their own'.
- Extraordinary revenue came from the subject's obligation to help the king in time of need. By the fifteenth century this usually meant taxation levied in Parliament, which came as a 'grant' that the king had to request from his subjects. Less frequently it could also be money which came to the king as feudal overlord, a right which belonged to any feudal lord; this was known as a 'feudal aid' and was levied on specific occasions. For example, if the king was captured and held to ransom, he could demand an aid to raise the money necessary to obtain his release. It could also be money raised by borrowing from his richer subjects in an emergency, or gifts from other rulers, often granted as part of a favourable peace treaty. The Church too was asked to contribute, through clerical taxes, towards the financial well-being of the kingdom.

Ordinary revenue

There were four principal sources of income available to Edward:

- Crown lands. The most important way in which Edward increased his ordinary revenue was by maximising the income from Crown lands. This was partly because they were collected more efficiently. These lands included

Edward's own personal estates as Duke of York, the lands of the Duchy of Lancaster and all properties confiscated or forfeited for treason such as those owned by Clarence. It has been estimated that by 1482–3 Edward was enjoying an annual income of £30,000 (£15 million in today's money).

- Customs duties. At the beginning of Edward's reign customs duties on imported goods made up the largest part of the king's income. The principal duties or taxes levied were on wool, leather, cloth and wine, but many of these (such as the duties on cloth) had not changed since 1347. Under Edward the average annual yield had increased from £25,000 to a little over £35,000 (£12.5–17.5 million in today's money) owing to his encouragement of trade and a tighter administration, which cut down on fraud and embezzlement.
- Profits of justice. As head of the judicial system Edward was, therefore, entitled to its profits. The law courts yielded income in two ways: fees and fines. The fees paid by those involved in a court case for the legal writ or summons necessary for any case to begin, which provided the king with a continuous income that varied between £300 and £800 per annum (£150,000–400,000 in today's money). The fines were levied by the courts as punishment. The amount raised by fines was irregular because it depended on the number of cases heard in court but the sums involved were often considerable.
- Feudal dues. Feudal dues were paid by those who held land from the king. As the greatest feudal lord, the king was owed certain obligations by his tenants-in-chief (those holding their land directly from the king), just as they in turn were owed the same duties by their tenants. These included wardship, **marriage**, livery and the fine known as '**relief**'. It is thought that Edward collected around £550 per annum (£275,000 in today's money) from this source of income.

Extraordinary revenue

Edward could count on four principal sources of income:

- Parliamentary grants. The main form of extraordinary revenue was a sum of money granted by Parliament for emergencies, such as war or defence. Edward was aware that his subjects were prepared to help him when the national interest was threatened and he was careful not misuse this right. He was reluctant to tax unless absolutely necessary. This was because the Lancastrian kings had encountered difficulties with Parliament which, realising it had a bargaining position, had demanded restrictions on the king's power in exchange for grants of money. The usual type of tax levied was a **national assessment**. This was a fifteenth (in the countryside) and a tenth (in the towns) of the value of a subject's income. Several of these grants could be levied in one session of Parliament, depending on how much the king needed. In 1473, the fifteenth and tenth brought in £30,000 (£15 million in today's money). This was not really satisfactory as it was based on town and county assessments carried out by royal commissioners, which were out of date and, therefore, did not tap anything approaching all

KEY TERMS

Marriage The royal right to arrange the marriage, for a fee, of heirs and heiresses.

Relief A payment the king received on the transfer of lands through inheritance.

National assessment Country-wide system of assessing people's wealth for purposes of taxation.

the available taxable wealth of the country. So, when he needed money to finance the French war, in 1472–3, Edward tried another method – a form of income tax. Unfortunately for him, it failed. Only half of the expected £60,000 (£30 million in today's money) was collected. This directly assessed **subsidy** was viewed with suspicion and hostility in Parliament, which insisted that no precedents were to be set and no returns were to be recorded.

- Loans and benevolences. The king could also rely on loans from his richer subjects in times of emergency. However, if these were not forthcoming Edward turned to a different method called the **benevolence**, a kind of forced loan. Introduced in 1475, when he was preparing to invade France, the benevolence was a general tax more far-reaching than the fifteenth and tenth. Subjects were asked to contribute to the king's expenses as a sign of their goodwill towards him at a time of crisis. If not overused, it was an effective way of raising money. Edward collected nearly £22,000 (£11 million in today's money) by this method.
- French pension. The Treaty of Picquigny brought the Crown an annual pension of £10,000.
- Clerical taxes. The king was entitled to tax the Church but Edward did not fully exploit this source of income. In an effort to keep the Church on his side, he made no demands other than that **Convocation** collect and pay the usual clerical tenths. Between 1472 and 1475 the Church paid Edward £48,000 (£24 million in today's money).

Financial administration

In order to manage the collection of money more efficiently, Edward turned his mind to reform of the financial institutions.

Exchequer and Chamber

Since the twelfth century the centre of the Crown's financial administration had been the Exchequer. This had two functions:

- to receive, store and pay out money
- to audit the accounts.

To organise this department and prevent fraud and embezzlement, there was a complex hierarchy of officials. Although it worked in an honest and reliable fashion, it did have flaws. The system was slow and cumbersome, outstanding sums often taking years to collect, and audits being equally behind time. It was because of this that Edward developed the Chamber as his chief financial department.

The Chamber was a more informal and flexible system, partly because it had not been involved in royal finance for so long. It had originated from the accounting system used on the estates of the great nobles, who appointed officials called **receivers** and **auditors** from within their household to run certain groups of their estates in their absence. Edward IV had been familiar with this practice on the Yorkist estates, so, when he became king in 1461, he applied it to the royal estates. He had chosen to use the King's Chamber, the innermost part of the king's household, to handle his finances in an attempt to exert more personal control over what happened. The result was that money now went directly to the king and not through an inefficient bureaucracy.

There is no doubt that Edward deserves credit for the way he made the financial system more flexible. As a result of the more efficient methods of identification and collection of revenue, the Crown's income rose to just under £70,000 per annum (£35 million in today's money). Although still underfunded when compared with some of the wealthier European monarchies, Edward had succeeded in restoring the Crown's finances to the extent that he could now act independently of both Parliament and the nobility. His greatest achievement was that he died solvent, the first monarch to do so for more than a century.

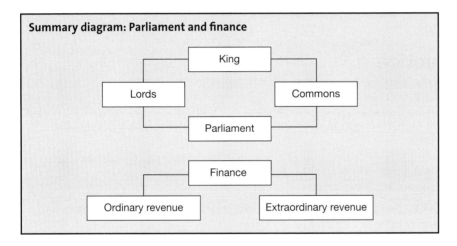

Summary diagram: Parliament and finance

King

Lords — Commons

Parliament

Finance

Ordinary revenue — Extraordinary revenue

Chapter summary

In 1471 Edward returned from exile and achieved victory in battle to reclaim the throne. Warwick was killed and Henry VI was executed soon after. Having restored his authority, Edward set about the task of establishing his dynasty. He healed the rift between himself and his brother, Clarence, whom he restored to power within the kingdom. However, he had to manage the tense relationship between his brothers, Gloucester and Clarence. In order to strengthen his hold on power, Edward initiated reforms in government and administration. Control at the centre was extended to the outlying regions of the kingdom through trusted noble governors. Edward also made use of Parliament by exploiting its power to make laws and raise revenue. Finance was a key issue for Edward, who was determined to improve the Crown's revenue. Parliament passed an Act of Resumption which enabled Edward to reclaim royal lands previously granted out. In foreign policy, Edward enjoyed some notable successes such as the signing of a treaty with King James of Scotland and the conclusion of a treaty (Picquigny) with France. A more ruthless Edward was determined to crush any signs of opposition and in 1478 Clarence was executed for treason.

Refresher questions

Use these questions to remind yourself of the key material covered in this chapter.

1 How was Edward IV able to reclaim the throne in 1471?

2 Why was Henry VI put to death?

3 Why did Edward pardon his brother Clarence for his earlier betrayal?

4 What caused Gloucester and Clarence to quarrel?

5 To what extent was Edward responsible for the tense relationship between his brothers?

6 How successful was Edward's foreign policy?

7 Why was Clarence executed by Edward IV?

8 How successful was Edward's government of the kingdom?

9 What was the nature of Edward's relationship with the nobility?

10 Why did Edward IV seek to reform the nation's finances?

11 What was the reason for and how effective was the Act of Resumption?

 Question practice

ESSAY QUESTIONS

1 'The murder of Henry VI was the main reason why Edward IV was able to re-establish his power in 1471.' Assess the validity of this view.

2 To what extent was the rivalry between George, Duke of Clarence, and Richard, Duke of Gloucester, the main reason for instability in England in the years 1468–78?

3 How successful was the foreign policy of Edward IV?

4 'The most important reason for Edward IV's success in establishing royal authority in the period 1471–83 was the absence of "over-mighty subjects".' How far do you agree?

SOURCE ANALYSIS QUESTION

1 Study Source 1. Assess the value of the source for revealing the character of King Edward IV and the reasons for the downfall of the Duke of Clarence. Explain your answer using the source, the information given about its origin and your own knowledge about the historical context.

SOURCE I

From the Act of Attainder of George, Duke of Clarence, in January 1478. This Act was passed by Parliament to confirm the Duke's conviction for treason. Parliament was dominated and controlled by Edward IV.

The King declares his tender love for George, Duke of Clarence, the large grants he has given him, and how he has forgiven his brother's past offences. The Duke of Clarence, nevertheless, has shown no increase in love to the King but has grown daily in hatred. He hath not ceased to plot new treasons; for the Duke hath falsely and traitorously intended the destruction and disinheriting of the King and his heirs. He has sought to undermine all the good rule of this realm, by force using both forces from this realm and abroad.

To bring about this wicked purpose, he attempted to find the means to induce the King's subjects to withdraw their affections from the King by many contrived ways. The Duke was fully intending to raise himself and his heirs to the throne and crown of England, and clearly intending to put aside for ever from the said crown and throne, the King and his heirs. To achieve this he intended falsely to say, that the King our sovereign lord was a bastard and not born to reign.

And in addition, the Duke obtained and got a charter under the great seal of King Henry VI, who claimed to be, but was not in right, King of this land. In the deed were contained all such agreements recently made between the said Duke and Margaret, who being the wife of King Henry called herself Queen of this land; the charter stated that, if the said Henry and his first born son died without male heirs, then the said Duke and his heirs should be King of this land. This charter of agreement the said Duke hath kept secret, not letting the King Edward IV, his brother, to have any knowledge thereof. In this he caused harm to the King's true subjects, the better to achieve his false purpose.

For which reasons the King, by the advice and assent of this present Parliament assembled, and by the authority of the same, commands that George, Duke of Clarence, be convicted and attainted of high treason and shall forfeit from him and his heirs for ever the honour, estate, dignity, and name of Duke and all his properties and possessions.

CHAPTER 7

'Triumph and tragedy': Richard III 1483–5

If Henry VI's weak and irresponsible rule resulted in civil war, Richard III's seizure of the throne led to rebellion, battle and ultimately his own death. Richard had the potential to be a good, if not a great, king but his unpopularity encouraged claimants like Henry Tudor to challenge him for the crown. These developments are examined as four themes:

★ Richard, Duke of Gloucester, and the overthrow of Edward V

★ Challenges to Richard's rule

★ Politics and government in the reign of Richard III

★ Bosworth Field and the overthrow of Richard III

Key dates

1483	**9 April**	Death of Edward IV and succession of Edward V
	30 April	Richard and Buckingham took custody of Edward V
	16 June	Edward V's brother handed over to Richard and Buckingham
	20 June	Lord Hastings executed

1483	**26 June**	Parliament petitioned Richard to take the throne
	6 July	Richard III crowned king
	2 Nov.	Buckingham rebelled and was executed when rebellion failed Princes disappeared
1484	**Jan.**	Parliament met
1485	**Aug.**	Battle of Bosworth; Richard killed

 ## 1 Richard, Duke of Gloucester, and the overthrow of Edward V

▶ *Why was Richard able to seize the throne?*

Richard, Duke of Gloucester: historical reputation

Richard is, arguably, one of England's most controversial monarchs, whom history has seen fit to label a monstrous deformed villain. History's assessment of Richard owes much to the pen of the Tudor playwright William Shakespeare, whose play *Richard III* portrayed him as evil personified. 'The royal Satan', as historian Roger Lockyer (writing in 1993) so memorably described him, has that rare distinction of being the only monarch with what some have described as a modern-day 'fan club' – the Richard III Society – dedicated to clearing his name.

The primary reason why the Richard III Society believes his name needs clearing is because of his supposed involvement in the murder of his young nephews, Edward and Richard, the so-called Princes in the Tower. Their disappearance and disposal during his seizure of power have cast a shadow over his short reign ever since. Indeed, so dark has that shadow become that he is credited with being involved in the murders of others: his elder brother George, Duke of Clarence, Prince Edward, the seventeen-year-old son of Henry VI, Henry VI himself and even his own wife, **Anne Neville**, Countess of Warwick. Yet on each count there is insufficient evidence to accuse him, let alone convict him, because:

- insufficient physical evidence has survived
- Tudor propaganda has influenced our perception of him
- he divided opinion even in his own day
- in the 500 years since his death some of the stories surrounding him have solidified into apparent fact.

Richard, Duke of Gloucester: the man behind the myth

Richard's birth and upbringing were entirely conventional and give no hint of the controversies to come. He was the youngest of the three sons of Richard, Duke of York, and was still a child when his elder brother Edward seized the throne in 1461. Until recently there had been no firm evidence to suggest that he was the deformed hunchback portrayed by Tudor historians and Shakespeare. However, the discovery of Richard's skeleton under a Leicester car park (the site of the Greyfriars monastery) in 2012 revealed a man suffering from scoliosis or curvature of the spine. Although Richard was five foot eight inches (173 cm) tall, the curvature would have made him appear much shorter. Thus, the descriptions of Richard as being 'little of stature, ill-featured of limbs, crooked back' were not simply literary inventions to signify evil: they contained some truth. While he may not have been kind-hearted or unambitious, there is nothing to suggest that he was anything like the 'malicious, wrathful, envious' creation of Shakespeare (see Source A, overleaf). Yet, we have to acknowledge, that, despite the propaganda efforts of the modern Ricardians, he may have been.

Richard entered the political world in 1469 in the midst of national crisis. The seventeen-year-old duke witnessed at first hand Warwick's betrayal and the deposition of his brother Edward. These episodes may have affected him deeply and influenced his thinking. They may have taught him to strike first rather than be struck down by his enemies. This may help to explain why he was complicit in the judicial murder of Henry VI (1471) and execution of Clarence (1478). It may be argued that these acts were pragmatic and necessary solutions to problems that threatened him and his brother's security. Yet it should be

KEY FIGURE

Anne Neville (1456–85)

Anne was the daughter and co-heiress of Richard Neville, Earl of Warwick (the 'Kingmaker'). She first married Edward, Prince of Wales, the son and heir of Henry VI. After his death she married Richard, Duke of Gloucester. Her elder sister Isabel was married to Richard's brother George, Duke of Clarence. Anne became queen when Richard III ascended the throne in June 1483. Anne predeceased her husband by five months, dying in March 1485. Her only child, Edward of Middleham, predeceased her.

Lancastrians, Yorkists and the Wars of the Roses 1399–1509

SOURCE A

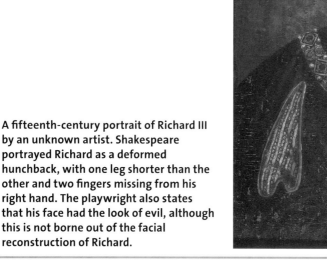

Study Source A. How far does the portrait of Richard III match Shakespeare's description?

A fifteenth-century portrait of Richard III by an unknown artist. Shakespeare portrayed Richard as a deformed hunchback, with one leg shorter than the other and two fingers missing from his right hand. The playwright also states that his face had the look of evil, although this is not borne out of the facial reconstruction of Richard.

remembered that Richard did not act on his own initiative (see pages 91 and 103) but was following the instructions issued by his brother, the king.

Edward and Richard: king and protector

Historians have long debated the reasons why Richard acted so aggressively in seizing the throne from his nephew. Having been so loyal to Edward IV throughout his reign, Richard's behaviour and actions in the months following his brother's death seem all the more puzzling. When Edward IV's brother, George, Duke of Clarence, joined the Earl of Warwick in rebellion against the Crown, Richard remained loyal. He distinguished himself at the Battle of Barnet in 1471, led the war against Scots in 1480 and recovered the city of Berwick from Scotland in 1482. Richard was handsomely rewarded by Edward, who granted him vast estates and royal offices in the north of England.

Edward had all but set his brother up as a prince of the north by granting him, in January 1483, a great **palatine** comprising the counties of Cumberland and Westmorland. In a gesture of generosity rarely displayed by English kings, including even the profligate Henry VI, Edward invested his brother with the power and freedom to conquer Scottish territory to add to his palatinate. Without realising it, Edward had elevated Richard to a position of power that warrants the description of an 'over-mighty subject'. Arguably, Richard's power and influence were greater than those enjoyed by Warwick back in the early 1460s.

Richard and the Woodvilles

Clearly, Richard was a man in whom the king had complete trust but this caused resentment at court, where the queen's family, the Woodvilles (see pages 82 and 86–7), became jealous and fearful of his growing power. Richard probably distrusted, if not hated, them also and it is notable that he rarely ventured to court in the last four years of his brother's reign (see Source B). Nevertheless, so long as Edward remained alive to keep the peace between them, the balance of power within the political establishment could be maintained. However, Edward's sudden and unexpected death in April 1483 upset the balance of power and put Richard's future in doubt. Richard was in the north when his brother died, making it impossible for him to influence, much less control, events at court. The Woodvilles, and their supporters, were keen to isolate Richard and deny him access to his nephew, Edward V.

Edward V was in the care of his uncle Anthony, Earl Rivers, at Ludlow and it was proposed to bring him to London at the head of an army. On arrival, Edward would be quickly crowned king so as to prevent any interference from Richard or anyone else who might oppose them. As King Edward V, the twelve-year-old monarch could then exercise his authority, in consultation with the Woodville-dominated council, to appoint a Protector of his choice to rule the kingdom while he grew to manhood. Unfortunately for the Woodvilles, they were unpopular and had few friends among the nobility. The first to turn against them was William, Lord Hastings, who had been one of Edward IV's most loyal friends and servants. He advised Richard to make his way to court as quickly as possible to support him in opposing the Woodville plan to seize control of the crown.

SOURCE B

Adapted from Dominic Mancini, *The Usurpation of Richard the Third*, 1483. Mancini was an Italian visitor living in England in 1482–3. He described the events leading to Richard's seizure of the throne in his book.

The problem of the government during the royal minority was referred to the consideration of the barons. Two opinions were discussed: one that the Duke of Gloucester should govern, because Edward in his will had so directed. The

KEY TERM

Palatine A territory ruled by a person invested with princely or royal authority.

Study Source B. To what extent was Richard III justified in regarding the Woodvilles as a threat to his safety and security?

other was that the government should be carried on by many persons among whom the duke should be accounted the chief. All who favoured the queen's family voted for this proposal as they were afraid that, if Richard took upon him the crown or even governed alone, they, who bore the blame for Clarence's death [see page 103], would suffer death or at least be ejected from their high estate.

Richard as Lord Protector

Edward IV's will has not survived, so it is impossible to say whether he intended his brother to rule on behalf of his son as Protector. However, the fact remains that as the only living close male relative, Richard had a better claim to that role than anyone else. Richard wrote to the queen to reassure her that his intentions were honourable and that his sole objective was to see his nephew safely upon the throne. Rivers appears to have believed Richard, and the two men met at Northampton. All appeared well, but following a night's revelry, Richard, aided by Henry Stafford, Duke of Buckingham, had Rivers, Sir Thomas Vaughan, Sir Richard Grey and other key members of the young king's household arrested, after which he took Edward into custody.

KEY TERM

Sanctuary A place of safety within the walls of a religious institution such as a monastery or church.

Bewildered and confused, the Woodvilles, led by the queen's son, the Marquis of Dorset, tried to raise an army but failed. They fled into **sanctuary** at Westminster Abbey when they realised there was nothing they could do to stop Richard entering the capital. Richard's success and conduct thus far – he promised to have Edward V crowned on 22 June – had earned the respect if not the whole-hearted support of the nobility. John, Lord Howard, Francis Lord Lovel and Henry Percy, Earl of Northumberland, were among the few that openly threw in their lot with Richard.

The overthrow of Edward V

Historians remain sharply divided in their opinion of the nature and cause of the usurpation. Some argue that it was carefully planned and skilfully executed by Richard and his chief supporter, the Duke of Buckingham. Others view Richard's seizure of the throne as a haphazard sequence of ill-considered impulsive reactions. The most widely held view is that Richard acted on the spur of the moment to prevent the queen's family from robbing him of the position of Protector. Richard feared that the Woodvilles might try to destroy his power by turning his nephew against him. He may even have feared assassination. Therefore, self-preservation rather than ambition is thought to be the most likely cause of the usurpation.

The events leading up to the usurpation began on 4 May 1483 when Richard, Buckingham and Edward V entered London in triumph. Within days, the king's council had confirmed Richard's appointment as Protector and had invested him with greater powers than those enjoyed by his father, Richard of York, during his protectorates in the 1450s. Almost immediately, Richard promoted Buckingham, Howard and Lovel to positions of power within the government. This would certainly have worried the Woodvilles, but it seems also to have caused Hastings some anxiety. Whether or not they combined to plot Richard's downfall is not known, but, on 10 June, the Protector requested the military assistance of his northerners to crush what he called a Woodville conspiracy to 'murder and utterly destroy' himself and Buckingham.

Three days later, on 13 June, Hastings was arrested and accused of treason; a week later he was executed. On the same day, 20 June, Edward IV's most loyal and trusted ecclesiastical servants, Thomas Rotherham, Archbishop of York, and John Morton, Bishop of Ely, were removed from the council. Thomas, Lord Stanley, was also arrested but later released by Richard. On 16 June a reluctant Thomas Bourchier, Archbishop of Canterbury, was pressured into forcing the queen to release her younger son, Richard, from sanctuary so that he could join his brother in the Tower of London.

The *Crowland Chronicle* records the usurpation

Following these events, Richard of Gloucester and Buckingham, according to the Crowland chronicler, 'did thereafter whatever they wanted'. Written at the Benedictine Abbey of Crowland, in Lincolnshire, the *Crowland Chronicle* is an important source for events in late fifteenth-century England. The section that covers the years 1459–86 was written in April 1486 (after Henry Tudor ascended the throne as Henry VII) by someone who had access to information from the court of Richard III. Some historians believe that the author was John Russell, Bishop of Lincoln, who was Richard's chancellor for most of his reign (until Richard dismissed him in July 1485) but others conclude that the work was written by an unknown Crowland monk.

On the day appointed for Edward's coronation, sermons were preached at St Paul's Cathedral calling into question Edward IV's legitimacy and that of his son. The carefully orchestrated event was clearly designed to declare publicly Edward IV a bastard while at the same time highlighting Richard's legitimacy and claim to the throne. Four days later, on 26 June, in another choreographed event, a petition was submitted by Parliament calling on Richard to take the crown. On 6 July 1483 Richard was crowned king of England. The overthrow had taken a little over eight weeks. The princes lodged in the Tower were never seen alive again and it is thought they had been disposed of some time between July and October 1483.

SOURCE C

Study Source C. Why did the artist deliberately romanticise the fate of Edward and Richard?

'The Princes in the Tower'. This nineteenth-century painting of the princes by J.E. Millais is perhaps the most famous depiction of the unfortunate royal siblings.

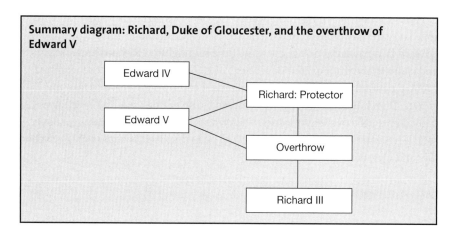

Summary diagram: Richard, Duke of Gloucester, and the overthrow of Edward V

Challenges to Richard's rule

▶ *Why did nobles such as Buckingham challenge Richard's rule?*

The elimination of rivals

All was not to run smoothly for Richard. He lost much support in the aftermath of his usurpation or overthrow of Edward V, and court and country became disunited again. Richard's ruthless disposal of his enemies, the leader of the Woodvilles, Earl Rivers, and former allies, William, Lord Hastings, deeply divided the nobility. Earl Rivers was accused of plotting to remove Richard as Protector and make his sister, the queen, regent. Hastings shared Richard's fear and distrust of the Woodvilles, so he supported the execution of Earl Rivers. He also supported Richard's protectorship but he would not agree to the deposition of Edward V. Hastings' refusal to support the usurpation made him a threat to Richard, so he was eliminated.

Buckingham's rebellion

The Duke of Buckingham, who was ruthlessly ambitious, encouraged Richard to dispose of Earl Rivers and Hastings and to seize the throne for himself. Buckingham disliked the Woodvilles and was jealous of Hastings' power and

Henry Stafford, Duke of Buckingham

1455	Birth of Henry Stafford
1458	His father was killed at the Battle of St Albans
1460	Created Duke of Buckingham, aged four, by Henry VI
1472	Became a member of the king's council
1478	Served briefly as lord high steward of the Kingdom of England
1483	Supported Richard's usurpation of the throne
1483	Executed for treason

Henry's parents were Humphrey Stafford, Earl of Buckingham, and Margaret Beaufort, daughter of Edmund Beaufort, Duke of Somerset (killed in battle on 22 May 1455). He had a distinguished bloodline, being descended from Edward III. In 1465 the ten-year-old Henry was married to Katherine Woodville, sister of Edward IV's queen.

In 1471 Edward IV appointed him to serve on a series of royal commissions of the peace. His role was to help pacify resentful Lancastrians after the battles of Barnet and Tewkesbury. In 1475 Buckingham was commissioned to serve as a captain of soldiers in Edward IV's campaign against the French. In 1476 he may have fallen out with Edward IV for he was dismissed from the council and kept out of office. On the death of Edward IV, Buckingham allied himself to Richard, Duke of Gloucester. He was instrumental in putting Richard III on the throne. In 1483 he rebelled against Richard III, and was captured and executed.

Buckingham was among the best connected and most powerful noblemen in the kingdom. He was ambitious for power and during Richard III's reign he became an 'over-mighty subject'. Buckingham's attempt to remove Richard III from the throne weakened the king's position, which encouraged usurpers like Henry Tudor to challenge for the crown.

influence. Edward IV had judged Buckingham to be dangerously untrustworthy and kept him out of power. Buckingham struck up a friendship with Richard which saw them plot the usurpation together. Buckingham was lavishly rewarded and became the most powerful noble in the kingdom. However, within four months of Richard's coronation, this 'over-mighty' subject rebelled. He failed and was executed in November 1483.

SOURCE D

Adapted from the *Crowland Chronicle*, which records the rebellion of the Duke of Buckingham in 1483.

A public proclamation was made, that Henry, Duke of Buckingham, who at this time was living at Brecon in Wales, had repented of his former conduct, and would be the chief mover in the rebellion, while a rumour was spread that the sons of King Edward had died a violent death, but it was uncertain how. Accordingly, all those who had agreed to join this insurrection, seeing that if they could find no one to take the lead in their designs, the ruin of all would speedily ensue, turned their thoughts to Henry, earl of Richmond, who had been for many years living in exile in Brittany. To him a message was sent, by the Duke of Buckingham, by advice of the lord bishop of Ely, John Morton, who was then his prisoner at Brecon, requesting him to hasten over to England as soon as he possibly could, for the purpose of marrying Elizabeth, the eldest daughter of the late king, and, at the same time, together with her, taking possession of the throne.

? How does Source D suggest that Richard's enemies did not fully trust Buckingham?

The reasons for Buckingham's rebellion

The reasons for Buckingham's rebellion are a matter for debate. For example, there has been a great deal of speculation about the fate of the two young sons of Edward, the 'Princes in the Tower', neither of whom was seen alive again. Some historians have argued that their murder by Richard may have turned Buckingham against him. Others have accused Buckingham of murdering them himself. The real reason why Buckingham rebelled will probably never be known but the following may have been possible motives:

- dissatisfaction with the rewards and position of power given to him by Richard
- conversion to Henry Tudor's cause (for self-preservation)
- ambition to take the crown for himself.

Of course, Buckingham could simply have been swept along with the rising tide of opposition to Richard, so that self-preservation was the primary motive for his rebellion. It is known that rising resentment among the gentry classes in the southern counties of England had begun to grow. In common with many of the southern-based nobility, the gentry of Kent, in particular, resented the power and influence of Richard's **'northern affinity'**. The result was a rebellion in which Henry Tudor, the exiled Lancastrian claimant to the crown, was invited

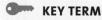

KEY TERM

'Northern affinity'
Used to describe the noble and gentry supporters of Richard III who came from northern England.

to take the throne. He had been in exile in Brittany and France for over twelve years but had still been able to communicate with Buckingham, who now pledged his support.

In light of the events in Kent and Henry Tudor's preparations to land in England at the head of an army, Buckingham might have reasoned that Richard III's days were numbered and that he himself should be seen to support the winning side. In the event, his judgement on Richard was misplaced: Lord Howard crushed the rising in Kent while the king dealt swiftly and ruthlessly with the rebels. Henry Tudor's invasion did not took place, for, on hearing the news of Buckingham's failure, the fleet, hampered by bad weather, turned back to France.

Richard and the nobility

It has been said that only under-mighty kings have over-mighty subjects, but this does not apply to Richard III, who was anything but 'under-mighty'. Nevertheless, Richard's relationship with the Duke of Buckingham points to a dependency that reveals the weakness of his position. The success of Richard's kingship relied on maintaining the loyalty of a small group of powerful nobles:

- Henry Stafford, Duke of Buckingham
- John, Lord Howard
- Henry Percy, Earl of Northumberland
- Thomas, Lord Stanley
- John de la Pole, Earl of Lincoln
- William Herbert, Earl of Huntington.

As his reign wore on, Richard came increasingly to rely on the support of John, Lord Howard, whom he created Duke of Norfolk as a reward for crushing the Kent rebellion. As for the others:

- Buckingham had rebelled and been executed.
- Henry Percy, Earl of Northumberland, gradually grew resentful at Richard's failure to confirm him as his successor in the north.
- Lord Stanley's loyalty had to be secured by Richard's taking of his eldest son, George, as a hostage.
- Lincoln and Huntington offered their support and were rewarded with positions on the council, but for much of the reign the latter remained lukewarm.

The bulk of Richard's core support came from northerners, men such as Sir Richard Ratcliffe and Sir William Catesby, which made him unpopular in the south. This southern resentment of northern interference in the affairs of state and the operation of patronage is expressed in **William Collingbourne**'s famous rhyming couplet:

> *The Cat, the Rat and Lovel our dog*
> *Rule all England under the* **Hog**

 KEY FIGURE

William Collingbourne (c.1436–85)
Collingbourne was a Wiltshire landowner and commissioner of the peace. He opposed the usurpation of Edward V. He sided with Buckingham and corresponded with Henry Tudor. He was arrested and convicted of treason. A contemporary reported that having been hanged Collingbourne was cut down immediately and his 'entrails were then extracted and thrown into the fire, and all this was so speedily done that when the executioners pulled out his heart he spoke and said, "Oh Lord Jesus, yet more trouble"'!

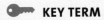 **KEY TERM**

Hog Refers to Richard's emblem, the white boar.

The Hog (Richard) did his best to widen his support base but he met with limited success. In return for his not ungenerous patronage, a few nobles, such as Walter Devereux, Lord Ferrers, John Brooke, Lord Cobham and Lord Henry Grey of Codnor, offered their service, but many were unwilling to commit to a usurper.

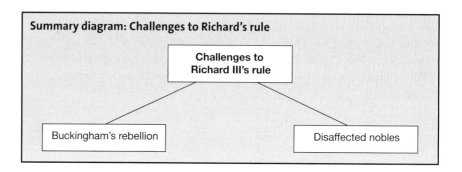

Summary diagram: Challenges to Richard's rule

3 Politics and government in the reign of Richard III

▶ *How able a king was Richard?*

Richard III and the government of England

The government of medieval England was in the hands of the king and whomever he chose to advise him and to sit on his council. It was an age of personal monarchy. This meant the country prospered or stagnated depending on the ability of the ruler. Richard proved to be a capable and energetic king. He was determined to stamp his authority on the kingdom by promising to outlaw corruption, restore peace and reform the legal system. He participated in government and moved around the kingdom to show himself to his subjects. He was also prepared to retain, and reward, talented councillors who had served his brother. Of the 54 councillors employed in Richard's government, 24 had once been in service to Edward IV. Richard was also prepared to innovate if the reason for doing so was sufficiently strong. In July 1484 he transformed his household council into a more formal Council of the North with full powers to govern the region on behalf of the king. Its first president was John de la Pole, the Earl of Lincoln. More significantly, the king founded a new body called the Council of Requests and Supplications, which was intended to help poor people in search of justice.

SOURCE E

Adapted from the *Rous Roll*, written by John Rous between 1483 and 1485. Rous was a contemporary historian and author of two books, the *History of England* and the *History of the Earls of Warwick*.

The most mighty prince Richard by the grace of God king of England and of France and lord of Ireland all avarice [greed] set aside, ruled his subjects in his realm full commendably, punishing offenders of his laws, especially extortioners and oppressors of his commons, and cherishing those that were virtuous; by the which guidance he got from God and the love of his subjects rich and poor and great praise of the people.

Study Source E. Why might historians question the reliability of Rous's praise of Richard III's rule?

Restoring the Crown's authority

In 1471 Sir John Fortescue (see page 97), chief justice of the king's bench under Henry VI, wrote *The Governance of England*, in which he offered Edward IV advice on how to restore the Crown's authority, political strength and stability. Fortescue identified two major problems and the means to deal with them:

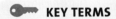

KEY TERMS

Retrenchment Cutting down on expenditure.

Re-endowment Reinvestment, or finding other ways of raising money for the Crown.

- The financial weakness of the Crown. To solve this problem, Fortescue advocated **retrenchment** to halt the decline in royal revenue and **re-endowment** to increase the monarchy's income.
- The increasing power of the nobility. To combat the power of the nobility, especially the 'over-mighty' subject, Fortescue advocated a code of strict discipline mixed with reward and punishment.

When Richard became king he tried to follow this advice. He sought stability by continuing the financial policies of his brother Edward IV and raised much needed revenue from the forfeited estates of people attainted for treason. This enabled Richard to grant revenues worth around £12,000 (£6 million in today's money) per annum as rewards for loyal service. He also tried to improve the efficiency of revenue collection in Crown lands. Although he did not rule long enough to solve the financial weakness of the Crown, Richard had introduced a measure of stability and efficiency in collection of royal revenue.

Richard hoped to stabilise the government by recruiting the nobility. He won many of them over by offering financial rewards, grants of land and important offices. Although this added to his financial problems, he thought that gaining noble support was worth the risk. He relied on the likes of the Duke of Norfolk, the Earl of Huntington and the Earl of Lincoln to advise him in council and provide stability in the provinces. The execution of Buckingham showed that he was not afraid to punish nobles who betrayed him. Although most of his support came from northern lords, it is a measure of his success that no English peers declared their support for Henry Tudor until after the Battle of Bosworth.

Richard III's Parliament

Richard's only Parliament has been held up as an example of how great a king he might have been had he been given the time. Meeting in January 1484, Parliament was required to fulfil five basic aims:

- To ratify Richard's claim to the throne.
- To pass legislation leading to the attainder of 114 traitors and the confiscation of their lands.
- To enact reforming legislation to end the abuse of power by local officials.
- To improve the operation of justice in local courts.
- To tighten up the rules on those chosen for jury service and to end benevolences or forced loans.

Richard also offered individuals the opportunity to submit private bills to Parliament, mainly in connection with disputed property rights. Although short lived, Richard's Parliament hints at the direction in which the king wished his government to go – down the path of reform.

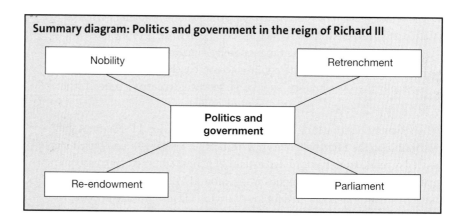

Summary diagram: Politics and government in the reign of Richard III

 Bosworth Field and the overthrow of Richard III

▶ *Why did Bosworth lead to the overthrow of Richard III?*

The road to Bosworth

It is important to remember that Henry could never have contemplated invading England without financial and military assistance from abroad. Charles VIII of France was willing to provide this in the hope that it would distract Richard III from sending help to Brittany. This would enable the French to annex the duchy. Henry set sail, in ships provided by the French, from Harfleur on 1 August

1485. He was accompanied by between 400 and 500 loyal exiles who had joined him, and at least 1500 French soldiers. Although half the French troops lacked quality, the remainder were tough mercenaries hired to provide some military professionalism to the army's ranks.

The expedition sailed for Wales, hoping for a good reception in Henry's homeland. He landed at Mill Bay near Dale in Pembrokeshire on 7 August and marched northwards along the Cardiganshire coast, turning inland through the Cambrian mountains and along the River Severn to the border with England. By 12 August Henry had won over Rhys ap Thomas, the most influential landowner in south Wales, with the promise of the Lieutenancy of Wales should Richard be defeated. According to one eyewitness, Thomas brought with him 'a great band of soldiers' some 800 strong. From north Wales, Henry was joined by William ap Gruffudd, who led the largest of several contingents, totalling some 500 men.

Henry reached Shrewsbury on 15 August with an army swollen to around 5000 men, mainly Welsh recruits, but could not hope to win a battle unless he obtained more support from the English nobility. Henry's main hope lay with two brothers – his stepfather, Thomas, Lord Stanley, and Sir William Stanley – whose lands included much of north Wales, Cheshire and the Borders. They sent money, but did so secretly since Richard held Lord Stanley's eldest son, George, as a hostage to ensure his father's good behaviour. However, Henry was confident enough of their support to march further into England, gaining the additional support of Gilbert Talbot, the powerful uncle of the Earl of Shrewsbury, and 500 of his men.

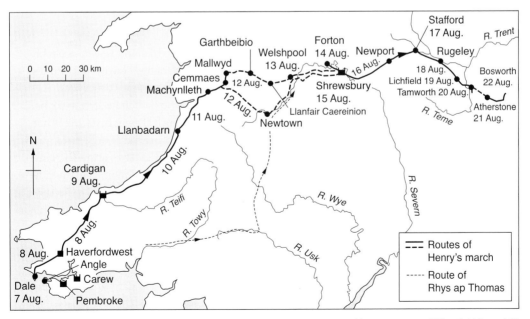

Figure 7.1 Map of Henry VII's march through Wales and the gathering of his supporters. Why did Henry VII land in Wales and spend a week marching through it?

Preparing for battle at Bosworth

Richard was in residence at Nottingham Castle when he learnt of the invasion. He did not act immediately because he thought that his rival would be defeated in Wales by either Rhys ap Thomas in the south or the Stanleys in the north. When he realised his mistake, he moved his troops to Leicester. The two armies confronted each other just outside the small village of Market Bosworth in Leicestershire on 22 August. Henry's forces now numbered between 5000 and 6000 men, Richard's forces outnumbering them two to one. The records do not make clear whether or not this included the Stanleys' force of 3000, which remained on the sidelines for most of the battle. Neither Richard nor Henry knew for certain on whose side the notoriously unreliable Stanleys intended to intervene.

Henry's army

The majority of the recruits to Henry's army were not professional soldiers, but they had probably seen some active service during the civil wars. For the most part they were tenant farmers recruited by their landlords to serve for a limited period. They were lightly armed and tended to fill the ranks as archers and spearmen. The more professional troops or retainers and mercenaries fought as men-at-arms, with sword, shield and pike. The landowners, the majority of whom were nobles, knights and squires, wore armour and fought on horseback. They were the cavalry which provided Henry's army with the necessary mobility on the battlefield. Henry relied on the military expertise of his uncle Jasper and John de Vere, Earl of Oxford, to guide him in battle.

Richard's army

Since England had no regular standing army, Richard's troops were probably similar in quality and background to those of his enemy. However, Richard's troops were better equipped and he had considerably more cavalry than Henry. They were fresher than Henry's troops, who had had a fortnight's hard marching, whereas Richard's army had come a much shorter distance. What **artillery** Henry had been able to bring with him consisted of light **field guns**, certainly inferior to the heavier artillery available to Richard's army. Richard had vastly more experience of warfare and military command than Henry and he had had ample time to prepare his defences. This enabled Richard to occupy the more favourable tactical position on the battlefield, the high ground on Ambion Hill with marshland protecting the flank.

It soon became apparent that some of those around Richard were ready to betray him. Richard's closest allies urged him to flee but according to an eyewitness he refused, stating that 'God forbid I yield one step. This day I will die a King or win.' The identity of the eyewitness is not known, nor can Richard's words be verified. The king's defiant statement was reported in a letter dated 1 March 1486 by Spanish merchants in England who returned home to Spain a few months after the battle.

KEY TERMS

Artillery Used to describe wheeled cannons of various sizes.

Field guns Small cannons mounted on wheels.

The Battle of Bosworth and the death of Richard III

No eyewitness account of the battle exists but, by piecing together later accounts, we learn that fighting began early in the morning with Henry's forces charging across a marshy area towards the king's army. The battle lasted about three hours, but was bitterly contested with heavy casualties on both sides. According to Polydore Vergil, Henry fought bravely and 'bore the brunt longer than his own soldiers … who were almost out of hope of victory'. The turning point came when Richard suddenly decided to strike at Henry himself. This apparently reckless action – Richard could have fled the field to fight another day – was caused in part by the Earl of Northumberland's refusal to move his reserve up in support. Having spotted Henry riding towards the Stanleys in the company of a relatively small band of men, Richard, accompanied by no more than 100 men, launched a furious assault on him. He almost succeeded, slaughtering Henry's standard-bearer before Henry's personal guard closed ranks.

At this crucial moment, Henry's step-uncle, Sir William Stanley, waiting in the wings to see the direction the battle would go, rushed to his rescue. Stanley's cavalry, perhaps some 500 strong, overwhelmed Richard, who refused to quit the battlefield (see Sources F and G). Accounts note that Richard was surrounded by Stanley's men and killed. It was said that the blows were so violent that the king's helmet was driven into his skull. The Burgundian chronicler Jean Moulet stated that a Welshman, Rhys ap Maredudd of Ysbyty Ifan, struck the death-blow while Richard's horse was stuck in the marshy ground.

Richard's death concluded the battle and the leaderless Yorkists fled. The most prominent Yorkist, the Duke of Norfolk, was killed in the battle but the Earl of Northumberland survived. Northumberland's betrayal of Richard III did not earn the respect of the victor Henry Tudor, who had him arrested and imprisoned after the battle. The crown was picked up by Lord Stanley from the field of battle and it was placed on Henry Tudor's head. Richard's naked body was tossed over a mule and taken to Leicester to be buried. The long years in exile were over for Henry.

SOURCE F

Adapted from the *Crowland Chronicle*, which describes the Battle of Bosworth in 1485.

There now began a very fierce battle between the two sides; Henry, Earl of Richmond with his knights advanced directly upon King Richard. In the end a glorious victory was granted by heaven to the Earl of Richmond, now sole king, together with the priceless crown which King Richard had previously worn. As for King Richard he received many mortal wounds, and like a spirited and most courageous prince fell in battle on the field and not in flight.

Study Source F. Why might the *Crowland Chronicle* be accused of bias?

The end of the Wars of the Roses

Bosworth was the final act in the conflict known as the Wars of the Roses (unless one counts the Battle of Stoke in 1487), which had dominated England's political, social and economic life throughout the second half of the fifteenth century. For this reason, 1485 is often seen as a turning point in the history of England. It is a date frequently used as a division between what historians call the medieval and the early modern periods. The reign of Henry VII ended the civil war and heralded the foundation of a new dynasty, the Tudors.

SOURCE G

? Study Source G. Why might Vergil be accused of bias towards Richard III?

Adapted from Polydore Vergil, *Anglica Historia*, 1513. Vergil, an Italian scholar who arrived at the English court in 1501, described the battle.

King Richard alone was killed fighting manfully in the thickest press of his enemies … such great fierceness and such courage huge force of mind he had … his courage also strong and fierce which failed him not in the very death which when his men forsook him, he rather yielded to take with the sword than by foul flight to prolong his life.

SOURCE H

? How useful is Source H as evidence to a historian studying the Battle of Bosworth?

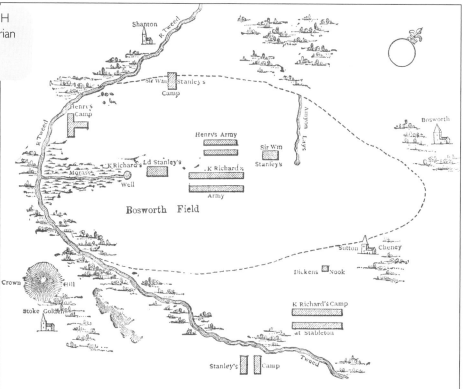

A historic map of the Battle of Bosworth. The plan shows the location of the opposing armies and, more importantly, the key positions occupied by the forces of the Stanley brothers.

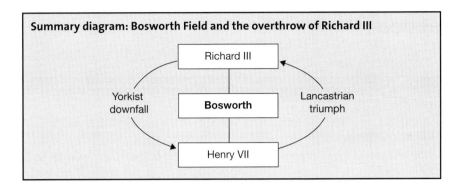

Summary diagram: Bosworth Field and the overthrow of Richard III

Richard III → Bosworth → Henry VII

Yorkist downfall

Lancastrian triumph

Chapter summary

In 1483 Edward IV died unexpectedly, leaving his twelve-year-old son, Edward, as his heir. A regency council was formed to govern on behalf of the young king until he came of age. Prominent among the councillors chosen by the late king to administer the government was Richard, Duke of Gloucester. Gloucester became the effective head of the council as Lord Protector but he feared the threat posed by the Woodvilles, whom he believed intended to destroy him. To protect himself, Richard seized the throne from his nephew and disposed of the Woodvilles and others such as William, Lord Hastings, who might challenge his position. Richard III was assisted by his chief ally, the Duke of Buckingham, who rebelled within weeks of the successful *coup d'état*. The rumoured murder of Richard III's young nephews, the so-called 'Princes in the Tower', undermined the new king's rule. In the short time he was king, Richard called a Parliament and managed the affairs of government efficiently. However, he was brought to battle at Bosworth by his enemy Henry Tudor, who defeated and killed him.

Refresher questions

Use these questions to remind yourself of the key material covered in this chapter.

1 Why did Richard seize the throne from his nephew, Edward V?

2 What made Richard's usurpation of the throne appear so easy?

3 Why did Richard fear the Woodvilles?

4 Why was Lord Hastings executed?

5 Why has Richard III been accused of murdering his nephews?

6 Why did Buckingham first support Richard and then turn against him?

7 How effective was Richard as a king and ruler of England?

8 Why did Richard summon Parliament?

9 Which leader had the advantage going into the Battle of Bosworth?

10 Why might Henry's victory at the Battle of Bosworth be attributed to the Stanleys?

 Question practice

ESSAY QUESTIONS

1 'Richard III's failure to consolidate his position as king in the years 1483–5 was due to his own mistakes.' Assess the validity of this view.

2 'The most important reason for Richard III's failure to establish his authority in the period 1483–5 was the constant fear of invasion.' How far do you agree?

3 'Richard III faced rebellion in the first year of his reign because of his illegal seizure of the crown.' How far do you agree with this statement?

4 How significant was the challenge posed by the Duke of Buckingham's rebellion to the government of Richard III?

SOURCE ANALYSIS QUESTION

1 With reference to Sources 1–3, and your understanding of the historical context, assess the value of these three sources to a historian studying Richard, Duke of Gloucester's seizure of the throne in 1483.

SOURCE 1

From *De Occupatione Regni Anglie per Riccardum Tercium* (*The Occupation of the Throne of England by Richard III*). This account was written by Dominic Mancini, an Italian who visited England in 1483–5.

In claiming the throne Richard was motivated not only by ambition but also by lust for power, for he also claimed that he was goaded by the ignoble family of the queen and the affronts of Edward's relatives by marriage. In 1478 the then Richard Duke of Gloucester was so overcome with grief for his brother's death that he was overheard to say he would one day get his revenge. From then on he very rarely came to court, preferring to keep within his own lands and set out to acquire the loyalty of his people through favours and justice. All were afraid that if Richard then went on to take the throne and governed alone, that those who bore the blame for Clarence's death would suffer death or at least be ejected from their high estate. No sooner had the death of Edward IV become known, when Richard had established the attitude of everyone, and with the help of friends in the capital, Richard and the young King entered London with 500 soldiers. But, after Hastings was removed, all of the attendants that had waited on the King were denied access to him. The King and his brother were withdrawn into the inner apartments of the Tower and day by day began to be seen less, till at length they ceased to appear altogether.

SOURCE 2

From 'The Great Chronicle of London'. The chronicle was written in c.1484 by a London merchant.

The Sunday following the execution of Lord Hastings at Paul's Cross, and in the presence of the Lord Protector and the Duke of Buckingham, it was declared by the brother of the mayor that the children of King Edward were not the rightful inheritors of the Crown, and that King Edward was not the legitimate son of the Duke of York, as the Lord Protector was. By this declaration and many other reports and allegations, he then alleged that the Lord Protector was worthy to be king and no other. The following Tuesday, at the Guildhall and in the presence of a multitude of citizens, the Duke of Buckingham gave a speech in which he talked of the excellency of the lord protector and the rightful claim he had to the crown. The following Thursday, the Lord Protector himself went to the Great Hall at Westminster where he was set in the king's seat and called before him all of the judges of the kingdom and demanded that they should administer his laws justly to which they all agreed. He then went to the Abbey where he prayed at the shrine. Following this a hasty arrangement was made for the new king's coronation.

SOURCE 3

From the *Historia Regum Angliae* (*History of the Kings of England*), written by John Rous between 1485 and 1492. Rous was an Oxford-educated priest based in Warwick.

Richard of Gloucester imprisoned King Edward V, king indeed but not crowned, with his brother Richard, taken from Westminster under promise of safety, so that it was afterwards known to very few by what death they were martyred. Then he ascended to the throne of the dead princes, whose protector he had been, the tyrant King Richard who was in his mother's womb for two years and emerged with teeth and hair down to his shoulder. Like a scorpion he had a stinging tail. He received Edward V blandly, with embraces and kisses, yet within three months he had killed him and also his brother. And Lady Anne, his queen, daughter of the Earl of Warwick, he poisoned. And what was most detestable to God and to all Englishmen, indeed to all nations to whom it became known, he caused others to kill the holy man King Henry VI, or as many think, did so by his own hands. He was small of stature with a short face and unequal shoulders, the right higher and the left lower.

CHAPTER 8

'The son of prophecy': Henry VII 1485–1509

A nation's government, security and well-being depend on the character and strength of its ruler. This was particularly true during the Middle Ages, when kings had the power to pass laws, raise revenue and make war. Following Henry's victory at the Battle of Bosworth, he sought to establish and consolidate his dynasty. Henry was determined to re-establish 'good governance' after the turmoil of the Wars of the Roses. To enable him to govern effectively he sought to make the Crown solvent in the hope that financial security would help him to consolidate his power. Henry pursued an energetic foreign policy but this was marked more by diplomacy than by war. The means by which Henry established the dynasty, governed the kingdom, restored the nation's finances and pursued an effective foreign policy are examined as five themes:

★ Establishing the dynasty: pretenders, protests and threats

★ Government, law and the maintenance of order

★ Seeking solvency: financial policy

★ Seeking security: foreign policy

The key debate on *page 178* of this chapter asks the question: What was the 'New Monarchy' theory and why did it lead to so much debate among historians?

Key dates

1485		Henry crowned as King Henry VII Henry's first Parliament met	1496		Trade agreement known as *Magnus Intercursus* signed
1486	Jan.	Marriage of Henry and Elizabeth of York	1497		Rebellion in Cornwall. Truce of Ayton signed
	Sept.	Birth of a son and heir, Arthur	1499		Warbeck and the Earl of Warwick executed
1487		First law passed against illegal retaining	1501		Marriage of Arthur and Catherine of Aragon
	June	Battle of Stoke	1502		Death of Prince Arthur. Treaty of Ayton
1489		Rebellion in Yorkshire. Treaty of Medina del Campo	1504		Second law passed against illegal retaining. Sir Richard Empson appointed head of the Council Learned in the Law
1492		Treaty of Étaples			
1494		Sir Edward Poynings appointed Lord Deputy of Ireland			
1495		Council Learned in the Law established	1509		Death of Henry VII

1 Establishing the dynasty: pretenders, protests and threats

▶ How was Henry able to secure the throne in the face of serious threats and opposition?

The weakness of Henry VII's claim to the throne

Henry VII was by right and just title of inheritance, and by divine providence, crowned and proclaimed king.

Writing in 1542 in his chronicle, *The Union of the Two Noble and Illustre Families of Lancastre and Yorke*, Edward Hall was convinced that there was no problem with Henry's claim to the throne. However, the legitimacy of Henry's right to the kingship of England was not always so clear or so certain. To the majority of Henry's contemporaries, the Battle of Bosworth on 22 August 1485 was just one more battle in the long dynastic struggle for the crown that dominated the second half of the fifteenth century. On this occasion the victor happened to be the obscure Lancastrian claimant, the 28-year-old Henry, Earl of Richmond. It was only victory in battle that had brought Henry to power, as his claim to the throne by inheritance was weak.

Maternal claim to the throne

Henry's claim came through his mother, Margaret Beaufort, who was a direct descendant of Edward III by the marriage of his third son, John of Gaunt, Duke of Lancaster, to Katherine Swynford (see the family tree on page 17). Their children had been born prior to the marriage, when Katherine was Gaunt's mistress, so there was some uncertainty about their legal standing.

Paternal claim to the throne

Henry VII also inherited royal blood, although not a claim to the throne, from his father, Edmund Tudor. This was because Edmund's mother, Catherine, was a French princess who had been married to Henry V of England before she became the wife of Edmund's Welsh father, Owen Tudor. After the death of her husband, Henry V, Queen Catherine had no claim to the throne. By virtue of this marriage, Edmund and his brother Jasper were the half-brothers of the king, Henry VI. In 1452 Henry VI raised his half-brothers to the peerage by creating Edmund Earl of Richmond and Jasper Earl of Pembroke. Therefore, Henry VII was the half-nephew of the king of England and a member of the extended royal family.

Acutely aware of the weakness of his claim to the throne, Henry determined to enhance and magnify his royal credential by pursuing a ruthless policy of propaganda. The policy was so thorough and successful that by the time Hall

SOURCE A

Study Source A. Why might Henry VII have approved of this painting?

A portrait of Henry VII, painted in 1505 by an unknown artist.

wrote his chronicle few would have questioned (or dared to question) the legitimacy of the Tudors. Hall was one in a long line of writers and chroniclers who embraced, and willingly spread, Tudor propaganda.

Henry VII's aims

Henry VII had one essential aim: to remain king and establish his dynasty by handing on an unchallenged succession to his descendants. His policies at home and abroad were shaped and dictated by this aim. Therefore, his goals were simple: to secure and strengthen his dynasty. He knew that if he was to prove himself a strong king and retain full control of his realm he would have to establish effective government, maintain law and order, control the nobility and secure the Crown's finances. He would also need good advice, friends abroad and a considerable amount of luck.

Character and personality of the new king

The character and personality of Henry VII fascinated his contemporaries because they knew so little about him. He had lived for nearly half his life abroad, so was unknown even to the majority of his nobility. Among the more interesting descriptions of the new king is by Polydore Vergil, a brilliant Italian scholar who arrived at the English court in 1501. Henry was so impressed by his understanding of history that he urged him to write a history of England.

SOURCE B

Henry VII is described by Vergil in his book *Anglica Historia*, published in 1513.

His appearance was remarkably attractive and his face was cheerful, especially when speaking; his eyes were small and blue, his teeth few, poor and blackish; his hair was thin and white; his complexion sallow.

In government he was shrewd and prudent so that no one dared get the better of him through deceit and guile … He well knew how to maintain his royal majesty …

> Study Source B. Is Vergil's description a truthful reflection or a distorted picture of what Henry VII was really like?

Francis Bacon's *History of the Reign of King Henry the Seventh*, published in 1622, remained the major work on the reign until the twentieth century. He described Henry as 'one of the best sort of wonders: a wonder for wise men', but 'for his pleasures, there is no news of them'. This implies that Henry was admired for his intellectual ability but that his lifestyle was rather colourless. Bacon wanted his contemporaries and future generations to learn from his *History*, which is why he was prepared to pass judgement on those who came under his scrutiny. Henry is portrayed as rather a cold man, but his warmer, more human side was revealed on the death of his eldest son, Prince Arthur, when he rushed to comfort his wife. When Elizabeth herself died, Bacon explains that 'he privily departed to a solitary place and would no man should resort unto him'.

First steps to securing the throne

Henry's first actions revealed his concern about the succession and his desire to stress the legitimacy of his position, regardless of defeating Richard or his marriage to Elizabeth of York. For example:

- He dated the official beginning of his reign from the day before Bosworth. Therefore, Richard and his supporters could be declared traitors. This was doubly convenient because it meant that their estates became the property of the Crown by act of attainder.
- He deliberately arranged his coronation for 30 October, before the first meeting of Parliament on 7 November. Thus, it could never be said that Parliament made Henry VII king.
- He applied for a papal dispensation to marry Elizabeth of York. This was necessary because they were distant cousins. Henry and Elizabeth were married on 18 January 1486, finally uniting the Houses of Lancaster and York.

After Bosworth, Henry's most immediate and perhaps greatest problem was ensuring that he kept the crown. Although many potential candidates had been eliminated from the succession during the Wars of the Roses and their aftermath, it was not until 1506 that Henry could feel really secure on his throne. By that time, the most dangerous claimants to the crown were either dead or safely locked away.

Rival claims to the throne

In 1485 there were still a number of important Yorkists alive with a strong claim to the throne. The most direct male representative of the family was Richard III's ten-year-old nephew, Edward, Earl of Warwick (son of his brother Clarence). Henry successfully disposed of him, at least temporarily, by sending him to the Tower of London. Although it was a royal stronghold, the Tower was also a royal residence, so Warwick lived in relative comfort, although without the freedom to come and go as he pleased. Richard had named another nephew, John de la Pole, the Earl of Lincoln, as his heir. However, both he and his father, the Duke of Suffolk, professed their loyalty to Henry and the king accepted this. Lincoln was invited to join the government and became a member of the king's council.

The surviving Yorkist nobility

Although Richard's supporters at Bosworth were naturally treated with suspicion, Henry was prepared to give them a second chance as long as he could be persuaded of their loyalty to him. The Earl of Surrey had fought on the Yorkist side with his father, the Duke of Norfolk, who died at Bosworth, and Henry kept him in prison until 1489, by which time he was convinced of his good intentions. However, another of Richard's allies, the Earl of Northumberland, was released even sooner, at the end of 1485, and was given the opportunity to prove his loyalty by resuming his old position in control of the north of England. Ex-Yorkists were, therefore, not automatically excluded from the Tudor court: loyalty was the new king's only requirement for them to regain royal favour.

Lovel and Stafford rising

In spite of his precautions, Henry faced minor risings before the first anniversary of his accession. Although, with hindsight, they appear rather insignificant, they still proved alarming for Henry. Trouble broke out while the king was on royal progress to his northern capital of York. This was a public relations exercise in an unruly area, whereby the king showed himself to his people in an attempt to secure their support. Since Bosworth, Francis, Lord Lovel, and the Stafford brothers, Thomas and Humphrey, faithful adherents of Richard, had been in sanctuary at Colchester. The Church offered protection from the law for up to 40 days but, by the fifteenth century, sanctuaries were becoming a source of dispute with the Crown.

As Henry travelled north in April 1486, the three lords left sanctuary. Lovel headed north and planned to ambush the king, while the Staffords travelled to Worcester to stir up rebellion in the west. Henry continued with his progress, but sent an armed force to offer the rebels the choice of pardon and reconciliation or, if they fought and lost, excommunication and death. The rebels dispersed, but Lovel evaded capture and fled to Flanders. The Staffords were arrested and sent to the Tower. Humphrey was executed but Thomas was pardoned and remained loyal thereafter.

Henry's policy of 'calculated mercy' – severity towards the major ringleaders and clemency to the rank and file – proved successful. The royal progress to the disaffected areas provoked the required reaction of loyalty and obedience, and Henry was seen as the upholder of justice and order. As if to put the seal on this success, the queen gave birth to a healthy son at Winchester, England's ancient capital. Evoking memories of the country's great past, the baby was christened Arthur. These events helped towards securing the dynasty by giving it an air of permanence.

Rebellions in Yorkshire (1489) and Cornwall (1497)

These rebellions stemmed not from dynastic causes but from the king's demands for money. However, they did influence the way in which Henry responded to dynastic challenges and showed how delicate the balance was between public order and lawlessness.

Yorkshire

Henry planned to go to the aid of Brittany and the Parliament of 1489 granted him a subsidy of £100,000 to pay for it. The tax caused widespread resentment because it was raised in a new way, as a sort of income tax. The king appears to have received only £27,000 of the total granted. The tax was particularly badly received in Yorkshire, which was suffering the after-effects of a poor harvest the previous summer. The people also resented the fact that the counties to the north of them were exempted from the tax because they were expected to defend the country from the Scots. Henry Percy, Earl of Northumberland, put their case to the king, but Henry refused to negotiate. When the earl returned north with the news he was murdered. The Earl of Surrey defeated the rebels outside York. The king travelled north to issue a pardon to most of the prisoners as a gesture of conciliation, but he failed to collect any more of this tax. Henry appointed the Earl of Surrey as his lieutenant in this area.

Cornwall

It was another request for money that ignited a rebellion in Cornwall. In January 1497 Parliament voted a heavy tax to finance an expedition north to resist the expected invasion of the Scottish king, James IV, and the pretender Perkin Warbeck. The Cornish refused to contribute to the defence of the northern part of the kingdom. In May the rebels set out from Bodmin and marched through the western counties, acquiring their only leader of any significance, the impoverished Lord Audley, at Wells. On 16 June, about 15,000 strong, they reached the outskirts of London and encamped on Blackheath. The Cornishmen were confronted by a royal army under the command of Lord Daubeney and Sir Rhys ap Thomas.

Historians estimate that about 1000 rebels were killed in the battle and that the rest swiftly fled. Only Audley and the two original local leaders were executed. Despite the fact that the rising had been defeated, it was worrying that the rebels had been able to march as far as London before facing any opposition. The rebellion hardly endangered his throne, but it had shown that he could not afford a serious campaign against Scotland. Henry now attempted to come to terms with James.

The Pretenders: Lambert Simnel and Perkin Warbeck

Henry was king because he had defeated Richard III in battle. The nature of the usurpation meant that a rising from Richard's Yorkist followers was almost inevitable. The careers of the two pretenders, Lambert Simnel and Perkin Warbeck, were of great significance to Henry VII. They presented such a dangerous challenge to his hold on the crown both because of their entanglement with other European states, particularly Burgundy, and because they lingered for such a long time.

Lambert Simnel 1486–7

Trouble began in the winter of 1486 when conflicting rumours circulated about the fate of the Earl of Warwick. Many concluded that he must be dead, as he had not been seen for some time. In this unsettled climate, a priest from Oxford, Richard Symonds, seized his opportunity. Symonds passed Simnel off as the younger boy, Richard of York. However, in the light of fresh rumours about the Earl of Warwick, he seems to have changed his mind and to have decided that Simnel, the ten-year-old the son of an organ maker, would now impersonate Warwick.

Symonds took Simnel to Ireland, a centre of Yorkist support, where the Lord Lieutenant, the Earl of Kildare, and other Irish leaders, readily proclaimed Simnel king in Dublin. The pretender was also supported by Edward IV's sister, Margaret, Dowager Duchess of Burgundy, who was always ready to seize any opportunity to strike at Henry. She sent money and a force of 2000 German mercenaries to Ireland, commanded by the capable Martin Schwartz. This formidable support led the Irish to go as far as to crown Simnel as King Edward VI in Dublin in May 1487.

Although the conspiracy had begun in the autumn of 1486, Henry himself does not appear to have been aware of it until New Year 1487. The real Earl of Warwick was exhibited in London to expose the imposter. However, the sudden flight of the Earl of Lincoln to join Lord Lovel in Flanders at the court of his aunt,

Margaret of Burgundy, made clear the gravity of the situation. Lincoln then accompanied Lovel and Schwartz to Ireland in May 1487. It is probable that the earl had been involved from an early stage. Lincoln knew that Simnel was an imposter, but possibly planned to put forward his own claim to the throne when he judged the time to be right.

The Battle of Stoke 1487

On 4 June 1487 Lincoln and his army landed in Lancashire, marched across the Pennines and then turned south. He received less support than he expected because people were weary of civil strife. The king was prepared and the two armies met just outside Newark at East Stoke on 16 June 1487. Lincoln's 8000 men faced a royal army of some 12,000 strong.

The Yorkist forces were decisively defeated. Lincoln, Schwartz, and Kildare's younger brother, Thomas, all perished, along with nearly half their army. It is likely that Lovel, too, was killed. Lambert Simnel and Richard Symonds were both captured. Symonds was sentenced to life imprisonment in a bishop's prison. Recognising that Simnel had been merely a pawn in the hands of ambitious men, Henry made him a turnspit in the royal kitchen. He was later promoted to be the king's falconer as a reward for his good service.

Henry's calculated mercy was apparent yet again. He could afford to be generous to Simnel because Symonds was now in prison and the real ringleaders were dead. As a deterrent to others in the future, those nobles who had fought at Stoke were dealt with swiftly in Henry's second Parliament, which met from November to December 1487. Twenty-eight of them were **attainted** and their lands were confiscated.

Henry never again faced an army composed of his own subjects on English soil, although further rebellions did follow. Indeed, Stoke could have been a second Bosworth (see pages 134–6), with Henry this time in the role of Richard III. What was most important was that Henry was victorious. However, the fact that such a ridiculous scheme almost succeeded indicates that the country was still unsettled and shows the fragility of Henry's grasp on the crown.

Perkin Warbeck 1491–9

Further troubles arose for Henry in the autumn of 1491 when Perkin Warbeck, a seventeen-year-old from Tournai in France, arrived in Cork, Ireland, on the ship of his master, a Breton merchant. He seems to have deeply impressed the townsfolk, who assumed that he might be the Earl of Warwick. Warbeck denied this, claiming instead to be Richard, Duke of York, whose murder in the Tower was assumed but had never been proved. The known figures behind Warbeck were men of humble origin. However, S.B. Chrimes (writing in 1972) believes that Warbeck's appearance in Ireland was 'no accident but was the first overt action in the unfolding of a definite plan'. He thinks that Charles VIII of France, and probably Margaret of Burgundy, wanted to use Warbeck to put pressure on Henry.

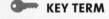 **KEY TERM**

Attainted Accused and declared guilty of treason by a vote of Parliament.

Warbeck and France

The conspiracy achieved international recognition from the predictable trouble spots of Ireland, Scotland and France. Charles VIII welcomed Warbeck at the French court and by the summer of 1492 approximately 100 English Yorkists had joined him in Paris. However, the Treaty of Étaples, which Henry VII negotiated with France in November, meant that he had to find a new refuge, so he fled to Flanders, where he was accepted by Margaret of Burgundy as her nephew.

Warbeck and Burgundy

It is unlikely that Margaret believed Warbeck to be who he claimed to be but, in the absence of any genuine Yorkist claimant at liberty, supporting him would have been her best opportunity to dislodge Henry. Margaret calculated that faithful Yorkists would be prepared to back anyone in order to gain their revenge on Henry VII. Margaret's support of Warbeck worried Henry to the extent that in 1493 he temporarily broke off all trade with Flanders, even though this jeopardised the cloth trade which was so important to the English economy.

Warbeck and the Holy Roman Empire

Not content with Margaret's support alone, Warbeck found an even more influential patron when Maximilian, the newly elected Holy Roman Emperor, recognised him as Richard IV in 1494. However, Maximilian did not have the resources available to finance an invasion of England.

The conspiracy of Stanley and Lord Fitzwalter

In the meantime, Henry's intelligence network had informed him who was implicated in plotting treason, both at home and abroad, and in the Parliament of 1495 a number of acts of attainder were passed. The most important victim was Sir William Stanley, Henry's step-uncle and the man who had changed the course of the Battle of Bosworth. As chamberlain of the king's household, he was one of Henry's most trusted officials. Henry must have been disappointed and frightened by his betrayal. His execution showed that Henry would spare no one, no matter how eminent. Lord Fitzwalter, his steward, was also executed. It appears that a supposed adherent of the conspiracy, Sir Robert Clifford, revealed vital names to the king. It is probable that Clifford was in Henry's service from the beginning, for he received a pardon and rewards for breaking the conspiracy.

Warbeck and Scotland

The efficient work of Henry's agents and the king's swift reaction meant that Warbeck's attempted landing at Deal in Kent in July 1495 was a fiasco. He failed to gather sufficient local support and he set sail for Ireland, ruthlessly abandoning those of his men who had already gone ashore. He laid siege to the town of Waterford for eleven days without success. Warbeck then departed for Scotland, where he met with more encouragement when James IV gave him refuge and support. It is difficult to be certain how far James was convinced by Warbeck, if at all, but he did go so far as to give him his cousin in marriage together with an annual pension of £1200.

These actions were enough to challenge Henry's government and to threaten the marriage alliance with Spain, between Catherine of Aragon and Arthur, Prince of Wales. King Ferdinand and Queen Isabella would not contemplate sending their daughter to marry the heir to a contested crown. Fortunately for Henry, the Scottish invasion of England was a disaster. Warbeck received no support south of the border and retreated, horrified at the manner in which the Scots raided and pillaged the countryside. James did not take advantage of the rebellion in Cornwall to attack again. Disillusioned with Warbeck, he thought that Henry's conciliatory offer of his eldest daughter, Margaret, in marriage was more to Scotland's long-term advantage. In September 1497 a seven-year truce was agreed at Ayton which was formalised in 1502 – the first full peace treaty with Scotland since 1328.

Warbeck's failure

Warbeck himself eased the situation by returning to Ireland in July 1497, hoping for more success there. However, he found that even Kildare was temporarily loyal to Henry, so he set sail for the south-west of England hoping, as a last resort, to find support from this traditionally rebellious area. Again he was to be bitterly disappointed; having landed in Devon, he was driven out of Exeter and Taunton and only a few thousand people joined him. Within a fortnight it was all over, and Warbeck once again abandoned his followers. This time he fled to the sanctuary of Beaulieu Abbey in Hampshire. In August 1497 he was persuaded to give himself up and to make a full confession.

Since he was a foreigner, it would have been difficult at this stage to accuse him of treason under English law. Henry allowed him to remain at court with his young Scottish bride, but Warbeck was not content with this and foolishly escaped in 1498. He was recaptured, publicly humiliated by being forced to sit in the stocks, and was then imprisoned in the Tower. As for his wife, she remained at court and became a lady-in-waiting to the queen.

The plot and execution of Warbeck and Warwick

Historians have long argued over the truth of whether Warbeck and Warwick entered into a plot to escape the Tower and murder the king. Some suggest that the prisoners were the victims of a cynical attempt by the king's agents to manipulate them into conceiving a plot. Others believe that Warwick, weary of imprisonment, was persuaded by Warbeck to enter into a conspiracy. The pretender, and his powerful foreign backers, had succeeded in causing Henry eight years of considerable anxiety and expense that the king could well have done without. Consequently, in 1499, Warbeck was charged with trying to escape yet again and this time he was hanged.

The Earl of Warwick was found guilty of treason and was executed a week later. Although Warwick himself might not have been dangerous, he was always there for others to manipulate and weave plots around. Very probably, pressure from Spain forced Henry to act in this way. Ferdinand and Isabella wanted to ensure that their daughter was coming to a secure inheritance.

De la Pole

On the death of Warwick, the chief Yorkist claimant to the throne was Edmund de la Pole, Earl of Suffolk, brother of the rebellious Earl of Lincoln who had died at Stoke. Suffolk appeared reconciled to Henry's rule, but there was underlying tension because the king refused to allow him to inherit his father's dukedom. Suddenly, in July 1499, Suffolk took flight to Guisnes, near Calais. Henry, fearing a further foreign-backed invasion by a rival claimant to his throne, persuaded him to return and he remained on amicable terms with the king until 1501. In that year he fled with his brother, Richard, to the court of Maximilian.

What remained of the old Yorkist support once more gathered in Flanders. That Henry now acted more ruthlessly than ever before reveals how insecure he must have felt. Suffolk's relations who remained in England were imprisoned and, in the Parliament that met in January 1504, 51 men were attainted. This was the largest number condemned by any Parliament during his reign. The most famous victim was Sir James Tyrell, once constable of the Tower, and latterly governor of Guisnes, where Suffolk had sought shelter. Before his execution, Tyrell conveniently confessed to murdering the two young princes, the sons of Edward IV, thus discouraging any further imposters.

The end of Yorkist threats 1499–1506

Henry was determined to pursue and destroy Suffolk, but so long as the latter remained on the Continent protected by foreign princes there was little he could do. However, Henry's luck changed in 1506 when a storm caused Philip of Burgundy and his wife to take refuge in England. Henry persuaded Philip to surrender Suffolk. He agreed to do so on condition that the earl's life would be spared. Henry kept his promise; Suffolk remained in the Tower until his execution by Henry VIII in 1513. Meanwhile, his brother, Richard de la Pole, remained at large in Europe trying in vain to muster support for his claim to the English throne. The Yorkist threat died with Richard when he was killed in battle in Europe in 1525.

Was Henry secure?

It was not until 1506 that the persistent threat of Yorkist claimants was, for the most part, eliminated. Even then, the security of the dynasty rested on the heartbeat of his only surviving son, Prince Henry. It is a credit to Henry's clear, decisive judgement and diplomatic skill that he managed to hand on his throne intact to his son, when the previous three kings of England had failed to do so.

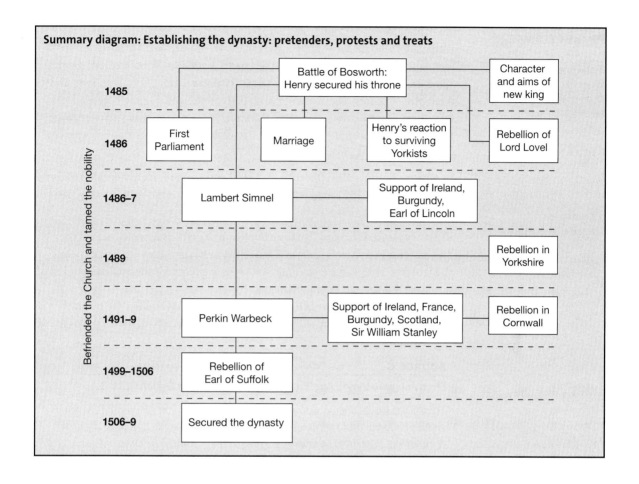

Summary diagram: Establishing the dynasty: pretenders, protests and treats

Government, law and the maintenance of order

▶ *How effective and successful was Henry's government of the kingdom?*

Central government: the king's council

The centre of medieval English government was the king himself and the men he chose to sit on his council. The functions of the council were to advise the king over matters of state, to administer law and order, and to act in a judicial capacity. During Henry's reign there was a total of 227 councillors, but there were not more than 150 at any one time, most of whom rarely attended meetings. When all the active members were present, the council totalled about 40.

The difficulty in controlling this led Henry to rely on a small, core group of councillors who met with the king regularly (see Source C). This elite group included the chief officers of state, the **Lord Chancellor**, John Morton, the **Lord Privy Seal**, Richard Fox, the **Lord Treasurer**, John, Lord Dynham, and a handful of others. These men gave stability to the new regime because Henry kept them in power for so long. For example, Morton served as lord chancellor for fourteen years until his death in 1501, while Fox served as lord privy seal for 22 years until the king's death in 1509.

In order to improve the efficiency of central government, Henry decided to use smaller committees formed from within the council, as his Yorkist predecessors had done. For example:

- Henry revived Richard III's Court of Requests, which was nicknamed the 'Court for Poor Men's Causes'. One of the first committees to be set up by Henry, in 1487, was one to undertake responsibility for the implementation of the act of livery and maintenance.
- Another was the Court of General Surveyors, which audited the revenues coming in from the Crown lands and from those of which the king was feudal overlord.

SOURCE C

From Polydore Vergil, *Anglica Historia* (*The History of England*), 1513.

Henry VII established a Council in his household by whose opinion all things should be justly and rightly governed and causes brought to it to be decided without the bitterness of lawsuits. And for this Council, he chose men renowned for their shrewdness, loyalty and reliability, John, Earl of Oxford; Jasper, Duke of Bedford; Thomas Stanley, Earl of Derby; John Morton, Bishop of Ely; Richard Fox, Edward Poynings. And he chose other wise men to council for specific business among whom were Rhys ap Thomas, a Welshman; Thomas Grey, Marquis of Dorset, a good and prudent man; George Talbot, Earl of Shrewsbury, wise and moderate in all things; Thomas, Earl of Ormond, an Irishman; William Say, a prominent knight; Thomas, Earl of Surrey, a man of great wisdom, reliability and loyalty.

❓ Study Source C. Why did Henry think it was important to rely on such a small group of councillors?

The Council Learned in the Law

The Council Learned in the Law (normally referred to simply as the Council Learned) was a small and very professional body. Its name derived from the fact that most of its members had some sort of legal training or experience. This council came into being in 1495 to defend the king's position as a feudal landlord. It was responsible for keeping up to date with the wardship, marriage and relief of all the king's tenants, and the collection of the feudal dues that were owed to him. Contemporaries criticised it because it operated without a jury, but this was true of all the conciliar committees. In fact, it was done deliberately because of the frequent charges of bribery brought against juries. The Council

Learned was particularly hated because of its connection with **bonds and recognisances** (see pages 169–70) as it supervised the collection of these financial agreements. By the end of the reign it had become the most detested but the most important of all Henry's institutions of government.

The Council Learned became increasingly feared after the promotion of Sir Richard Empson to the chancellorship of the Duchy and the presidency of the Council Learned in 1504. Under the joint leadership of Empson and his colleague, Edmund Dudley, royal rights were scrupulously enforced. Henry's disciplinary use of financial penalties, such as bonds and recognisances, was certainly an effective way of keeping the peace, but under the management of these two councillors the practice seems to have become much more widespread. As Henry was by this time more secure than ever before, the harsh enforcement of such penalties by Empson and Dudley, through this court, was bitterly resented. So hated had the pair become that, upon Henry's death, they were toppled in a palace coup led by the king's other servants.

SOURCE D

Study Source D. What impression of Henry VII is the artist attempting to convey through this painting?

Henry VII (centre) in conference with Sir Richard Empson (left) and Edmund Dudley (right), in a fifteenth-century painting by an unknown artist.

The personnel of government: clerics, nobles and the 'new men'

The membership of Henry's council differed very little from that of the Yorkists. The majority of its members came from the Church and the nobility. It has been argued that the most important members of Henry's council came not from the Church or from the nobility but from a third group, the gentry. Some historians have referred to this group as being 'middle class' because they were lower in degree than the nobility and higher than the masses. Others, such as Steven Gunn (writing in 2001), have dubbed them the 'new men' serving a 'new monarchy'.

Clerics

The largest social grouping on the council was the clerics, who accounted for about half of the total membership between 1485 and 1509. Among the most favoured of them were John Morton, whom Henry VII appointed his chancellor or chief minister in 1487, and Richard Fox, who became the king's principal secretary. Morton was a doctor of civil law and he had practised in the Church courts, while Fox had a degree in theology and had studied in Paris. This sort of education and legal expertise proved ideal for administrators, which is why Henry appointed men like Morton and Fox to his council.

Nobles

There were also a substantial number of nobles. Unlike his Yorkist predecessors, Henry demanded real service from those who sat on his council, so that what counted was not noble blood but how loyal and useful a councillor proved to be. Those nobles who served him well were amply rewarded. Among these was John de Vere, Earl of Oxford, and Jasper Tudor, Duke of Bedford. Henry tried not to alienate the former Yorkists, who, once they had paid in some way for their 'treachery', were given opportunities to prove their loyalty. The Earl of Lincoln was a member of the council until he joined the Simnel rebellion, while Thomas, Earl of Surrey, became a councillor after his release from the Tower and was appointed lord treasurer of England in 1501.

'New men'

Henry did not rely on a particular nobleman or family; instead, his chief advisers and servants were drawn from the ranks of the lesser landowners or gentry, and from the professional classes (especially lawyers) – men like Sir Reginald Bray, Edmund Dudley and Sir Edward Poynings. This has led some historians to label them the 'new men' because they were not noble and they did not come from families with a tradition of royal service. Although Henry made less use of the nobility in central government than his predecessors, there was nothing particularly 'new' about his reliance on the gentry rather than on the aristocracy. The ancestors of these 'new men' had generations of experience in local government, justice and landowning. As Henry was exploiting his lands through more efficient methods of estate management, he needed servants who understood auditing and property laws and had administrative skills. Real ability in these areas was what mattered to Henry, not social class.

Regional government

Like his predecessors, he recognised the nobles' importance to him in controlling the provinces in the absence of a standing army. He never attempted to interfere with their authority in the localities and they continued to dominate local government. Henry continued the medieval practice of granting the overlordship of the outlying areas of his kingdom to the greater **magnates** as a gesture of goodwill. But, wherever possible, he stopped individuals building up too much power and he always insisted on their absolute loyalty to the Tudor dynasty.

Supporters of Richard III found it virtually impossible to regain the positions that they had enjoyed under the Yorkists. Although Henry Percy, Earl of Northumberland, was allowed to continue in his former role of lord lieutenant of the north, his powers were greatly restricted and, on his death in 1489, Henry appointed **Thomas Howard**, Earl of Surrey, to the lieutenancy. In 1501 the northern families were once again overlooked when Surrey was replaced by a council under the Archbishop of York, Thomas Savage. Savage's uncle was Thomas Stanley, Earl of Derby.

The same pattern emerged in Wales after the deaths of Jasper Tudor (he died in 1495) and the Prince of Wales (died 1502). Control was in the hands of a council under the presidency of William Smyth, Bishop of Coventry and Lichfield, who had no power base in the Principality. So, by the end of his reign Henry was moving away from the idea of appointing a local magnate to control a particular region. This prevented the growth of magnate power and over-mighty subjects in the provinces and in doing so forged far stronger links between central and regional government.

The Council of the North

The Council of the North differed from the conciliar committees in having a clearly defined function dating from the time of Richard of Gloucester's period as governor. Yet it was closely linked to the main council, enjoying similar administrative and judicial power to enable the law to be enforced swiftly and efficiently, and, of course, it was ultimately subordinate to the king. Unlike his predecessors, Henry required his council in London to keep a close watch on the activities of his provincial council. In addition, Henry made sure that key members of the council were appointed by him rather than by his lieutenants. For example, one of the most important officials on Surrey's council, William Sever, Bishop of Carlisle, was appointed by the king to enforce his prerogative rights in the north. Sever was also required to keep in regular contact with Sir

KEY TERM

Magnate A powerful nobleman.

KEY FIGURE

Thomas Howard, Earl of Surrey (1443–1524)

Former Yorkist who governed the north of England on behalf of Henry VII. He was the richest and most powerful nobleman in England after the death of Jasper Tudor in 1495.

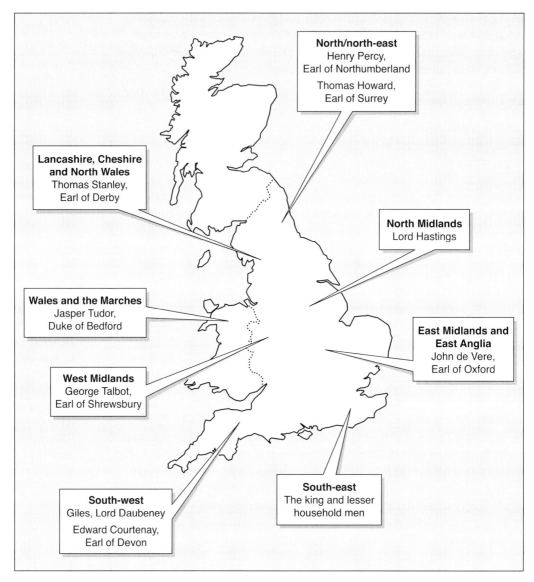

North/north-east
Henry Percy,
Earl of Northumberland

Thomas Howard,
Earl of Surrey

**Lancashire, Cheshire
and North Wales**
Thomas Stanley,
Earl of Derby

North Midlands
Lord Hastings

Wales and the Marches
Jasper Tudor,
Duke of Bedford

**East Midlands and
East Anglia**
John de Vere,
Earl of Oxford

West Midlands
George Talbot,
Earl of Shrewsbury

South-east
The king and lesser
household men

South-west
Giles, Lord Daubeney

Edward Courtenay,
Earl of Devon

Figure 8.1 Divisions of power: localities governed by the nobility. Why did Henry VII entrust the government of the localities to the nobles mentioned in the map?

Reginald Bray in London, with whom he worked closely to ensure the smooth running of the north.

The Council in Wales and the Marches

Like Edward IV, Henry appreciated the need for administrative order. This is why he appointed his uncle, Jasper Tudor, to govern Wales, and why, later in about 1493, he revived the council, appointing his seven-year-old son Arthur as its nominal head as Prince of Wales. Although Henry's own experience pointed out to him the danger of an invasion of England through Wales, unlike Richard III, he did not have to worry too much about a possible threat to his position from the Welsh. His family links and Welsh connections, highlighted and celebrated by native poets and writers, ensured for him the support of the people. He rewarded their faith in him by trusting them to see to their own affairs, hence his policy of appointing Welshmen to key positions in Wales. For example, Sir Rhys ap Thomas was appointed to govern south-west Wales. Henry's control of Wales was helped by the fact that, by 1495, he governed a larger proportion of Wales than any king had done before.

The Council of Ireland

Henry quickly learnt the danger that Ireland could pose when Simnel and Warbeck received considerable support there. In 1492, after the Earl of Kildare had recognised Perkin Warbeck's claim to the throne, the king deprived him of his position as lord deputy. Only after he had sought the king's pardon in person was Henry willing to restore his title.

In 1494 Henry set about reorganising Irish government. He created his infant son, Prince Henry, Lord Lieutenant, so as to echo the nominal headship exercised by his elder son in Wales, and appointed Sir Edward Poynings, one of his most trusted advisers, as deputy. Poynings' main task was to bring the most rebellious areas under the king's control and to impose a constitution on Ireland that would ensure its future obedience to the English Crown.

Poynings succeeded in establishing a constitution at the Parliament which met at Drogheda in 1494. Poynings' Law, as it became known, decreed that only the king had the power to summon an Irish Parliament and approve the passing of laws. No future legislation was to be discussed unless it had first been agreed by the king and his council. In addition, any law made in England would automatically apply to Ireland. This gave the king far greater control over Ireland by destroying the independent legislative power of the Irish Parliament.

In the short term, he hoped to prevent the calling of an unauthorised Irish Parliament, which might recognise another pretender. In the long term, it proved to be largely a theoretical victory. The expense of attempting to rule Ireland directly soon proved to be unsustainably high, and the experiment was abandoned. Henry returned to his earlier policy of ruling through the Irish chieftains. Kildare was reinstated as lord deputy and, for much of the rest of the reign, Ireland ceased to be a problem for Henry.

Local government

Supervision from the centre was the key feature of the exercise of law and government in the localities. This did not mean that Henry made royal progresses around the kingdom involving himself in cases in a personal way as Edward IV had done. Instead, Henry was the central figure directing all operations from London and making his commands felt in three ways:

- through the exploitation of Crown lands
- by encouraging more frequent use of the royal council and its offshoots for the settlement of local lawsuits
- by increasing the powers of the justices of the peace (JPs).

Henry's more efficient management and exploitation of the Crown lands had extended the authority of the monarch to all parts of the country, as well as increasing the income that he received in rents. In developing the role of the royal council and JPs, Henry was also exerting his control more effectively over the localities. This arrangement worked relatively well under a strong king, who could ensure that his instructions were obeyed and that the local nobility did not develop too much power, or seize the opportunity to pursue their private feuds. Although the problem of keeping the peace had not been completely solved, Henry had gone a long way to extending his control of local government.

The sheriffs and justices of the peace

The sheriff and the JP continued to be the two most important royal officials in each county. As the power of the JP increased, that of the sheriff continued to decline. Nevertheless, the sheriffs were given a new lease of life in the Tudor period insofar as:

- They became the Crown's representatives in every county throughout England. In effect, they became the 'eyes and ears' of the monarch.
- They took on greater responsibility for the conduct and management of parliamentary elections.

Unlike the JPs, who were appointed to the commission of the peace for life, the sheriff was selected annually so that the Crown could exert greater control over these local officials.

After 1485 JPs, like sheriffs, continued to be selected from the landowning county elite. They met and dispensed justice in local courts known as Quarter Sessions (meeting four times a year). For more serious offences the JPs sent criminal to the senior courts or Courts of Assize, which were staffed by judges appointed by the Crown. The highest criminal court was the Court of the King's Bench, which could override decisions made at the Quarter Sessions and Courts of Assize. After 1485 JPs were commanded to read out a proclamation at the beginning of each session stating that grievances against justices could be taken either to an assize judge or to the king.

Hundred and parish

Just as the king was dependent on sheriffs and JPs for the maintenance of law and order in the counties, so they were dependent on lesser officials in the countryside to bring offenders to them. By law, every hundred (a subdivision of a county) had to provide itself with a high constable and every parish with a petty constable.

Weakness of local government

The possible weakness in this type of local government was that the king was dependent on the goodwill of his officials. Henry had to rely on the JPs' own self-interest as leaders of society for the upholding of law and order. Virtually his only control over them was the threat of removal from the commission of the peace if they acted improperly, which would be regarded by most JPs as a considerable social disgrace. What Henry wished to avoid was the fate that befell the Crown on the sudden usurpation of Richard III, when some nobles seized their opportunity to take authority into their own hands and deliberately chose to ignore royal commands. A system of paid servants, as existed in France, would have been more efficient but, given the financial constraints on the English Crown, the system adopted by Henry VII worked relatively well by late medieval standards.

Parliament

In the 24 years of Henry VII's reign Parliament was summoned on only seven occasions, and five of those were in his first decade as king when he was relatively insecure in his possession of the throne. Several reasons have been advanced to explain why Henry so rarely summoned Parliament:

- He did not need to ask for war taxes very often because his foreign policy was based on avoiding expensive campaigns abroad.
- He did not wish to strain the loyalty of his subjects by too many requests for grants of money, so he found other ways of filling his Treasury.
- He did not feel the need to initiate legislation on a large scale. The government bills most frequently passed were acts of attainder designed to subdue the more troublesome of his political opponents.

The king might not have summoned Parliament frequently but, by the way he used it, he continued its traditional role as an institution where the most important business of the kingdom was transacted. This is clear not only in the number of attainders (see page 167) against individual nobles that he requested Parliament to pass, but in the way he used it to ratify his claim to the throne in 1486.

Legislation was also used to carry out his policies against riots and retaining, and ten per cent of all statutes dealt with the responsibilities of the JPs and the control of the provinces. Further acts dealt with social discipline, such as that of 1495 which laid down rules on wages and hours of work. Henry's use of Parliament emphasised the fact that all power derived from the Crown. So, although Parliament did not meet on a regular basis during Henry's reign, there was no threat of its ceasing to exist as a political institution. The king used it as and when circumstances demanded, just as his predecessors had done.

Table 8.1 List of parliamentary meetings under Henry VII. What does the list of meetings reveal about Henry's use of Parliament?

Year	Date of session	Approximate length of session
1485–6	07/11/85–04/03/86	3 months
1487	09/11/87–10/12/87	1 month
1489	13/01/89–23/02/90	1.5 months
1491	17/10/91–04/11/91	0.5 month
1495	14/10/95–22/12/95	2 months
1497	16/01/97–13/03/97	2 months
1504	25/01/04–01/04/04	2.5 months

Henry VII and the nobility

A wise king recognised the importance of keeping control of the nobility because they had the wealth and power to challenge the monarchy. In order to safeguard the throne Henry employed a number of strategies to combat and master the disaffected nobleman.

The stability and security of the realm rested on the nature of the relationship between the king and his nobility (and with the localities), and their ability to co-operate. According to the teachings of the Church, the nobility had a duty to serve their social superior the king, who was held to be God's deputy on earth. By the same token, the king too was obliged to protect them, to reward them for their loyalty and service and, above all, to rule wisely and fairly. This theory of obligation, known as the Great Chain of Being (see page 5), was the natural order of society. However, this theory did not always work well in reality.

 **KEY TERM**

Faction Political groupings that formed around and followed a particular noble leader.

The Wars of the Roses had temporarily upset this natural order of society with the crown being fought over by rival **factions**. This damaged and reduced the status of the monarchy. The nobles had profited most from this, seizing the opportunity to take the law into their own hands. Although they had always tried to control their localities, they now took this a step further, using their servants and retainers as private armies to settle their petty quarrels and to make or unmake kings on the battlefields of the recent civil wars.

Asserting control over the nobility

In 1485 it was this class over whom Henry had to assert his authority if he was to restore the dignity and authority of the monarchy. His problem was how to prevent the magnates' abuse of their power while preserving the power itself. A great nobleman had the power to provoke disorder and even revolt, but he could also quell rebellion and act as a mediator between the people and central government. Henry hoped that by imposing his will by ruthless impartiality the nobles might learn to accept that their position was one of obedience, loyalty and service to the Crown. If this was achieved the rest of his subjects would follow suit because the nobility were the natural leaders of society. In this context it can be argued that Henry's reign marks the end of an independent **feudal** nobility and the beginning of a service nobility.

Over-mighty subjects

Henry was fortunate that he faced fewer of the over-mighty nobles who had so troubled Edward IV. One reason for this was his lack of close male relatives. Whereas Edward had had to cope with two powerful brothers, the Dukes of Clarence and Gloucester, Henry, apart from his step-brothers, had none. The other was the king's cautious policy in rewarding his followers. The lands that came to the Crown from extinct peerage families were not given away again. They were mostly retained by the Crown, particularly the great estates that were acquired from the extinct Yorkist families of Warwick, Clarence and Gloucester.

Henry also controlled the marriages of his nobles, carefully ensuring that leading magnates did not link themselves to great heiresses in order to create dangerous power blocks. He was able to do this because, as their feudal lord, his permission was necessary for them to marry.

Some of these over-mighty subjects, such as the Percy Earls of Northumberland and the Stafford Dukes of Buckingham, still remained, but such families were kept under surveillance. Even closely related families with the potential to become over-mighty, like the Stanley Earls of Derby, were kept firmly in check. So, partly through good fortune and partly through a carefully thought-out policy, the greater magnates posed less of a threat to Henry than they had in previous reigns.

Thomas Howard, Earl of Surrey

The career of Thomas Howard, Earl of Surrey, illustrates clearly how Henry was prepared to forget past mistakes if their perpetrators subsequently performed loyally for him. The earl's father had enjoyed the title of Duke of Norfolk, an honour bestowed on him by Richard III, and he had died fighting for his king at Bosworth. After Henry's accession, the earl was imprisoned in the Tower and both he and his father were attainted. However, he was released in 1489 and put in charge of maintaining law and order in the north, probably because he had impressed the king by turning down the chance to escape from the Tower during the Simnel plot. The attainder was revoked and his title was restored, but Henry only returned some of his lands.

After his success in suppressing the Yorkshire rebellion, Surrey was given back more but not all of the Howard estates. The ducal title was also denied him and Henry kept this final prize to ensure his loyalty to the end. It was not until 1513 that Henry VIII finally rewarded Surrey with the dukedom for his leading role in defeating the Scots.

KEY TERM

Feudal/feudalism The medieval social and political system.

Henry frequently used acts of attainder to punish disobedient magnates. After a period of time he would often arrange for Parliament to revoke them, but he would only gradually restore the confiscated lands as rewards for actions of particular loyalty and support.

Financial threats imposed on the nobility

Henry also used financial threats to strengthen royal authority and curb the power of the nobility, particularly where he was suspicious of an individual but could not prove treason. In such cases he manipulated the existing system of bonds and recognisances for good behaviour to his advantage. These were written agreements in which a person who offended the king in a particular way was either forced to pay up front or promised to pay a certain sum of money as security for their future good behaviour. Henry used the system not only to act as a financial threat against potentially disloyal magnates but to raise much needed revenue for the Crown. The sums stipulated in these agreements ranged from £400 for a relatively insignificant person to £10,000 for a peer.

As with his policy over acts of attainder, the greater the magnate, the more likely Henry was to bring him under this type of financial pressure. Typical was the case of Lord Dacre, who was forced to make a bond of £2000 for his loyalty in 1506. Even the lords of the Church were not spared the king's ruthless treatment: the Bishop of Worcester had to promise to pay a bond of £2000 as well as agreeing not to leave the country. But the most important noble to suffer in this way was Edward IV's step-son, the Marquis of Dorset. The king had believed him to be implicated in the Simnel plot and, after further treachery in 1491, his friends signed bonds totalling £10,000 as a promise of his good behaviour. When Henry was planning the invasion of France in 1492 he even went so far as to take the marquis's son as hostage in case he seized this opportunity to rebel again.

Livery and maintenance: Henry VII's attitude towards retaining

Henry VII openly condemned retaining at the beginning of his reign and two laws were passed against it in 1487 and 1504. However, he still relied on the nobles' armies to protect the interests of the Crown in times of emergency. In 1486 it was the Earl of Northumberland's force which rescued the king from ambush in Yorkshire. In the first months of the reign the king forced the members of both Houses of Parliament to swear that they would not retain illegally. The statute of 1487 paid far greater attention to the actual interpretation of the law. The loophole over 'lawful' retaining was partly closed by interpreting it strictly and was accompanied by a recognisance to ensure that the retinue was not misused.

Henry took this further in the legislation of 1504. This act introduced a novel system of licensing whereby men could employ retainers for the king's service alone. To do this, a lord had to have a special licence and the entire retinue had to be listed for royal approval. It was only valid during the king's lifetime.

Curbing the practice of retaining

Evidence of Henry's success in this matter is seen in the reduction of the numbers of retainers that magnates maintained. Those magnates who did break the law and were found out were made examples of. In 1506 Lord Bergavenny was fined the statutory £5 per month per retainer, which amounted to the enormous sum of £70,550. Although Henry suspended this in favour of a recognisance, the culprit had learnt his lesson and was an example to other would-be offenders.

Unlike Edward IV, who turned a blind eye towards the misdemeanours of those close to him, Henry treated everyone alike. Among those **indicted** for illegal retaining in 1504 were the Duke of Buckingham, the Earls of Derby, Essex, Northumberland, Oxford (see Source E) and Shrewsbury, and even the king's mother, Lady Margaret, Countess of Richmond and Derby! Henry did not eliminate the practice, but he controlled it to a far greater extent than his predecessors and prevented it from being a significant problem.

KEY TERM

Indicted Legal term used to describe those charged with a crime.

SOURCE E

From Sir Francis Bacon, *The History of the Reign of King Henry the Seventh*, 1622. Bacon was a statesman, philosopher and author.

The king was entertained by the Earl of Oxford at his castle of Heningham [in 1504]. The king called the Earl of Oxford to him and said 'My Lord, are these gentlemen which I see on both sides of me your servants?' The earl smiled and said, 'it may please your Grace that most of them are my retainers'. The king was surprised and said, 'I thank you for my entertainment but I cannot have my laws [against retaining] broken in my sight. My attorney must speak with you'. And for this offence the Earl of Oxford had to pay a fine of 15,000 marks (£10,000).

Study Source E. Why did Henry consider it important that he punish his friend and royal councillor?

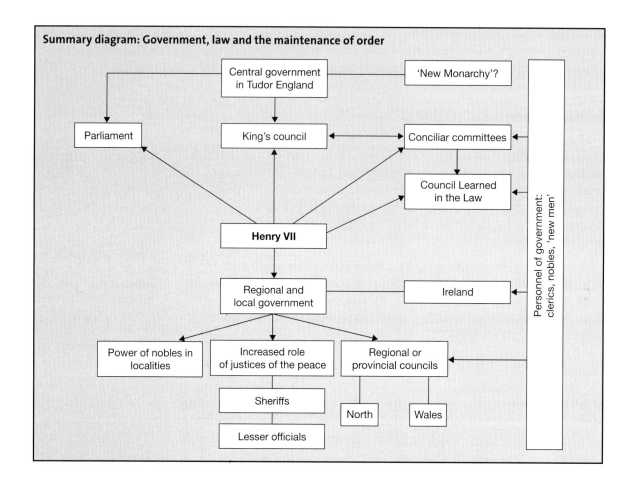

Summary diagram: Government, law and the maintenance of order

3 Seeking solvency: financial policy

▶ *Why did Henry consider finance to be so important?*

Henry's financial aims

Henry VII's financial aims were quite simple: to achieve solvency by increasing royal income, decreasing expenditure and thereby restoring the Crown's financial strength.

Henry VII has been described as 'the best businessman ever to sit upon the English throne', and on his death he was credited with being the 'richest lord that is now known in the world'. However, the truth is Henry lacked experience in government and was untried and untested in the rigours of financial administration and diplomacy. Nevertheless, in spite of his shortcomings he was acutely aware of the importance of strong finances if he was to remain safely on his throne. His usurpation of the Crown meant there was always the possibility of others putting forward their own claim. The availability of revenue together with financial stability was essential if he was to be able to raise an army to defeat them.

Henry did not feel secure unless he was rich: he could use his wealth to reward loyal service, bribe potential opponents and fund armies if necessary. It helped him to consolidate the dynasty because if the succession was still challenged at the time of his death, a full Treasury would provide his heir with the resources to fight to retain the throne. However, Henry was well aware that his determination to make the collection of revenue more efficient would encounter opposition from those who would be expected to pay.

Financial administration

The centre of royal finance, handling an annual turnover well in excess of £100,000, was the Chamber. It dealt with the transfer of all revenue from the following:

- Crown lands
- profits of justice
- feudal dues
- French pension.

In fact, it dealt with all sources of income except custom duties and the accounts of the sheriffs (the officials responsible for the maintenance of law and order in the shires). These remained under the control of another financial department, the Exchequer, because their collection involved detailed information and a complex organisation of officers and records not available to the head of the Chamber, known as the **treasurer of the chamber**.

The financial resources of the Crown

Ordinary revenue

Ordinary revenue was the regular income on which the Crown could rely to finance the costs of monarchy.

Crown lands

Henry inherited all the lands which had belonged to the Houses of York and Lancaster, including the Earldoms of Richmond, March and Warwick, the Duchy of Lancaster and the Principality of Wales. On the deaths of his uncle and his wife, their lands reverted to him as well. He also further enriched the Crown through **escheats** and attainders.

Henry was fortunate in having few relatives who expected to benefit from his territorial acquisitions. He had no brothers; his uncle, Jasper Tudor, died in 1495, and his elder son, Arthur, in 1502. This left only Prince Henry requiring provision. Henry had no obvious favourites, nor was he inclined to shower

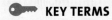 **KEY TERMS**

Treasurer of the chamber Chief financial official responsible for overseeing the royal finances.

Escheat When a landholder died without heirs, his lands passed by right to the king.

honours on his supporters. Therefore, on his death, the Crown lands were more extensive than they had ever been. Efficient management, a thrifty nature and good fortune meant that the annual income from Crown lands had increased from £29,000 in 1485 to £42,000 in 1509.

Henry recognised the importance of land from the start, encouraging his first Parliament of 1486 to pass the Act of Resumption, which recovered for the Crown all properties granted away since 1455. However, having stated his claim, he did not take back all the estates involved because he did not wish to antagonise the majority of noble families affected by the act. Henry knew that if he was to consolidate the dynasty he must try to gain the support of the nobility by showing them that he was prepared to compromise.

The most valuable of Henry's Crown lands was the Duchy of Lancaster. It had its own organisation, centred on its chancellor, and had adopted new methods of estate management. At the beginning of Henry's reign it brought in £650 per year to the Chamber, but by 1509 this had increased tenfold (to nearly £7000) under the skilful management of Sir Reginald Bray.

Customs duties

By 1509 the revenue derived from customs duties had been overtaken by the revenue from Crown lands. However, customs duties were still providing a third of the Crown's ordinary revenue. Henry tried to block many of the loopholes

---

Sir Reginald Bray

1440	Born in St John Bedwardine, Worcestershire, the second son of Sir Richard Bray. Educated at the Royal Grammar School in Worcester
1465	Appointed steward of the Stafford household
1485	Knighted by Henry VII and appointed chancellor of the Duchy of Lancaster
1492	Appointed to serve on the king's council as chief financial adviser
1494	Appointed high steward of Oxford University
1497	Participated in the defeat and dispersal of the Cornish rebels at Blackheath, London
1499	Presided over the Council Learned in the Law
1501	Elected a knight of the garter
1503	Died

Bray's royal contacts may have been as a result of his father, who is reported to have been a physician to Henry VI. Bray first found employment in the household of Sir Henry Stafford, second husband of Margaret, mother of Henry VII. His successful stewardship earned for him promotion to the chancellorship of the Duchy of Lancaster. His skill and expertise in estate management and financial administration impressed Henry VII, who appointed him a royal councillor.

Bray was one of the most powerful of Henry VII's councillors. His importance for the history of the reign of Henry VII lies in his long and loyal service to the king, whom he served as chief financial adviser. His close relationship with the king was such that he alone (with the possible exception of Jasper Tudor) had the freedom to rebuke as well as to influence Henry. As chancellor of the Duchy of Lancaster he presided over the novel institution of the Council Learned to direct a penal system of bonds, and the enforcement of the prerogative rights of the king. Bray is credited with restructuring the revenue system and restoring the financial health of the Crown. His financial management enhanced the financial power of the Crown, ensuring it became solvent by the end of Henry's reign.

in the custom system. For example, from 1487 merchants involved in coastal trading, shipping merchandise from one English port to another, were required to produce a certificate from the first port specifying the duties paid. In 1496 he tried to reduce some of the privileges enjoyed by foreign merchants, for example immunity from English taxation. Twice during his reign he updated the Book of Rates of customs duties to be paid in London.

Despite Henry's efforts, income from customs did not greatly increase. The average annual receipts were about £33,000 for the first ten years of the reign and about £40,000 thereafter (between £16 million and £19 million today). Smuggling seems to have continued, in spite of stricter control, and even Henry could not manipulate international trade, which was dependent on the fragile and changing relationships of all the European powers.

Feudal dues

Henry was determined to enforce these traditional rights to the full and to extract the maximum income possible from them. Initially, the proceeds from wardship and marriage were small, amounting to only £350 in 1487, but after 1503 a new officer (the master of the king's wards) was appointed to supervise them, and by 1507 the annual income had risen to £6000 (£3 million today).

Profits of justice

Legal fines made a significant contribution to Henry's income because he ensured that most criminal acts, including treason, were punished by fines rather than by imprisonment or execution. This brought him much more profit, as happened with his treatment of the rebels after the insurrection in Cornwall in 1497. Another type of fine that the king used as punishment against opponents was that of attainder. Sir William Stanley brought the Crown £9000 in cash (in income from his lands) and £1000 per annum in this way after his treason in 1495. There was only one Parliament during the reign that omitted to pass any attainders and the highest number in any session was 51.

Table 8.2 Attainders passed during the reigns of Edward IV, Richard III and Henry VII. What does this table reveal about the use of attainders?

Attainders	Number
Passed by Edward IV	140
Reversed	42
Passed by Richard III	100
Reversed	1
Reversed by Henry VII directly after Bosworth	99
Passed by Henry VII	138
Reversed	46

John Guy, *Tudor England*, Oxford University Press, 1990.

Extraordinary revenue

Extraordinary revenue was money which came to the Crown on particular occasions and therefore with no regularity.

Parliamentary grants

Henry was cautious in his demands to Parliament. However, he did request financial assistance in 1487 to pay for the Battle of Stoke, in 1489 to go to war against the French, and in 1496 to defend the throne against attack from the Scots and Perkin Warbeck. Historians have accused Henry of cheating his subjects by raising money for wars that never actually took place, as in 1496. However, it could be argued that the money was still needed in the event of a Scottish attack some time in the future. In the event, there was no further trouble from Scotland, but some of the money was used to suppress the Cornish rebellion.

Loans and benevolences

In 1491 Henry raised a forced loan when he intended to take his army across the Channel to protect Brittany from French aggression; this produced £48,500 (£23 million today), a considerable amount when compared with the sums yielded by direct taxation. Royal commissioners were stringent in its collection.

In 1496 Henry was desperate for extra cash to defeat Warbeck and the Scots. He appealed to his landholding subjects for financial support. Such requests were virtually impossible to decline, even though they were traditionally in the form of 'agreements'. Henry seems to have asked for only modest sums, around £10,000, and there is no evidence of any resentment, probably as most of the loans appear to have been repaid. In truth, Henry had little choice but to repay them because those subjects who were owed money by the king were more likely to support a rival claimant to the throne.

SOURCE F

Adapted from an extract of a letter sent by the king to Sir Henry Vernon requesting a loan in 1492.

Letting you know that from our spies we understand that our enemies of France prepare themselves to do all the hurt and annoyance that they can. For the defence of our realm and subjects we desire and heartily pray you that you will lend unto us the sum of £100 and to send it to our Treasurer of England by some trusty servants of yours.

? Study Source F. Why might it have been unwise for Vernon to refuse the king's request for a loan?

Clerical taxes

Henry received quite substantial sums from the Church, although smaller amounts than those collected after the Reformation, when, in 1534, the Church came under the control of the state. On several occasions, usually when Parliament made a grant, the Convocations followed suit with their own contributions. In 1489 they voted £25,000 towards the cost of the French war.

Henry also made money from **simony**, charging £300 for the Archdeaconry of Buckingham on one occasion. Like many of his predecessors, the king kept bishoprics vacant for many months before making new appointments so that he could pocket the revenue in the meantime. Owing to a rash of deaths among the bishops in the last years of the reign, Henry received over £6000 per annum in this way.

Feudal obligations

Another type of extraordinary revenue was connected with feudal obligations. As the chief feudal lord, the king had the right to demand feudal aid on special occasions, such as the knighting of his eldest son, the marriage of his eldest daughter, and his own ransom if he were ever captured in war, a fate which Henry avoided. He was also able to levy **distraint of knighthood**, the medieval practice of forcing those with an annual income of £40 or more to become a mounted knight to fight for the king in time of war.

The French pension

As part of the Treaty of Étaples in 1492, Henry negotiated a pension from the king of France. The pension was a bribe offered by the French king so that the English armies would be removed from French soil. Henry was promised £159,000 to compensate him for the cost of the war, a sum to be paid in annual amounts of about £5000.

Bonds and recognisances

In general terms, bonds and recognisances meant the practice of subjects paying a sum of money to the Crown as a guarantee of their future good behaviour. However, there was a subtle difference between the two:

- Bonds were written obligations in which people promised to perform some specific action on pain of paying money if they failed to carry out their promise. Bonds had long been used as a condition for the appointment of officials, particularly customs staff, but in the later fifteenth century their use was extended to private individuals as a way of keeping the peace and ensuring loyalty to the government.
- Recognisances were formal acknowledgements of actual debts or other obligations that already existed. Under Henry, recognisances became the normal way of ensuring payment of legal debts owed to the Crown. Such was Henry's personal interest in such matters that none was issued without his explicit agreement. Almost immediately after Bosworth, he demanded a recognisance of £10,000 from Viscount Beaumont of Powicke and a similar sum from the Earl of Westmorland as guarantees of their future loyalty.

At its best, and certainly in those early insecure years of his reign, this financial screw was an effective way of restoring law and order and the evidence shows that, in most cases, it brought in the revenue Henry wanted. In the first decade of the kingship, 191 bonds were collected, rising to well over 200 in the later

KEY TERMS

Simony The selling of Church appointments and privileges.

Distraint of knighthood The dubbing of a knight based on annual income – more than £40 per annum.

years of his reign. This is reflected by the fact that the receipts from bonds rose from £3000 in 1493 to £35,000 in 1505 (between £2 million and £17 million today). Those who fell behind in these payments were hounded by the king's officials, particularly those from the Council Learned in the Law, which was made responsible for bonds and recognisances. The Council became greatly feared because of the efficiency of two of its officials, Richard Empson and Edmund Dudley, in pursuing defaulters.

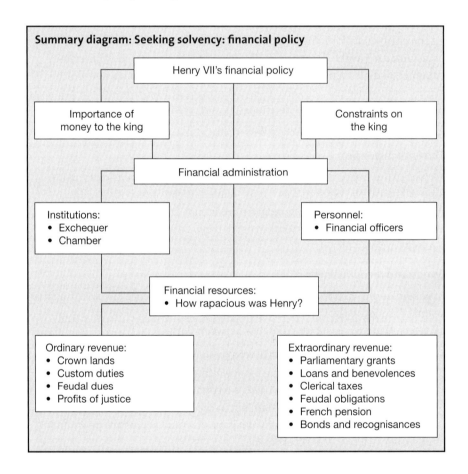

Summary diagram: Seeking solvency: financial policy

- Henry VII's financial policy
  - Importance of money to the king
  - Constraints on the king
- Financial administration
  - Institutions:
    - Exchequer
    - Chamber
  - Personnel:
    - Financial officers
- Financial resources:
  - How rapacious was Henry?
  - Ordinary revenue:
    - Crown lands
    - Custom duties
    - Feudal dues
    - Profits of justice
  - Extraordinary revenue:
    - Parliamentary grants
    - Loans and benevolences
    - Clerical taxes
    - Feudal obligations
    - French pension
    - Bonds and recognisances

 # Seeking security: foreign policy

▶ *What were Henry's aims in foreign policy and how successful was he in achieving them?*

Henry's aims

Polydore Vergil (see page 143) wrote that Henry was 'more inclined to peace than to war'. Henry's vulnerable position in dynastic and financial terms made non-intervention on the Continent the most sensible approach. Henry's foreign policy was very obviously subordinated to his domestic policies of enriching the monarchy and ensuring the obedience of his subjects. Dynastic threats dominated his dealings with foreign rulers, which is why the issue of security lay at the heart of the treaties he concluded with France, Spain, Scotland and Brittany.

Consequently, Henry's aim in foreign policy was defensive because of the nature of his succession, by usurpation. As we have seen, there were several claimants to his throne who successfully sought aid from foreign powers, and Henry had to be constantly on his guard against possible invasion. The most vulnerable border was the northern one with Scotland; as Pope Sixtus V remarked, England was 'only half an island'. Scotland was traditionally the back door into England, and one with which the French were particularly familiar. However, Henry could not afford to ignore Wales, through which his own armed invasion had come, or Ireland, which was volatile and prone to challenging the authority of the English Crown.

Consolidating support

In the first three years of his reign (1485–8) Henry's actions in foreign affairs were deliberately designed to give him time to consolidate support. He had to ensure that he had at least nominal support abroad if he was to secure his throne at home:

- As France had helped to finance the expedition which had led directly to Bosworth, Henry seized the opportunity to maintain good relations with England's traditional enemy. He immediately negotiated a one-year truce with France, which was subsequently extended to January 1489.
- In July 1486 he succeeded in persuading James III of Scotland to agree to a three-year truce.
- In July 1486 Henry negotiated a commercial treaty with Brittany, the other country to offer him hospitality during the long years in exile.
- In January 1487 he concluded a treaty with Maximilian, king of the Romans, the heir to the Holy Roman Emperor, for one year.

So, Henry had done his best to ensure that he would not suffer invasion from his principal foreign rivals while he was securing his throne at home. For the time being at least, he was fairly confident that they would not offer assistance to the other claimants to the throne. Perhaps most importantly for Henry, these treaties revealed that he was accepted as king of England by his European counterparts.

Problems caused by the Simnel Rising

The pretender Lambert Simnel caused various diplomatic problems because he received support from Ireland and Burgundy. Whereas Irish antagonism was not unusual, that from Burgundy was. Throughout the Hundred Years' War against France, Burgundy had been England's main ally. It was also the main outlet for the sale of English cloth. However, Margaret, the Dowager Duchess of Burgundy, the sister of Edward IV, had supported the Yorkists in the recent civil war and was only too willing to provide 2000 mercenaries for Simnel's cause. Fortunately for Henry, other support for Simnel was very limited, which enabled him to defeat the rebels at the Battle of Stoke in 1487. However, the episode acted as a warning to Henry as it showed how vulnerable his kingship was, particularly when claimants had support from outside the country.

Brittany

The first major foreign problem of the reign focused on France and Brittany. Until 1487 relations between France and England had remained harmonious, but Henry was forced to take up an aggressive stance towards his French neighbour when it threatened Brittany's independence.

Henry could not allow France to take over Brittany unopposed because he believed that it would pose an increased threat to England's security. On the other hand, he did not want to provoke his French neighbour, so he compromised. He sent several hundred volunteers to assist Duke Francis of Brittany while attempting to act as a mediator between the two courts. However, as the Bretons refused to listen, Henry renewed the truce with France and disowned Duke Francis. In July 1488 the Bretons were defeated by the French at the Battle of St Aubin du Cormier. The duke finally capitulated and signed the Treaty of Sablé in which he promised that his daughter and heir, Anne, would not marry without the permission of the French king. Three weeks later Duke Francis died and the twelve-year-old Anne became Duchess of Brittany. The French immediately claimed custody of her and the French annexation of Brittany seemed imminent.

Brittany and the Treaty of Redon 1489

Again Henry tried to use diplomacy to resolve the situation by finding allies to deter the French from going to war. Henry enlisted the support of Maximilian, the Holy Roman Emperor, and Ferdinand of Spain. A treaty was also made with Brittany at Redon in February 1489 in which the Bretons promised to pay for the cost of the 6000 men Henry undertook to send to them. Henry dispatched an army to defend Brittany in April but, despite an initial success, he found himself let down by his allies. Maximilian's support was rather unreliable while the Spanish sent a force of 2000 in 1490. Finally, in December 1491, the Bretons accepted defeat and the Duchess Anne was married to King Charles. Their marriage spelled the end of Brittany's independence.

France and the Treaty of Étaples 1492

In October 1491 Henry summoned a Parliament which made a formal grant of two subsidies. Having spent the year preparing for the invasion of France, the English army, an imposing force of 26,000 men, crossed the Channel in October

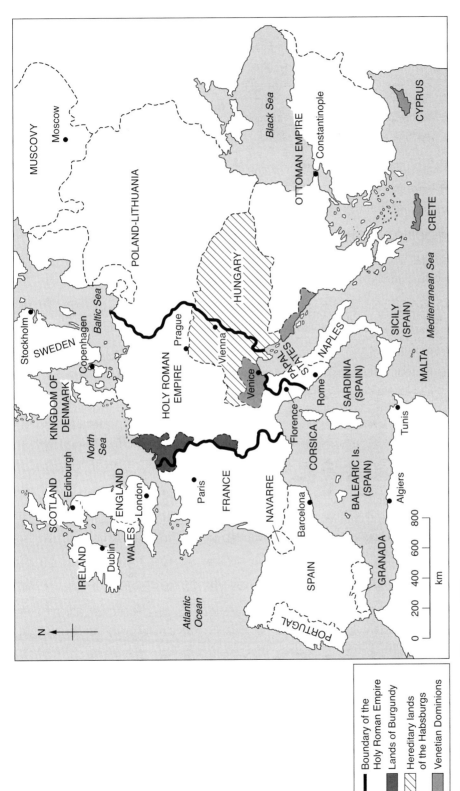

Figure 8.2 A political map of Europe c.1505.

1492 and laid siege to Boulogne. The French king, Charles, was eager to be rid of his English aggressor, so nine days after Henry had set foot on French soil he was offered peace and on 3 November the Treaty of Étaples was concluded. Charles's only concerns were to keep Brittany and to get rid of Henry. Therefore, he promised to give no further aid to English rebels, particularly Warbeck, and to pay most of Henry's costs of intervening in Brittany. This totalled 745,000 gold crowns, payable at the rate of 50,000 crowns a year. In contemporary English currency this equalled about £5000, approximately five per cent of the king's annual income. Henry had not won a glorious victory but he had prevented Charles VIII from helping Perkin Warbeck and he had secured a lucrative pension from the French.

Spain and the Treaty of Medina del Campo 1489

The most significant achievement of Henry VII's foreign policy was the alliance negotiated with Spain in the Treaty of Medina del Campo signed in March 1489. Spain emerged as a major power in the late fifteenth century after the unification of the country in 1479. Initially, England and Spain were commercial rivals, but both were willing to sink their differences in a common animosity towards France.

Early in 1488 Henry suggested a marriage between his eldest son, Prince Arthur, and Ferdinand and Isabella's youngest daughter, Catherine of Aragon, when they reached marriageable age. Catherine, then aged three, was six months older than her intended husband! The negotiations were laborious as both fathers wanted to secure the best possible terms. Finally, Ferdinand agreed to Henry's demands about the size of Catherine's dowry and promised not to help any English rebels.

The fact that the Tudor dynasty had been recognised as an equal by one of the leading royal families of Europe was of major importance to a usurper who was desperately keen to secure international recognition of the legitimacy of his position as king.

The Holy League and *Magnus Intercursus* 1496

Henry's involvement with the Holy League was as a result of Charles VIII's successes in Italy. The other European rulers feared that France was becoming too powerful and in 1495 the Pope, Ferdinand of Spain, Maximilian of the Holy Roman Empire, Venice and Milan formed the League of Venice with the aim of driving Charles out of Italy. England was not included because the theatre of conflict was outside the country's usual sphere of interest, but by 1496 Ferdinand suspected that Henry wished to preserve good relations with France and was fearful of losing England's goodwill to the French. Certainly Charles appeared to be ingratiating himself with Henry by offering assistance against Warbeck.

In October 1496 Ferdinand and Henry concluded an agreement for the marriage of Catherine and Arthur. Also in the same year Ferdinand secured England's entry into the revamped League of Venice, now called the Holy League. However, Henry showed that he was no one's puppet by joining the League only on condition that England would not be obliged to go to war against France; Ferdinand agreed to this. To Henry's credit he also managed to make a commercial treaty with France while maintaining good relations with his allies in the League. So 1496 was a successful year for Henry, particularly as he also concluded the **Magnus Intercursus**, the basis on which good trading relations were resumed between England and Burgundy.

Problems caused by the Warbeck rising

The significance of Warbeck's career to Henry in the field of foreign affairs was that he involved other rulers in England's dynastic problem. Warbeck received support at different times from Ireland, France, Burgundy and Scotland. This greatly complicated Henry's foreign policy. This was particularly evident over the treaty with Spain, as Ferdinand and Isabella did not wish their daughter to marry the heir to an insecure crown. A further example was in 1493 when Henry went as far as disrupting England's cloth trade by placing a temporary embargo on commercial dealings with the Netherlands because Philip and Margaret were offering Warbeck aid. It also highlighted the long-term problem of possible invasion of England via Scotland. It came as something of a relief to Henry when, in 1497, Warbeck was finally captured and peace was made with Scotland.

Scotland and the Truce of Ayton 1497

Relations between Scotland and England were always tense, with the Scots taking any opportunity to cross the border and cause problems for their overlord, the king of England. The kings of Scotland traditionally owed allegiance to the English kings, although they resented this and were always looking for ways to avoid it. James IV of Scotland was no exception to the rule and, despite a truce made with Henry when he came to the throne in 1488, he took Perkin Warbeck into his favour when he arrived in Scotland in 1495. He even went as far as to give Warbeck his cousin in marriage, which must have appeared extremely threatening to Henry. However, Warbeck's invasion of England with Scottish help came to nothing; he gained no support south of the border and, when the Scots heard that Henry was sending an army to oppose them, they took flight.

James IV lost faith in Warbeck and accepted Henry's terms for peace. The Truce of Ayton was concluded in 1497, but it was not until Warbeck had been executed that it became a full treaty of peace. The treaty was sealed by the marriage of James to Margaret, Henry's eldest daughter, in August 1503. However, Scotland did not abandon her ancient pact with France; this meant that the peace depended on the continuation of good relations between England and France, but while Henry lived this did not pose a problem.

 **KEY TERM**

Magnus Intercursus Latin term used to describe the commercial treaty signed between England and Burgundy.

Marriage of Prince Arthur and Catherine of Aragon 1501

Another of Henry's diplomatic marriage alliances was also achieved in this period. In October 1501 Catherine of Aragon arrived in England with 100,000 crowns of her dowry. On 14 November she and Arthur were married in St Paul's Cathedral. This alliance was now of even greater significance than when it had originally been mooted. Not only did Henry hope that England would play a part in the growing Spanish empire in the New World, but the marriage of Catherine's sister, Joanna, to Philip of Burgundy tied their two countries closer together and provided the possibility of another ally for Henry if he were to need one. The two marriage alliances were the pinnacle of Henry's success in his foreign policy.

Death of Prince Arthur

The major blow to Henry's policy was the sudden death of Prince Arthur at Ludlow in April 1502, only five months after his wedding. It seemed that Henry's dynastic hopes had been shattered, but within five weeks of Arthur's death Ferdinand and Isabella were instructing their ambassador to conclude a marriage with Prince Henry, the new heir to the throne, and to settle the terms of the dowry. A formal treaty was confirmed in September 1502, but it recognised that a dispensation would be needed from the Pope because Catherine was considered to be too closely related to Henry because of her marriage to Arthur. The required papal document arrived in 1504.

SOURCE G

Queen Isabella writing in a letter to Duke de Estrada, the Spanish ambassador in England, 1502.

It is vital that there should be no delay in making an agreement for the marriage of the Princess of Wales, our daughter, to the new Prince of Wales. This is now even more urgent since we hear that the King of France is trying to stop the marriage.

After the marriage, our anxiety will cease and we will be able to get England's help in our war against France. Let King Henry know that the King of France is sending a force against us. Henry knows that, under the terms of the treaty signed between us, England and Spain agree to defend each other's possessions. So try to get King Henry to take part in our war with France. Tell him that we will never have such a good chance again of recovering his territories in France.

? Study Source G. Why was Henry VII so reluctant to enter the war against France?

Death of Queen Elizabeth

In February 1503 Henry suffered another personal loss when Queen Elizabeth died shortly after giving birth to a daughter. This provoked new dynastic worries. Two of Henry's three sons were already dead, and with the death of his wife he had no hope of more children. Henry began to consider the possibility of taking a second wife who might be able to bear him more heirs; he seems to have sought the hand of Joanna of Naples, Margaret of Savoy and Joanna of Castile and Burgundy in turn. His first choice in 1504 seems to have been the young widow, Queen Joanna of Naples, the niece of Ferdinand of Aragon. This match was encouraged from Spain because Ferdinand was keen to strengthen his links with England as his relations with France were worsening. However, these plans came to nothing because the parties could not agree terms.

Relations with Burgundy

In 1505 Henry attempted to establish more amicable relations with Philip in case of a possible break with France. He also wanted to ensure better trading links with Antwerp and to persuade Philip to surrender the Earl of Suffolk. Friendship with Philip at this time automatically made relations with Ferdinand more difficult, particularly after Henry had lent Philip money to finance his expedition to claim the throne of Castile. Henry also considered marrying Margaret of Savoy but she rejected his proposal. As the daughter of Maximilian and sister of Philip, Henry's marriage with Margaret would have jeopardised the prospective marriage of Prince Henry and Catherine of Aragon. Henry further antagonised Ferdinand by keeping the Princess's dowry, despite her father's requests to complete the marriage settlement or return the bride and her dowry to Spain. The young Prince Henry was even persuaded to register a formal protest that a marriage with the widow of his brother was against his conscience.

Henry now began to seek a French or a Burgundian bride for his son. In 1506 Philip was forced to take shelter at the English court because of storms and Henry seized this opportunity to negotiate a treaty with him. This stated that Suffolk should be handed over to the English and that Henry would marry Philip's sister. Isolated, Ferdinand sought an agreement with France, as Louis XII was glad to see the union between Spain and the Netherlands shattered. This was cemented in October 1505 when Ferdinand married Germaine de Foix, Louis' niece. However, the diplomatic scene was completely altered in September 1506 when Philip of Burgundy died. Henry's diplomacy had to alter direction rapidly to keep pace with these changes. Fearing that France would seize on the weakness of the Netherlands to take lands there, Henry repaired his relationship with Ferdinand and strengthened relations with Maximilian. By 1508 Henry had achieved a measure of stability in his foreign relations and his position on the throne was now secure from foreign intervention.

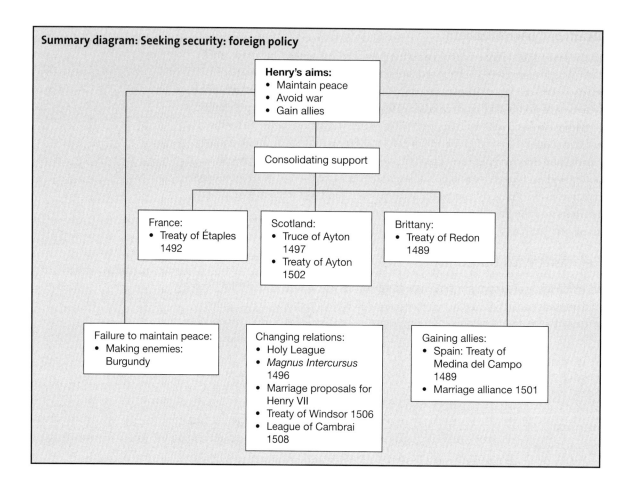

Summary diagram: Seeking security: foreign policy

Henry's aims:
- Maintain peace
- Avoid war
- Gain allies

Consolidating support

France:
- Treaty of Étaples 1492

Scotland:
- Truce of Ayton 1497
- Treaty of Ayton 1502

Brittany:
- Treaty of Redon 1489

Failure to maintain peace:
- Making enemies: Burgundy

Changing relations:
- Holy League
- *Magnus Intercursus* 1496
- Marriage proposals for Henry VII
- Treaty of Windsor 1506
- League of Cambrai 1508

Gaining allies:
- Spain: Treaty of Medina del Campo 1489
- Marriage alliance 1501

 # Key debate

▶ *What was the 'New Monarchy' theory and why did it lead to so much debate among historians?*

The nature of the restored monarchy after the dynastic civil war known as the Wars of the Roses was once hotly debated. The debate began with the publication, in 1874, of J.R. Green's *Short History of England*, in which he first outlined his theory of a 'New Monarchy'. The core of his thesis is that the period between 1471 and 1509 witnessed the creation of a new kind of monarchial authority. In Green's opinion, Edward IV and Henry VII (Richard III is largely overlooked owing to the brevity of his reign) were responsible for the restoration and centralisation of monarchial power, which was so thorough that it developed into despotism. In Green's opinion, the autocratic nature of this 'New Monarchy' was necessary because the image, status and authority of kingship had been tarnished during 30 years of civil and dynastic strife. In short, the dignity and power of monarchy required urgent restoration. The controversial nature of his theory naturally attracted the attention of other historians, some of whom were especially critical. Two years later, in 1876, J.S. Brewer wrote a critical article in which he dismissed Green's thesis as 'leftist, revolutionary, and highly dangerous reading for younger people'! Needless to say, not all historians were as critical of Green, although even those who supported him, such as A.F. Pollard, did so by seeking to modify his theory. As the debate developed, Pollard's modifications to the 'New Monarchy' theory were challenged by revisionist historians.

Pollard's 'New Monarchy' interpretation

Inspired by Green's theory, Pollard refined the interpretation by shifting his focus away from Edward IV towards Henry VII. Pollard believed that Henry VII innovated a whole new concept of monarchy that sought to establish peace and security after the disastrous Wars of the Roses. In basic terms, the 'new dynasty' brought with it a 'new monarchy', and this new style of organised, centralised and tightly controlled government saw the promotion of 'new men'. These 'new men' were drawn from the ranks of the gentry and the professional classes (especially lawyers), and became the king's chief advisers and filled the offices of central government. By employing these 'new men' the king was seeking to rely less on the nobility if not to deliberately undermine their power. By working alongside these men Henry succeeded in doing what his Yorkist predecessors had apparently failed to do, namely, deal with the serious problems arising out of the dynastic civil wars that had raged since 1455 – widespread lawlessness and disorder, aristocratic oppression and 'livery and maintenance'. To support their arguments, the 'New Monarchy' theorists pointed out how peaceful, solvent and well-governed the country was after 1485 compared to what had gone before.

EXTRACT I

From A.F. Pollard, *The History of England: A Study in Political Evolution*, Williams & Norgate, 1912, pp. 88–9.

National states were forming; the state which could best adapt itself to these changed and changing conditions would outdistance its rivals; and its capacity to adapt itself to them would largely depend on the strength and flexibility of its national organization. It was the achievement of the New Monarchy to fashion this organization, and to rescue the country from an anarchy which had already given other powers the start in the race and promised little success for England. Henry VII had to begin in a quiet, unostentatious way with very scanty materials. With a bad title and many pretenders, with an evil heritage of social disorder, he must have been sorely tempted to indulge in the heroics of Henry V. He followed a sounder business policy, and his reign is dull, because he gave peace and prosperity at home without fighting a battle abroad. He left to his son, Henry VIII, a stable throne and a united kingdom.

The revisionist interpretation

The case put forward by Green and refined by Pollard was compelling and influential until challenged in the 1950s. It was almost inevitable that a new generation of historians would seek to challenge and revise the 'New Monarchy' theory. Among the first to challenge the theory was G.R. Elton, who rejected the use of the term 'New Monarchy', but not the theory. He simply moved the idea of a restoration of monarchical power forward to the reign of Henry VIII, which he claimed witnessed an altogether more thorough reform of government. This was his 'revolution in government' theory, which was even more controversial than Green and Pollard's 'New Monarchy'. Elton did, at least, concede that the revolution in government undertaken by Henry VIII and his chief minister, Thomas Cromwell, owed something to the work of Henry VII, who restored the power of the Crown and stabilised the kingdom.

EXTRACT 2

From G.R. Elton, *The Tudor Revolution in Government*, Cambridge University Press, 1953, p. 424.

The true driving force of government continued to be with the king in person and the men who immediately surrounded him. The restoration of good government by the Yorkists, Henry VII and Wolsey, employing as they did the old methods of elastic household system proved that point. But the reforms of the 1530s did more than improve details of old practice. They cast off the central principle of centuries and introduced a new one. When an administration relying on the household was replaced by one based exclusively on bureaucratic departments and officers of state, a revolution took place in government.

Post-revisionist interpretation

Critics of Elton rejected the notion of a 'revolution' in government and upheld the idea of a 'New Monarchy', but the debate continued as to what this meant. In 1964 S.B. Chrimes stated that 'The foundations of what has commonly been called the "New Monarchy" were laid not by Henry VII but by Edward IV.' Thus, the term still had currency, as evidenced by the publication of Anthony Goodman's book in the late 1980s, *The New Monarchy: England 1471–1534*. In the mid-1990s Pollard, too, explored the theme of the 'New Monarchy' in which he described the period 1471–1509 as one in which 'royal authority recovered and normal politics were restored'. J.A.F. Thompson has further refined the post-revisionist interpretation.

EXTRACT 3

From J.A.F. Thompson, *The Transformation of Medieval England 1370–1529*, Routledge, 1983, p. 230.

Recent writing has played down the importance traditionally assigned to 1485 as a turning point in English history, and it has been shown that many of the methods of government employed in the early Tudor period had been foreshadowed under Edward IV. Indeed, it is fair to say that Henry VII's approach to government was strongly traditional. The search of historians for a 'New Monarchy' or a 'more modern' form of kingship, whether of the Yorkists or the Tudors, is in that sense the pursuit of a myth. In political terms, however, there is some justification in regarding Henry VII's accession as the start of a new epoch, because the dynastic change brought with it in the long run a more a more securely based royal authority than had previously existed.

In what sense, if any, did Henry VII found a 'New Monarchy' in England?

Chapter summary

The chaos of the Wars of the Roses enabled claimants like Henry Tudor to challenge Richard III for the crown. Once victorious, Henry VII's primary aim was to establish and consolidate his dynasty. His marriage to Elizabeth of York, followed by the birth of a son and heir, Arthur, contributed to the security of his throne. Nevertheless, he had to deal with pretenders such as Lambert Simnel and Perkin Warbeck, who challenged his kingship. Backed by disaffected Yorkists and funded by foreign rulers such as Margaret of Burgundy, the threat posed by the pretenders was dangerous. He was careful to cultivate the support of the nobility but was prepared to punish those who showed any signs of disloyalty. In order to secure his position on the throne, Henry VII pursued a policy of 'good governance'. Henry was especially determined to make the Crown solvent in the hope that financial security would help him to consolidate his power. The Crown ensured that its power was felt in the furthest corners of the kingdom, including Wales and Ireland. Henry's foreign policy was designed to support his kingship and secure his dynasty, which is why he pursued a policy marked more by diplomacy than by war.

Refresher questions

Use these questions to remind yourself of the key material covered in this chapter.

1 How did Henry VII secure the throne?

2 Why did the people of Yorkshire and Cornwall rebel?

3 How serious a challenge to Henry's kingship was Lambert Simnel's rebellion?

4 How significant a danger to Henry VII were Perkin Warbeck and his supporters?

5 When did Henry feel secure on the throne?

6 Who were the key men in Henry's government?

7 What was the Council Learned in the Law?

8 How effective was Henry's government of Wales and Ireland?

9 Why did Henry feel it was important to extend the power of the Crown into the localities?

10 What was Henry's attitude towards the nobility?

11 How far did Henry allow magnates to build up power in the localities?

12 What was Henry's attitude towards retaining and how did he deal with it?

13 Why did Henry call so few Parliaments?

14 Why did Henry consider it so important to improve the Crown's financial position?

15 What were Henry's aims in foreign policy?

 Question practice

ESSAY QUESTIONS

1 Explain why Henry was able to defeat Lambert Simnel's rebellion.

2 How successful was Henry in controlling the nobility?

3 How far can Henry be credited with the successful government and administration of England?

4 How far was Lambert Simnel's challenge responsible for Henry VII's insecurity?

5 How significant was the challenge posed by 'over-mighty subjects' to the government of Henry VII?

SOURCE ANALYSIS QUESTION

1 With reference to Sources 1–3, and your understanding of the historical context, assess how convincing the arguments in these three sources are in relation to the challenges to Henry VII's crown in the years 1485–1509.

SOURCE 1

Adapted from John Guy, *Tudor England*, Oxford University Press, 1990.

The dynastic threat to the Tudor regime must not be exaggerated. There was no one to cause rival political tensions amongst Henry VII's relations and no obvious focus for political discontent. It is true, the supporters of Simnel and Warbeck dressed their ambitions in dynastic clothes, but the most important revolts in Henry VII's reign, the Yorkshire and Cornish Risings of 1489 and 1497 respectively, were not dynastic. On the contrary, they were sparked by the demands of parliamentary grants. The tax revolts erupted in the south-west because Cornishmen refused to finance a campaign against Scotland for which, they believed had nothing to do with them.

SOURCE 2

Adapted from J.D. Mackie, *The Earlier Tudors*, Oxford University Press, 1987.

In May 1502 Sir James Tyrell was arrested and executed for treason. At the same time Lord William de la Pole, brother of Suffolk, and Lord William Courtenay, son of the earl of Devon, were taken into prison and were not released until after Henry's death. This is because Henry was suspicious and expected conspiracy. Henry's agents may have been guilty of inventing some of these threats in order to advance their own careers, but it is hard to avoid the conclusion that there was a growing spirit of disaffection among the nobility. No doubt the ambitions of the great families were also aroused by the deaths of the king's sons, Edmund in June 1500 and Arthur in April 1502, but even without the influence of dynastic interests there was wavering support for the King in the ranks of the old nobility.

SOURCE 3

Adapted from A.J. Pollard, *The Wars of the Roses*, Palgrave Macmillan, 2001.

Whilst Henry VII used every means at his disposal to reduce the power of mighty subjects, he also did his utmost to build up his own authority. The restoration of royal finances was a key element in this. The King recognised that the secret of recovering royal authority lay in making himself richer than his subjects. This was one reason why he retained possession of the Crown lands. But there was another reason. Land was the basis of local power. By keeping control of royal estates and administering them through his own household servants, Henry maintained a royal presence throughout his kingdom. In spite of his best efforts to protect himself Henry VII faced major rebellions, especially in 1497, and was never entirely secure on the throne. By ceaseless vigilance and unrelenting pressure on all his subjects, great and small, Henry made himself respected, feared and obeyed.

AQA A level History

Essay guidance

At both AS and A level for AQA Component 2: Depth Study: 2B The Wars of the Roses 1450–1499, you will need to answer an essay question in the exam. Each essay question is marked out of 25:

- for the AS exam, Section B: answer **one** essay (from a choice of two)
- for the A level exam, Section B: answer **two** essays (from a choice of three).

There are several question stems which all have the same basic requirement: to analyse and reach a conclusion, based on the evidence you provide.

The AS questions often give a quotation and then ask whether you agree or disagree with this view. Almost inevitably, your answer will be a mixture of both. It is the same task as for A level – just phrased differently in the question. Detailed essays are more likely to do well than vague or generalised essays, especially in the Depth Studies of Paper 2.

The AQA mark scheme is essentially the same for AS and the full A level (see the AQA website, www.aqa.org.uk). Both emphasise the need to analyse and evaluate the key features related to the periods studied. The key feature of the highest level is sustained analysis: analysis that unites the whole of the essay.

Writing an essay: general skills

- *Focus and structure.* Be sure what the question is asking and plan what the paragraphs should be about.
- *Focused introduction to the essay.* Be sure that the introductory sentence relates directly to the focus of the question and that each paragraph highlights the structure of the answer.
- *Use detail.* Make sure that you show detailed knowledge, but only as part of an explanation

being made in relation to the question. No knowledge should be standalone; it should be used in context.

- *Explanatory analysis and evaluation.* Consider what words and phrases to use in an answer to strengthen the explanation.
- *Argument and counter-argument.* Think of how arguments can be juxtaposed as part of a balancing act to give contrasting views.
- *Resolution.* Think how best to 'resolve' contradictory arguments.
- *Relative significance and evaluation.* Think how best to reach a judgement when trying to assess the relative importance of various factors, and their possible interrelationship.

Planning an essay

Practice question 1

To what extent was the success of the Yorkist seizure of power led by Edward, Duke of York, in 1461 due to the weakness of the Lancastrians under Henry VI?

This question requires you to analyse why the Yorkists were successful in seizing power. You must discuss:

- How the weakness of Henry VI and the Lancastrians helped the Yorkists to seize power (your primary focus).
- The other factors that allowed this to happen (your secondary focus).

A clear structure makes for a much more effective essay and is crucial for achieving the highest marks. You need three or four paragraphs to structure this question effectively. In each paragraph you will deal with one factor. One of these *must* be the factor in the question.

A very basic plan for this question might look like this:

- Paragraph 1: the effects of the weakness of Henry VI and the Lancastrians.
- Paragraph 2: the effects of events beyond the control of Henry VI and the Lancastrians, such as Henry VI's fragile mental health and the defeat of the Lancastrians in three successive battles.
- Paragraph 3: the dedication and growing organisation of the Yorkists under their charismatic leader, Edward, Duke of York, plus arrangements for the takeover.

It is a good idea to cover the factor named in the question first, so that you don't run out of time and forget to do it. Then cover the others in what you think is their order of importance, or in the order that appears logical in terms of the sequence of paragraphs.

The introduction

Maintaining focus is vital. One way to do this from the beginning of your essay is to use the words in the question to help write your argument. The first sentence of question 1, for example, could look like this:

The Yorkists were successful in seizing power in 1461 partly because of the defeat of the Lancastrians in battle, but there were other factors as well to explain this.

This opening sentence provides a clear focus on the demands of the question, though it could, of course, be written in a more exciting style.

Focus throughout the essay

Structuring your essay well will help with keeping the focus of your essay on the question.

To maintain a focus on the wording in question 1, you could begin your first main paragraph with 'weakness'.

The weakness of Henry VI and the Lancastrians was one very important factor in allowing the Yorkists to seize power.

- This sentence begins with a clear point that refers to the primary focus of the question (the Yorkists seizing power) while linking it to a factor (the weakness of Henry VI and the defeat of the Lancastrians in battle).
- You could then have a paragraph for each of your other factors.
- It will be important to make sure that each paragraph focuses on analysis and includes relevant details that are used as part of the argument.
- You may wish to number your factors. This helps to make your structure clear and helps you to maintain focus.

Deploying detail

As well as focus and structure, your essay will be judged on the extent to which it includes accurate detail. There are several different kinds of evidence you could use that might be described as detailed. These include correct dates, names of relevant people, statistics and events. For example, for sample question 1 you could use terms such as royal authority and noble factions. You can also make your essays more detailed by using the correct technical vocabulary.

Analysis and explanation

'Analysis' covers a variety of high-level skills including explanation and evaluation; in essence, it means breaking down something complex into smaller parts. A clear structure which breaks down a complex question into a series of paragraphs is the first step towards writing an analytical essay.

The purpose of explanation is to provide evidence for why something happened, or why something is true or false. An explanatory statement requires two parts: a *claim* and a *justification*.

In question 1, for example, you might want to argue that one important reason was the failure of the Lancastrians to defeat the Yorkists in battle. Once you have made your point, and supported it with relevant detail, you can then explain how this answers the question. For example, you could conclude your paragraph like this:

So the Lancastrians' failure to defeat the Yorkists in battle was important because Henry VI was captured and a number of powerful Lancastrian nobles were killed[1]. Lancastrian support gradually drained away because the people lost faith in Henry VI[2]. Some Lancastrians came to terms with the Yorkists and pledged their allegiance to the new King Edward IV[3].

1 The first part of this sentence is the claim while the second part justifies the claim.
2 'Because' is a very important word to use when writing an explanation, as it shows the relationship between the claim and the justification.
3 The justification of the claim.

Evaluation

Evaluation means considering the importance of two or more different factors, weighing them against each other, and reaching a judgement. This is a good skill to use at the end of an essay because the conclusion should reach a judgement which answers the question. Your conclusion to question 1 might read as follows:

Clearly, the weakness of Henry VI and his capture at the Battle of Northampton meant that the Yorkist seizure of power and Edward's elevation to the throne were grudgingly accepted. Therefore, the weakness of Henry VI and the defeat of the Lancastrians had provided an opportunity for the Yorkists.

Words like 'clearly', 'however' and 'therefore' are helpful to contrast the importance of the different factors.

Complex essay writing: argument and counter-argument

Essays that develop a good argument are more likely to reach the highest levels. This is because argumentative essays are much more likely to develop sustained analysis. As you know, your essays are judged on the extent to which they analyse.

After setting up an argument in your introduction, you should develop it throughout the essay. One way of doing this is to adopt an argument–counter-argument structure. A counter-argument is one that disagrees with the main argument of the essay. This is a good way of evaluating the importance of the different factors that you discuss. Essays of this type will develop an argument in one paragraph and then set out an opposing argument in another paragraph. Sometimes this will include juxtaposing the differing views of historians on a topic.

Good essays will analyse the key issues. They will probably have a clear piece of analysis at the end of each paragraph. While this analysis might be good, it will generally relate only to the issue discussed in that paragraph.

Excellent essays will be analytical throughout. As well as the analysis of each factor discussed above, there will be an overall analysis. This will run throughout the essay and can be achieved through developing a clear, relevant and coherent argument.

A good way of achieving sustained analysis is to consider which factor is most important.

Here is an example of an introduction that sets out an argument for question 1 (see page 184):

Henry VI's fragile mental health and his failure to lead or inspire his supporters in battle gave the Yorkists the opportunity to seize power[1]. However, this was not the only reason for the success of the Yorkists in the spring and summer of 1461. Successive defeats in battle had weakened and demoralised the Lancastrians and there was a move towards a peaceful resolution to the civil war[2]. But the most important reason why the Yorkists succeeded was because of Edward's charismatic and inspirational leadership[3].

1 The introduction begins with a claim.
2 The introduction continues with another reason.
3 Concludes with an outline of the argument of the most important reason.

- This introduction focuses on the question and sets out the key factors that the essay will develop.
- It introduces an argument about which factor was most significant.
- However, it also sets out an argument that can then be developed throughout each paragraph, and is rounded off with an overall judgement in the conclusion.

Complex essay writing: resolution and relative significance

Having written an essay that explains argument and counter-argument, you should then resolve the tension between the argument and the counter-argument in your conclusion. It is important that the writing is precise and summarises the arguments made in the main body of the essay. You need to reach a supported overall judgement. One very appropriate way to do this is by evaluating the relative significance of different factors, in the light of valid criteria. Relative significance means how important one factor is compared to another.

The best essays will always make a judgement about which was most important based on valid criteria. These can be very simple, and will depend on the topic and the exact question. The following criteria are often useful:

- Duration: which factor was important for the longest amount of time?
- Scope: which factor affected the most people?
- Effectiveness: which factor achieved most?
- Impact: which factor led to the most fundamental change?

As an example, you could compare the factors in terms of their duration and their impact. A conclusion that follows this advice should be capable of reaching a high level (if written, in full, with appropriate details) because it reaches an overall judgement that is supported through evaluating the relative significance of different factors in the light of valid criteria.

Having written an introduction and the main body of an essay for question 1, a concluding paragraph that aims to meet the exacting criteria for reaching a complex judgement could look like this:

Thus, the reasons for Yorkist success were complex with several interrelated factors. Even given Henry VI's failure as king and the defeat of the Lancastrians in battle, Yorkist success was not inevitable. It only became possible because of particular circumstances. Henry VI's fragile mental health and failure to rule the kingdom effectively for a number of years prior to his capture provided an opportunity for Edward to seize power. It was the total commitment and energy of the Yorkist leadership, Edward IV and his chief adviser, Richard, Earl of Warwick, the success they achieved in battle, and the plans they put in place to seize control of the government and ensure the coronation of a new, young, healthy king.

Sources guidance

Whether you are taking the AS exam or the full A level exam for AQA Component 2: Depth Study: 2B
The Wars of the Roses 1450–1499, Section A presents you with sources and a question which involves
evaluation of their utility or value.

AS exam	A level exam
Section A: answer question 1 based on two primary sources. (25 marks)	Section A: answer question 1 based on three primary sources. (30 marks)
Question focus: with reference to these sources, and your understanding of the historical context, which of these two sources is more valuable in explaining … ?	Question focus: with reference to these sources, and your understanding of the historical context, assess the value of these three sources to a historian studying …

Sources and sample questions

Study the sources. They are all concerned with Richard III's seizure of the throne in July 1483.

SOURCE I

From an account by Domenico Mancini of the usurpation of the throne by Richard III. Mancini was an Italian who visited England in 1483–5 and witnessed the usurpation of Richard III. It is unclear how Mancini acquired such detailed information.

In claiming the throne Richard was motivated not only by ambition but also by lust for power, for he also claimed that he was goaded by the ignoble family of the queen and the affronts of Edward's relatives by marriage. In 1478 the then Richard Duke of Gloucester was so overcome with grief for his brother's death that he was overheard to say he would one day get his revenge. From then on he very rarely came to court, preferring to keep within his own lands and set out to acquire the loyalty of his people through favours and justice. All were afraid that if Richard then went on to take the throne and governed alone, that those who bore the blame for Clarence's death would suffer death or at least be ejected from their high estate. No sooner had the death of Edward IV become known, when Richard had established the attitude of everyone, and with the help of friends in the capital, Richard and the young King entered London with 500 soldiers. But, after Hastings was removed, all of the attendants that had waited on the King were denied access to him. The King and his brother were withdrawn into the inner apartments of the Tower and day by day began to be seen less, till at length they ceased to appear altogether.

SOURCE 2

From 'The Great Chronicle of London'. The chronicle was written, shortly after the events described, by a London merchant.

The Sunday following the execution of Lord Hastings at Paul's Cross, and in the presence of the Lord Protector and the Duke of Buckingham, it was declared by the brother of the mayor that the children of King Edward were not the rightful inheritors of the Crown, and that King Edward was not the legitimate son of the Duke of York, as the Lord Protector was. By this declaration and many other reports and allegations, he then alleged that the Lord Protector was worthy to be king and no other. The following Tuesday, at the Guildhall and in the presence of a multitude of citizens, the Duke of Buckingham gave a speech in which he talked of the excellency of the Lord Protector and the rightful claim he had to the crown. The following Thursday the Lord Protector himself went to the Great Hall at Westminster where he was set in the king's seat and called before him all of the judges of the kingdom and demanded that they should administer his laws justly to which they all agreed. He then went to the Abbey where he prayed at the shrine. Following this a hasty arrangement was made for the new king's coronation.

SOURCE 3

From the *History of the English Kings* written by John Rous, sometime in the early years of the reign of Henry VII. Rous was a churchman who had written very positive accounts of Richard III during his reign.

Richard of Gloucester imprisoned King Edward V, king indeed but not crowned, with his brother Richard, taken from Westminster under promise of safety, so that it was afterwards known to very few by what death they were martyred. Then he ascended to the throne of the dead princes, whose protector he had been, the tyrant King Richard who was in his mother's womb for two years and emerged with teeth and hair down to his shoulder. Like a scorpion he had a stinging tail. He received Edward V blandly, with embraces and kisses, yet within three months he had killed him and also his brother. And Lady Anne, his queen, daughter of the Earl of Warwick, he poisoned. And what was most detestable to God and to all Englishmen, indeed to all nations to whom it became known, he caused others to kill the holy man King Henry VI, or as many think, did so by his own hands. He was small of stature with a short face and unequal shoulders, the right higher and the left lower.

AS style question

With reference to Sources 1 and 2 and your understanding of the historical context, which of these two sources is more valuable in explaining why Richard III was able to seize the crown?

A level style question

With reference to Sources 1, 2 and 3 and your understanding of the historical context, assess the value of these sources to a historian studying the reasons for Richard III being able to usurp the crown.

The mark schemes

AS mark scheme

See the AQA website (www.aqa.org.uk) for the full mark schemes. This summary of the AS mark scheme shows how it rewards analysis and evaluation of the source material within the historical context.

Level 1	Describing the source content or offering generic phrases.
Level 2	Some relevant but limited comments on the value of one source or some limited comments on both.
Level 3	Some relevant comments on the value of the sources and some explicit reference to the issue identified in the question.
Level 4	Relevant well-supported comments on the value and a supported conclusion, but with limited judgement.
Level 5	Very good understanding of the value in relation to the issue identified. Sources evaluated thoroughly and with a well-substantiated conclusion related to which is more valuable.

A level mark scheme

The A level mark scheme is similar to the AS one, but, of course, covers three sources, not two. Also the wording of the question means that there is no explicit requirement to decide which of the three sources is the most valuable. Concentrate instead on a very thorough analysis of the content and evaluation of the provenance of each source.

Level 1	Some limited comment on the value of at least one source.
Level 2	Some limited comments on the value of the sources or on content and provenance or comments on all three sources but no reference to the value of the sources.
Level 3	Some understanding of all three sources in relation to both content and provenance, with some historical context; but analysis limited.
Level 4	Good understanding of all three sources in relation to content, provenance and historical context to give a balanced argument on their value for the purpose specified in the question.
Level 5	As Level 4, but with a substantiated judgement on each of the three sources.

Working towards an answer

It is important that knowledge is used to show an understanding of the relationship between the sources and the issue raised in the question. Answers should be concerned with the following:

- provenance
- arguments used (and you can agree/disagree)
- tone and emphasis of the sources.

The two or three sources used each time will be contemporary – probably of varying types (for example, diaries, newspaper accounts, government reports). The sources will all be on the same broad topic area. Each source will have value. Your task is to evaluate how much – in terms of its content and its provenance.

You will need to assess the *value of the content* by using your own knowledge. Is the information accurate? Is it giving only part of the evidence and ignoring other aspects? Is the tone of the writing significant?

You will need to evaluate the *provenance* of the source by considering who wrote it, and when, where and why. What was its purpose? Was it produced to express an opinion; to record facts; to influence the opinion of others? Even if it was intended to be accurate, the writer may have been biased – either deliberately or unconsciously. The writer, for example, might have only known part of the situation and reached a judgement solely based on that.

Here is a guide to analysing the provenance, content and tone for Sources 1, 2 and 3 (see pages 188–9).

Analysing the sources

To answer the question effectively, you need to read the sources carefully and pull out the relevant points as well as add your own knowledge. You must remember to keep the focus on the question at all times.

Source 1 (page 188)

Provenance:

- The source is from an account written by Domenico Mancini, an Italian who visited England in 1483–5. He will have a particular view on the circumstances of Richard's seizure of the crown.
- It is taken from an account published after Mancini had left England – it will therefore be addressing a foreign audience with little knowledge of English affairs.

Content and argument:

- The source argues that Richard was motivated by ambition and lust for power.
- The family of the queen, the Woodvilles, was unpopular and especially hated by Richard. He blamed the family for the death of his brother George, Duke of Clarence.
- Richard was out for revenge on the Woodvilles, including his nephew the young king, Edward V.

Tone and emphasis:

- The tone is accusative. Richard is portrayed as a dangerous and vindictive plotter who was determined to secure power.

Own knowledge:

- Use your own knowledge to agree/disagree with the source, for example: details about how Mancini obtained his information on Richard, or evidence relating to why the author thought that Richard was an unscrupulous plotter with evil intentions.

Source 2 (page 189)

Provenance:

- The source is from a chronicle written at the time by an unnamed London merchant.
- It provides a contemporary account of what was thought to be happening at the time.

Content and argument:

- The source reports that the supporters of Richard had publicly proclaimed that the young king, Edward V, had no right to the crown because his father, King Edward IV, was illegitimate.
- Powerful noblemen such as the Duke of Buckingham had prepared the way for Richard to take the crown.

Tone and emphasis:

- The tone is matter-of-fact, no passion or bias, simply a recounting of events.

Own knowledge:

- Use your own knowledge to agree/disagree with the source, for example: evidence about the attitude of the chronicler, or the attitude of the public at large and of the other members of the nobility in particular.

Source 3 (page 189)

Provenance:

- The source is from a contemporary manuscript entitled *History of the Kings of England* and written by John Rous.
- It is written by a chronicler who has turned against Richard.

Content and argument:

- The source attacks Richard's seizure of the crown.
- The author portrays Richard as an evil tyrant.

Tone and emphasis:

- The tone is accusative. The writer is biased and very much against Richard.

Own knowledge:

- Use your own knowledge to agree/disagree with the source, for example: detailed knowledge about the circumstances in which the manuscript was written, such as the pressure or otherwise that might have been brought to bear during the reign of Henry VII, or knowledge about why Rous turned against a king he had once admired.

Answering AS questions

You have 45 minutes to answer the question. It is important that you spend at least one-quarter of the time reading and planning your answer. Generally, when writing an answer, you need to check that you are remaining focused on the issue identified in the question and that you are relating this to the sources and your knowledge.

- You might decide to write a paragraph on each 'strand' (that is, provenance, content and tone), comparing the two sources, and then write a short concluding paragraph with an explained judgement on which source is more valuable.
- For writing about content, you may find it helpful to adopt a comparative approach, for example when the evidence in one source is contradicted or questioned by the evidence in another source.

At AS level you are asked to provide a judgement on which is more valuable. Make sure that this is based on clear arguments with strong evidence, and not on general assertions.

Planning and writing your answer

- Think how you can best plan an answer.
- Plan in terms of the headings above, perhaps combining 'provenance' with 'tone and emphasis', and compare the two sources.

As an example, here is a comparison of Sources 1 and 2 in terms of provenance, and tone and emphasis:

The two sources have different viewpoints. In terms of their provenance, Source 1 is very one-sided as it is totally hostile to Richard III. The viewpoint is based on the desire to present the truth of the

events it describes to an audience unfamiliar with England and English politics. Source 2 is more studied in its analysis; it is taken from a chronicle written by a London merchant who simply describes the events without comment.

Then compare the *content and argument* of each source, by using your knowledge. For example:

Source 1 is arguing that Richard had intended to take the throne from the beginning. His coup was planned and skilfully executed. He was ruthless, determined and intent on satisfying his ambition for power.

Source 2, however, focuses on the events of the usurpation. The step-by-step description of the takeover is related in a dispassionate, objective and unbiased way. The chronicler avoids making any personal comments and does not reveal his attitude to the events he is describing.

Which is *more valuable*? This can be judged in terms of which is likely to be more valuable in terms of where the source came from; or in terms of the accuracy of its content. However, remember the focus of the question: in this case, why Richard III seized the throne.

With these sources, you could argue that Source 2 is the more valuable because it was written by an unbiased and objective observer who is a native of England and resident in London, whereas Source 1 is written by a foreign visitor who has no known connections with the royal court, which suggests that his information is based on report and rumour. Source 1 is therefore limited by the nature of its source material and the context in which that material was collected and/or disseminated.

Then check the following:

- Have you covered the 'provenance' and 'content' strands?
- Have you included sufficient knowledge to show understanding of the historical context?

Answering A level questions

The same general points for answering AS questions (see 'Answering AS questions', page 192) apply to A level questions, although of course here there are three sources and you need to assess the value of each of the three, rather than choose which is most valuable. Make sure that you remain focused on the question and that when you use your knowledge it is used to substantiate (add to) an argument relating to the content or provenance of the source.

If you are answering the A level question with Sources 1, 2 and 3 above (see pages 188–9):

- Keep the different 'strands' explained above in your mind when working out how best to plan an answer.
- Follow the guidance about 'provenance' and 'content' (see the AS guidance).
- Here you are *not* asked to explain which is the most valuable of the three sources. You can deal with each of the three sources in turn if you wish.
- However, you can build in comparisons if it is helpful, but it is not essential. It will depend to some extent on the three sources.
- You need to include sufficient knowledge to show understanding of the historical context. This might encourage cross-referencing of the content of the three sources, mixed with your own knowledge.
- Each paragraph needs to show clarity of argument in terms of the issue identified by the question.

Edexcel A level History

Sources guidance

Edexcel's Paper 3, Option 30: Lancastrians, Yorkists and Henry VII, *c*.1399–1509 is assessed by an exam comprising three sections:

- Section A is a source analysis assessment. It tests your knowledge of one of the key topics in depth.
- Section B requires you to write one essay from a choice of two, again testing your knowledge of key topics in depth (see page 199 for guidance on this).
- Section C requires you to write one essay from a choice of two. Questions relate to themes in breadth and test your knowledge of change over a period of at least 100 years (see page 202 for guidance on this).

The sections of the exam relate to the sections of the paper in the following way:

Section A and Section B	Test your knowledge of the key topics in depth	Kings challenged and kings triumphant: • The crises of 1399–1405 • Henry V and the conquest of France, 1413–21 • Renewed crises and challenges, *c*.1449–61 • The Yorkists divided, 1478–85 • Henry VII: seizing the throne and trying to keep it, 1485–97
Section C	Tests your knowledge of the themes in breadth	'The divinity which doth hedge a king': changes in royal authority, 1399–1509 • Changing relationships between the Crown and nobility: 'over-mighty subjects' • Changes in the sinews of power

The following advice relates to Paper 3, Section A. Paper 3 is only available at A level, therefore there is no AS level version of this paper.

Paper 3 Section A questions

Section A of Paper 3 comprises a single compulsory question which refers to one source.

The question

The Section A question will begin with the following stem: 'Assess the value of the source for revealing …' For example:

> Assess the value of the source for revealing the character of King Edward IV and the reasons for the downfall of the Duke of Clarence.

The source

The source will be a primary or contemporary source: it will have been written contemporary to *c*.1399–1509, the period that you are studying. The source will be around 350 words long. It will be accompanied by a brief passage which will set out the essential provenance of the source. Here is an example:

SOURCE 1

From the Act of Attainder of George, Duke of Clarence, in January 1478. This Act was passed by Parliament to confirm the Duke's conviction for treason. Parliament was dominated and controlled by Edward IV.

The King declares his tender love for George, Duke of Clarence, the large grants he has given him, and how he has forgiven his brother's past offences. The Duke of Clarence, nevertheless, has shown no increase in love to the King but has grown daily in hatred. He hath not ceased to plot new treasons; for the Duke hath falsely and traitorously intended the destruction and disinheriting of the King and his heirs. He has sought to undermine all the good rule of this realm, by force using both forces from this realm and abroad.

To bring about this wicked purpose, he attempted to find the means to induce the King's subjects to withdraw their affections from the King by many contrived ways. The Duke was fully intending to raise himself and his heirs to the throne and crown of England, and clearly intending to put aside for ever from the said crown and throne, the King and his heirs. To achieve this he intended falsely to say, that the King our sovereign lord was a bastard and not born to reign.

And in addition, the Duke obtained and got a charter under the great seal of King Henry VI, who claimed to be, but was not in right, King of this land. In the deed were contained all such agreements recently made between the said Duke and Margaret, who being the wife of King Henry called herself Queen of this land; the charter stated that, if the said Henry and his first born son died without male heirs, then the said Duke and his heirs should be King of this land. This charter of agreement the said Duke hath kept secret, not letting the King Edward IV, his brother, to have any knowledge thereof. In this he caused harm to the King's true subjects, the better to achieve his false purpose.

For which reasons the King, by the advice and assent of this present Parliament assembled, and by the authority of the same, commands that George, Duke of Clarence, be convicted and attainted of high treason and shall forfeit from him and his heirs for ever the honour, estate, dignity, and name of Duke and all his properties and possessions.

Understanding the question

To answer the question successfully you must understand how the question works. The question is written precisely in order to make sure that you understand the task. Each part of the question has a specific meaning.

Assess the value of the source[1] for revealing the character of King Edward IV[2] and the reasons for the downfall of the Duke of Clarence[3].

1 You must evaluate how useful the source could be to a historian. Evaluating the extent of usefulness involves considering its value and limitations in the light of your own knowledge about the source's historical context. Important information about the context of the source is included in the information given about the source.

2 The question focuses on two specific enquiries that the source might be useful for. The first is the character of King Edward IV.

3 The second enquiry is the reasons for the downfall of the Duke of Clarence.

In essence you should use the source, the information about the source and your own knowledge of the historical context to make a judgement about how far the source is useful to a historian engaged in two specific enquiries. Crucially, you must consider both enquiries; an answer which only focuses on one of the enquiries is unlikely to do well.

Source skills

Generally, Section A of Paper 3 tests your ability to evaluate source material. Your job is to analyse the source by reading it in the context of the values and assumptions of the society and the period from which it came.

Examiners will mark your work by focusing on the extent to which you are able to:

- Interpret and analyse source material:
  - At a basic level, this means you can understand the source and select, copy, paraphrase and summarise the source to help answer the question.
  - At a higher level, your interpretation of the source includes the ability to explain, analyse and make inferences based on the source.
  - At the highest levels, you will be expected to analyse the source in a sophisticated way. This includes the ability to distinguish between information, opinions and arguments contained in the source.
- Deploy knowledge of the historical context in relation to the source:
  - At a basic level, this means the ability to link the source to your knowledge of the context in which the source was written, using this knowledge to expand or support the information contained in the source.
  - At a higher level, you will be able to use your contextual knowledge to make inferences, and to expand, support or challenge the details mentioned in the source.
  - At the highest levels, you will examine the value and limits of the material contained in the source by interpreting the source in the context of the values and assumptions of the society from which it is taken.
- Evaluate the usefulness and weight of the source material:
  - At a basic level, evaluation of the source will be based on simplistic criteria about reliability and bias.
  - At a higher level, evaluation of the source will be based on the nature and purpose of the source.
  - At the highest levels, evaluation of the source will be based on a valid criterion that is justified in the course of the essay. You will also be able to distinguish between the value of different aspects of the source.

Make sure your source evaluation is sophisticated. Avoid crude statements about bias, and avoid simplistic assumptions such as that a source written immediately after an event is reliable, whereas a source written years later is unreliable.

Try to see things through the eyes of the writer:

- How does the writer understand the world?
- What assumptions does the writer have?
- Who is the writer trying to influence?
- What views is the writer trying to challenge?

Basic skill: comprehension

The most basic source skill is comprehension: understanding what the source means. There are a variety of techniques that you can use to aid comprehension. For example, you could read the sources included in this book and in past papers:

- Read the sources out loud.
- Look up any words that you don't understand and make a glossary.
- Make flash cards containing brief biographies of the writers of the sources.

You can demonstrate comprehension by copying, paraphrasing and summarising the sources. However, keep this to the minimum as comprehension is a low-level skill and you need to leave room for higher-level skills.

Advanced skill: contextualising the source

First, to analyse the source correctly you need to understand them in the context in which they were written. Source 1 (page 195) reflects Parliament's view. Your job is to understand the values and assumptions behind the source.

- One way of contextualising the source is to consider the nature, origins and purpose of the source. However, this can lead to formulaic responses.
- An alternative is to consider two levels of context. First, you should establish the general context. In this case, Source 1 was written at the time of the Duke of Clarence's conviction for treason. Second, you can look for specific references to contemporary events, people or debates in the source. For example, when considering the reasons for the downfall of the Duke of Clarence, the details in the source can be put in context in the following way:
  - 'Past offences'. This reveals that Clarence had a history of law-breaking.
  - 'Has shown no increase in love to the king but has grown daily in hatred.' 'He hath not ceased to plot new treasons.' Despite being forgiven for these 'past offences', Clarence has shown no remorse or gratitude for his pardon but has continued to plot against his brother, the king, the man who has done everything possible to rehabilitate him.
  - 'The Duke was fully intending to raise himself and his heirs to the throne and crown of England.' Clarence was clearly intending to depose the king and perhaps even murder him in order to take the crown for himself and his children.
  - 'He caused harm to the King's true subjects.' By plotting against the king, Clarence was guilty of putting the government of the kingdom in danger, which might lead to the renewal of civil war.
  - 'For which reasons the King, by the advice and assent of this present Parliament assembled, and by the authority of the same, commands that George, Duke of Clarence, be convicted and attainted of high treason.' This suggests that Edward IV had reluctantly declared his brother guilty of treason and that he was only acting on the advice of his Parliament.

Use context to make judgements

- Start by establishing the general context of the source:
  - Ask yourself: what was going on at the time when the source was written, or the time of the events described in the source?
  - What are the key debates that the source might be contributing to?
- Next, look for key words and phrases that establish the specific context. Does the source refer to specific people, events or books that might be important?
- Make sure your contextualisation focuses on the question.
- Use the context when evaluating the usefulness and limitations of the source.

For example:

Source 1 is valuable to a historian investigating the reasons for the Duke of Clarence's downfall because it highlights the nature and scale of his treason. First, there is considerable evidence in the source that Clarence had a track record of law-breaking and that he had deliberately plotted against his brother, the king. For example, Clarence had 'falsely and traitorously intended the destruction and disinheriting of the King and his heirs'. Indeed, he had 'sought to undermine all the good rule of this realm'. Therefore, Clarence was the author of his own downfall because of his ambition; he had not learned the lessons of his previous law-breaking. Second, that he intended to secure the crown 'by force using both forces from this realm and abroad' suggests that Clarence intended to internationalise the conflict with his brother by encouraging foreign intervention. It is possible to infer from the source that Clarence was motivated by ambition and an intense hatred of his brother.

Finally, Clarence had lived a privileged life – as the brother of the king he had vast estates and great wealth, and wielded considerable authority – but all this was not enough to satisfy his lust for power. In this sense, the source is extremely useful as it points to a variety of complementary reasons to explain Clarence's downfall, specifically that he was an experienced politician and power-broker at court and that, as a member of the royal family, it was only one short step to securing the crown. After all, his brother Edward had done the same thing to Henry VI by plotting and scheming his way to the crown.

This answer makes inferences from details in the source to uncover a variety of motives, showing that the passage is of considerable use for this enquiry. Significantly, in order to do well it would also have to deal with the other enquiry: the extent of the source's usefulness for revealing the character of Edward IV.

Essay guidance (1)

The following advice relates to Paper 3, Section B. Paper 3 is only available at A level, therefore there is no AS level version of this paper.

Essay skills

In order to get a high grade in Section B of Paper 3 your essay must contain four essential qualities:

- focused analysis
- relevant detail
- supported judgement
- organisation, coherence and clarity.

Section B: the nature of the question

Section B questions are designed to test the depth of your historical knowledge. Therefore, they can focus on relatively short periods, or single events. Moreover, they can focus on different historical processes or 'concepts'. These include:

- cause
- consequence
- change/continuity
- similarity/difference
- significance.

Some questions include a 'stated factor'. A common type of stated factor question would ask how far one factor caused something.

Planning your answer

It is crucial that you understand the focus of the question. Therefore, read the question carefully before you start planning. Check:

- The chronological focus: which years should your essay deal with?
- The topic focus: what aspect of your course does the question deal with?
- The conceptual focus: is this a causes, consequences, change/continuity, similarity/difference or significance question?

Consider the following question, for example:

> How significant[1] was the Battle of Stoke to the success of Henry VII in keeping the throne[2] between 1487 and 1509[3]?

1 Conceptual focus: significance, specifically to the Battle of Stoke.
2 Topic focus: the means by which Henry VII retained the throne.
3 Chronological focus: 1487–1509.

Your plan should reflect the task that you have been set. Section B asks you to write an analytical, coherent and well-structured essay from your own knowledge, which reaches a supported conclusion in around 40 minutes:

- To ensure that your essay is coherent and well structured, it should comprise a series of paragraphs, each focusing on a different point.
- Your paragraphs should come in a logical order. For example, you could write your paragraphs in order of importance, so you begin with the most important issues and end with the least important.
- In essays where there is a 'stated factor', it is a good idea to start with the stated factor before moving on to the other points.
- To make sure you keep to time, you should aim to write three or four paragraphs plus an introduction and a conclusion.

The opening paragraph

The opening paragraph should do four main things:

- answer the question directly
- set out your essential argument
- outline the factors or issues that you will discuss
- define key terms used in the question – where necessary.

Below is an example introduction in answer to the following question:

> 'Both Henry IV and Henry VII faced opposition and rebellion in the first decade of their reigns because of their violent overthrow of Richard II and Richard III, respectively.' How far do you agree with this statement?

There is no doubt that Henry IV and Henry VII faced opposition and rebellion because they had set bad examples by seizing the crown[1]. However, whereas Henry VII faced rebellion in the early years of his reign, Henry IV endured a series of rebellions throughout his[2]. Unlike Henry VII, who took the crown through bloody battle at Bosworth, Henry IV's overthrow of power was both peaceful and bloodless[3].

1 The essay starts with a clear focus on the question.
2 This sentence simultaneously defines the meaning of 'first decade' and provides an initial answer to the first part of the question.
3 This sentence simultaneously defines 'overthrow' and provides an initial answer to the second part of the question.

The opening paragraph: advice

- Don't write more than a couple of sentences on general background knowledge. This is unlikely to focus explicitly on the question.
- After defining key terms, refer back to these definitions when justifying your conclusion.
- The introduction should reflect the rest of the essay. Don't make one argument in your introduction, then make a different argument in the essay.

Deploying relevant detail

Paper 3 tests the depth of your historical knowledge. Therefore, you will need to deploy historical detail. In the main body of your essay your paragraphs should begin with a clear point, be full of relevant detail and end with explanation or evaluation. A detailed answer might include statistics, proper names, dates and technical terms. For example, if you are writing a paragraph on the way in which Henry VII won the throne at Bosworth, you might include the impact of reports in specific chronicles such as the *Croyland Chronicle*, or Edward's Hall's *The Union of the Two Noble and Illustre Families of Lancastre and Yorke*, or of specific stories such as that published by Shakespeare in his play *Richard III*.

Writing analytically

The quality of your analysis is one of the key factors that determines the mark you achieve. Writing analytically means clearly showing the relationships between the ideas in your essay. Analysis includes two key skills: explanation and evaluation.

Explanation

Explanation means giving reasons. An explanatory sentence has three parts:

- a claim: a statement that something is true or false
- a reason: a statement that justifies the claim
- a relationship: a word or phrase that shows the relationship between the claim and the reason.

Make sure of the following:

- The reason you give genuinely justifies the claim you have made.
- Your explanation is focused on the question.

Reaching a supported judgement

Finally, your essay should reach a supported judgement. The obvious place to do this is in the conclusion of your essay. Even so, the judgement should reflect the findings of your essay. The conclusion should present:

- a clear judgement that answers the question
- an evaluation of the evidence that supports the judgement.

Finally, the evaluation should reflect valid criteria.

Evaluation and criteria

Evaluation means weighing up to reach a judgement. Therefore, evaluation requires you to:

- summarise both sides of the issue
- reach a conclusion that reflects the proper weight of both sides.

So, for example, for the following question:

> How far was Henry IV's seizure of the throne responsible for the outbreaks of rebellion during his reign?

the conclusion might look like this:

In conclusion, Henry IV's seizure of the throne was largely responsible for the outbreaks of rebellion during his reign because his action set a bad example and led other equally ambitious nobles to attempt to do the same to him[1]. Clearly, Owain Glyndŵr and Henry Percy ('Hotspur') also played a part[2]. Glyndŵr's decade-long campaign against the English Crown undermined Henry IV's status and power and it caused political instability and financial problems. Henry's apparent inability to defeat the Welsh rebels encouraged the French to renew the

Hundred Years' War. Moreover, Percy's rebellion posed an even greater threat to Henry IV because he was a member of the English nobility and his fame and reputation commanded respect and attracted followers. Percy had the means, motive and opportunity to replace Henry IV as king[3]. However, Percy's threat was short lived, his death at the Battle of Shrewsbury in 1403 ended his challenge and encouraged Henry IV to believe that he was now secure on the throne. This was a mistake for he had yet to defeat Glyndŵr, and his complacency merely encouraged others to rebel against him, such as Percy's father, the Earl of Northumberland, and Lord Bardolf. While Henry fought to defend his throne he could not end the nagging doubt held by many noblemen that his kingship was illegal and a breach of divine law because of the way in which he had removed the 'rightful' king, his cousin, Richard II. Therefore, it can be argued with conviction that Henry IV was largely responsible for the rebellions against him[4].

1 The conclusion starts with a clear judgement that answers the question.
2 This sentence begins the process of weighing up the different factors involved in causing rebellion by acknowledging that others also played a role.
3 The conclusion summarises the roles of Glyndŵr and Percy.
4 The essay ends with a final judgement that is supported by the evidence of the essay.

The judgement is supported in part by evaluating the evidence, and in part by linking it to valid criteria. In this case, the criterion is the distinction between Henry IV's seizure of the throne in 1399 and the rebellions instigated and led by others such as Glyndŵr and Percy.

Essay guidance (2)

The following advice relates to Paper 3, Section C. Paper 3 is only available at A level, therefore there is no AS level version of this paper.

Essay skills

Section C is similar in many ways to Section B. Therefore, you need the same essential skills in order to get a high grade:

- focused analysis
- relevant detail
- supported judgement
- organisation, coherence and clarity.

Nonetheless, there are some differences in terms of the style of the question and the approach to the question in Sections B and C.

Section C: the nature of the question

Section C questions focus on the two themes in breadth:

- Changes in the relationships between the Crown and nobility: 'over-mighty subjects', c.1399–1509.
- Changes in the sinews of power c.1399–1509.

There are two questions in Section C, of which you must answer one. Questions can address either theme or both themes. However, you are not guaranteed a question on both of the themes, therefore you have to prepare for questions on either of the themes.

Section C questions are designed to test the breadth of your historical knowledge, and your ability to analyse change over time. Therefore, questions will focus on long periods, of no less than 100 years.

Section C questions have a variety of forms but they will focus on either:

- the causes of change: for example, the factors, forces or individuals that led to change.

or

- the nature of change: the ways in which things changed.

Significantly, the exam paper may contain two causes of change questions or two nature of change questions: you are not guaranteed one of each. Finally, questions can focus on different aspects of change over time:

- Comparative questions: ask you to assess the extent of change and continuity of an aspect of the period.
- Patterns of change questions: ask you to assess differences in terms of the rate, extent or significance of change at different points in the chronology.
- Turning point questions: ask you to assess which changes were more significant.

Comparative question:	'The key factor in promoting tension between the Crown and nobility in the period 1399–1509 was noble ambition.' How far do you agree with this statement?
Patterns of change question:	How accurate is it to say that there was a continuous growth in the power and influence of the Crown in the period 1399–1509?
Turning point question:	How far do you agree that the death of Warwick the Kingmaker in 1471 was the key turning point in the relationship between the Crown and nobility in the period 1399–1509?

Planning your answer

It is crucial that you understand the focus of the question in order to make an effective plan. Therefore, read the question carefully before you start planning. Different questions require a different approach. Here are suggestions about how to tackle some of the common types of question:

'The key factor in promoting tension between the Crown and nobility in the period 1399–1509 was noble ambition.' How far do you agree with this statement?

This is a comparative question which focuses on the causes of change. In this case you should examine the significance of 'noble ambition', the stated factor, and compare it to other possible causes of change.

How accurate is it to say that there was a continuous growth in the power and influence of the Crown in the period 1399–1509?

This is a patterns of change question which focuses on the nature of change. Here you should examine the pattern of the development of royal power in the period 1399–1509. You should consider how far development took place at an even rate, as opposed to developing in fits and starts.

How far do you agree that the death of Warwick the Kingmaker in 1471 was the key turning point in the relationship between the Crown and nobility in the period 1399–1509?

This is a turning point question which focuses on the nature of change. Therefore, you should examine the significance of the stated turning point, and compare it to two or three other turning points from the period 1399–1509. Significantly, you should not just focus on the Earl of Warwick's death or the year 1471; you must consider other possible turning points. Additionally, when considering how far an event was a turning point you must consider both the changes it caused and the ways in which things stayed the same.

Advice for Section C

In many ways a Section C essay should display the same skills as a Section B essay (see page 199). However, Section C essays focus on a much bigger period than Section B essays and this has an impact on how you approach them.

The most important difference concerns the chronology. In order to answer a Section C question properly you must address the whole chronology, in this case the period 1399–1509. In practice, this means choosing examples from across the whole range of the period. Specifically, it is a good idea to have examples from the early part of the period, the middle of the period and the end of the period. For example, if you were answering the question:

How far do you agree that the death of Warwick the Kingmaker in 1471 was the key turning point in the relationship between the Crown and nobility in the period 1399–1509?

the question states a possible turning point from 1471 – towards the latter half of the period. Therefore, if you are considering other possible turning points you should choose one from the early part of the chronology and one from the middle to make sure you cover the whole period.

Equally, if you are dealing with the question:

How accurate is it to say that there was a continuous growth in the power and influence of the Crown in the period 1399–1509?

you should analyse examples of the growth in the power and influence of the Crown throughout the whole period. This could include developments such as:

- early: military leadership and success in France by Henry V 1415–21
- middle: weakness and decline in royal power during the reign of Henry VI 1437–61
- late: assumption of power by Henry VII and the beginning of the Tudor dynasty 1485, development of a service nobility subordinate to the Tudor Crown 1485–1509.

In so doing, you would be addressing the full chronological range of the question.

OCR A level History

Essay guidance

The assessment of OCR Unit Y134 England 1377–1455; Y135 England: 1445–1509 depends on whether you are studying it for AS or A level:

- for the AS exam, you will answer one essay question and one two-part source question
- for the A level exam, you will answer one essay question and one source question.

The guidance below is for answering both AS and A level essay questions.

For both OCR AS and A level History, the types of essay questions set and the skills required to achieve a high grade for Unit Group 1 are the same. The skills are made very clear by both mark schemes, which emphasise that the answer must:

- focus on the demands of the question
- be supported by accurate and relevant factual knowledge
- be analytical and logical
- reach a supported judgement about the issue in the question.

There are a number of skills that you will need to develop to reach the higher levels in the marking bands:

- understand the wording of the question
- plan an answer to the question set
- write a focused opening paragraph
- avoid irrelevance and description
- write analytically
- write a conclusion which reaches a supported judgement based on the argument in the main body of the essay.

These skills will be developed in the section below, but are further developed in the 'Period Study' chapters of the *OCR A level History* series (British Period Studies and Enquiries).

Understanding the wording of the question

To stay focused on the question set, it is important to read the question carefully and focus on the key words and phrases. Unless you directly address the demands of the question you will not score highly. Remember that in questions where there is a named factor you must write a good analytical paragraph about the given factor, even if you argue that it was not the most important.

Types of AS and A level questions you might find in the exams	The factors and issues you would need to consider in answering them
1 Assess the reasons why there was so much unrest during the reign of Henry IV.	Weigh up the relative importance of a range of factors as to why there was so much unrest during Henry IV's reign.
2 To what extent was Lancastrian weakness the most important cause of the victory of the Yorkists in 1461?	Weigh up the relative importance of a range of factors, including comparing the importance of Lancastrian weakness with other factors.
3 'The leadership of Edward, Duke of York, was the most important reason for the victory of the Yorkists in seizing the throne in 1461.' How far do you agree?	Weigh up the relative importance of a range of factors, including comparing the importance of Edward's leadership with other issues, to reach a balanced judgement.

Planning an answer

Many plans simply list dates and events – this should be avoided as it encourages a descriptive or narrative answer, rather than an analytical answer. The plan should be an outline of your argument; this means you need to think carefully about the issues you intend to discuss and their relative importance before you start writing your answer. It should therefore be a list of the factors or issues you are going to discuss and a comment on their relative importance.

For question 1 in the table, your plan might look something like this:

- Accession of Henry IV: deposition of rightful king by a usurper.
- Military campaigns: link to resources and the impact of battles such as Shrewsbury (1403) and Bramham Moor (1408).
- Rebellions by powerful English nobles: Percy, Mortimer and Bardolf.
- Leadership: political weakness and lack of authority of a usurper king.
- Breakdown in law and order in Wales and in some English regions.
- Resources: Henry IV faced financial difficulties, unable to properly fund the war and reward servants for loyal service.
- International support for Glyndŵr: French army landing in Wales and marching to English Midlands.

The opening paragraph

Many students spend time 'setting the scene'; the opening paragraph becomes little more than an introduction to the topic – this should be avoided. Instead, make it clear what your argument is going to be. Offer your view about the issue in the question – why there was so much unrest during the reign of Henry IV – and then introduce the other issues you intend to discuss. In the plan it is suggested that the accession of Henry IV seriously undermined his kingship. This should be made clear in the opening paragraph, with a brief comment as to why – by seizing the crown and deposing

the rightful king, Henry was setting a dangerous precedent. He was flying in the face of tradition and the divine right of inherited kingship. This will give the examiner a clear overview of your essay, rather than it being a 'mystery tour' where the argument becomes clear only at the end. You should also refer to any important issues that the question raises. For example:

There are a number of reasons why there was so much unrest during the reign of Henry IV, including the nature of the accession, rebellion and lack of financial resources[1]. However, the most important reason was the way in which Henry seized the throne, in terms of both the violence of the deposition and the subsequent disposal of Richard II[2]. These were particularly important once Henry had been crowned king because other equally ambitious nobles thought they could do the same[3].

1 The student is aware that there were a number of important reasons.
2 The answer offers a clear view as to what the student considers to be the most important reason – a thesis is offered.
3 There is a brief justification to support the thesis.

Avoid irrelevance and description

It is hoped that the plan will stop you from simply writing all you know about the unrest in England and Wales during Henry IV's period in power between 1399 and 1413 and force you to weigh up the role of a range of factors. Similarly, it should also help prevent you from simply writing about the military events involving the battles and royal expeditions to Wales. You will not lose marks if you do that, but neither will you gain any credit, and you will waste valuable time.

Write analytically

This is perhaps the hardest, but most important skill you need to develop. An analytical approach can be helped by ensuring that the opening sentence of each paragraph introduces an idea, which directly answers the question and is not just a piece of factual information. In a very strong answer it should be possible to simply read the opening sentences of all the paragraphs and know what argument is being put forward.

If we look at question 2, on the importance of Lancastrian weakness (see page 204), the following are possible sentences with which to start paragraphs:

- Lancastrian weakness became an important factor once the Wars of the Roses had begun, but at the start of the war it was not an important factor. Henry VI was expected to remain as king irrespective of who ran his government.
- The failure of Henry VI to lead or inspire his Lancastrian supporters was a significant handicap.
- Yorkist strength, particularly in terms of military leadership, ensured that they were more likely to be successful.
- The political leadership of Richard, Duke of York, followed by that of his son and successor Edward, was important because they were able to keep their noble supporters working together.
- Richard, Earl of Warwick, and Edward, Duke of York, provided the Yorkists with the military leadership that they required if they were to defeat the king's forces.

You would then go on to discuss both sides of the argument raised by the opening sentence, using relevant knowledge about the issue to support each side of the argument. The final sentence of the paragraph would reach a judgement on the role played by the factor you are discussing in the victory of the Yorkists. This approach would ensure that the final sentence of each paragraph links back to the actual question you are answering. If you can do this for each paragraph you will have a series of mini-essays, which discuss a factor and reach a conclusion or judgement about the importance of that factor or issue. For example:

Continuity in political and military leadership was an important factor in securing Yorkist victory in 1461. The death of Richard, Duke of York, at the Battle of Wakefield in 1460, might have fatally weakened the Yorkist cause but the leadership shown by his teenage son, Edward, ensured that this did not happen[1]. Edward's cause was well supported by the leadership shown by Richard, Earl of Warwick, who proved to be a shrewd politician and an able military commander. Yorkist victories at the Battles of Northampton, Mortimer's Cross and Towton were logistical, political and psychological triumphs that broke the will of the Lancastrians[2].

1 The sentence puts forward a clear view that political and military leadership was clearly important for the Yorkist victory in the war.
2 The claim that it was important is developed and some evidence is provided to support the argument.

The conclusion

The conclusion provides the opportunity to bring together all the interim judgements to reach an overall judgement about the question. Using the interim judgements will ensure that your conclusion is based on the argument in the main body of the essay and does not offer a different view. For the essay answering question 1 (see page 204), you can decide what was the most important factor in the victory of the Yorkists, but for questions 2 and 3 you will need to comment on the importance of the named factor – Lancastrian weakness or Edward of York's leadership – as well as explain why you think a different factor is more important, if that has been your line of argument. Or, if you think the named factor is the most important, you would need to explain why that was more important than the other factors or issues you have discussed.

Consider the following conclusion to question 2: 'To what extent was Lancastrian weakness the most important cause of the victory of the Yorkists in 1461?'

Although the Lancastrians certainly had numerous weaknesses, such as poor leadership, an uninspiring king, an unpopular queen and the failure to take advantage of Richard of York's death at Wakefield, weakness was not the most important factor in their defeat[1]. After all, in the early years of the dynastic war the Lancastrians had been more than a match for the Yorkist armies on the battlefield. The Lancastrians tasted victory in the Battles of Ludford Bridge, the Second Battle of St Albans and Wakefield. After the death of their leader at Wakefield, it was therefore Yorkist morale that was crucial; as long as that held, and Edward of York's leadership was important in that respect, the superior resources, in terms of both manpower and war materials, along with the determination of Warwick as a military commander, would ensure that the Yorkists would win a long war[2].

1 This is a strong conclusion because it considers the importance of the named factor – Lancastrian weakness – but weighs that up against a range of other factors to reach an overall judgement.
2 It is also able to show links between the other factors to reach a balanced judgement, which brings in a range of issues, showing the interplay between them.

Sources guidance

Unit Y105 and Y135 England 1445–1509: Lancastrians, Yorkists and Henry VII are assessed through an essay and a source-based or enquiry question. There is no choice for the enquiry question. At AS level you will have to answer two source questions using three sources and for the A level you will answer one question using four sources.

AS question 1

The skills needed to answer this question are made very clear by the mark scheme, which emphasises that the answer must:

- focus on the question
- evaluate the source using *both* provenance and relevant contextual knowledge
- reach a supported analysis of its utility in relation to the issue in the question.

AS question 2 and A level question 1

The skills needed to answer this question are made very clear by the mark scheme, which emphasises that the answer must:

- focus on the question
- evaluate the sources using *both* provenance and relevant contextual knowledge
- uses detailed and accurate knowledge
- reach a supported analysis of the sources in relation to the question.

There are a number of skills that you need to develop if you are to reach the higher levels in the marking bands for both the AS and A level questions:

- You have to *interpret* the evidence. You need to link it to the issue in the question and decide what the evidence is saying about that issue.
- You need to consider *how useful* the evidence is. This involves thinking carefully about a range of issues concerning the provenance of the source; you might think about who wrote it, why it was written, whether the person who wrote was in a position to know and how typical it might be.
- You need to apply relevant contextual knowledge to the source to judge the validity of the source and its view. You therefore need a good knowledge of the topic in the question.
- You need to link your material to the issue in the question and not write a general essay about the topic.

These skills are illustrated in the guidance to answering the questions below, but are further developed in the 'Enquiry Study' chapters of the *OCR A level History* series (British Period Studies and Enquiries).

Practice questions

AS level

1 Use your knowledge of the events of 1450–1509 to assess how useful Source A is as evidence of the attitudes towards the king's advisers.

2 Using Sources A, B and C in their historical context, assess how far they support the view that monarchs chose their successors during this period.

A level

Using Sources A–D in their historical context, assess how far they support the view that Henry VI was chiefly responsible for losing his crown.

SOURCE A

From Jack Cade, *The Complaint of the Poor Commons of Kent*, 1450. Here, Cade gives his views about the government of England in an appeal to the people.

The king should have as his advisers men of high rank from his royal realm, that is to say, the high and mighty prince, the Duke of York, exiled from the service of the King by the suggestions of that traitor the Duke of Suffolk. He should also take advice from those mighty princes the Dukes of Buckingham and Norfolk, together with the earls and barons of this land.

SOURCE B

From *The Annals of the Kings of England* (*Annales rerum anglicarum*), May 1451. A chronicler reports on the debate in Parliament regarding the succession.

In Parliament Thomas Yonge, a lawyer from Bristol, stated that because the king had no offspring, it would be necessary for the security of the kingdom that it should be openly known who should be his heir. He named the Duke of York as the fittest man in the kingdom to be heir. For daring to do this, Thomas was afterwards imprisoned in to the Tower of London.

SOURCE C

From the anonymous *London Chronicle*, 1455. A chronicler describes the dispute between York and Somerset.

Soon after Easter 1455, another dispute arose between the noble Duke of York and the evil Duke of Somerset. Somerset was plotting the destruction of the noble Duke of York. He offered advice to the king, saying that the Duke of York wished to depose the king and rule England himself – which was false. Because of this, around the middle of May, the Duke of York and the Earls of Shrewsbury and Warwick approached London with seven thousand armed men. When the Duke of Somerset heard this, he suggested to the king that York had come to take the throne by force. For this reason Henry VI sided with the Duke of Somerset.

SOURCE D

From *A Chronicle of the Reigns of Richard II, Henry IV, Henry V and Henry VI*, c.1465. A chronicler comments on the government of England in 1459.

The realm of England was not well governed for King Henry VI was child-like and influenced by greedy advisors. His debts increased daily, but he made no payments; all the possessions and lordships that belonged to the crown the king had given away, some to lords and some to other lesser persons, so that he had almost nothing left of his own. And the money taken from the people was wasted, as all the taxes that came from them were spent in vain. The king did not have a proper household as a king should, nor was he able to maintain any wars.

The guidance for AS question 2 and A level question 1 (see page 208) is the same. The only difference is that for the A level question you have to use four sources, whereas for the AS question you must use three.

Answering AS question 1

The first question is worth ten marks and will ask you to:

> Use your knowledge of a particular topic or issue to assess how useful Source X is as evidence of …

In order to do well answering this type of question you should evaluate the source, using both its provenance (see page 208) and your own relevant knowledge of the historical context (see page 208) that is specified in the question. This will allow you to engage with the source and reach a supported analysis of its usefulness as evidence for the issue in the question. You should reach a judgement about its value. Remember it might be useful for some issues but not others.

First, it is important that you use the right source: it will not always be Source A, therefore double check before you start writing! To stay focused on the question set, it is important that you read the question carefully and remain focused on the key phrase 'as evidence of'. Unless you directly address the issue in the question you will not score highly. You can write separate paragraphs on the provenance of the source and the historical context, but the strongest answers will integrate them, often using the context to explain the provenance.

You should use short and appropriate quotations from the source to support the points you are making.

Although the mark scheme does not require you to reach a judgement about the value of the source in relation to the question, it would be helpful to summarise the strengths and weaknesses of the source as evidence for the issue in the question.

In answering the question 1, an answer might start as follows:

Source A is an extract from a manifesto produced and distributed by Jack Cade, in which he explains the primary reason for the rebellion. It is a powerful piece of propaganda intended to gather support for the rebellion. It presumably had to be read to the majority of those taking part given the level of illiteracy at the time[1].

The source is useful in that it explains why the people are unhappy and that their complaint is not so much against the king as against his chief adviser and favourite, Suffolk. The source is also useful because it suggests that the rebel leader, Cade, had some knowledge of the political situation and the struggle for power between York and Suffolk[2]. Additionally, it also begs the question of who may have been behind the rebellion. Was the exiled York involved or was it inspired by

Buckingham and/or Norfolk on his or their own behalf[3]?

1 The opening sentence explains the origin of the source and summarises it.
2 The answer considers the origin of the source and discusses the strengths and weaknesses of this in terms of its usefulness.
3 The answer considers the content of the source and whether it is useful in explaining the tense political situation in 1450 and the attitude of the commons to the nobility and the question of who should advise the king.

The answer should be further developed and might discuss issues such as why Suffolk was deemed to be a traitor. There might be some comment about it providing the names of the nobles considered fit for the purpose of advising the king. It might also be noted that no other complaint is mentioned in the extract apart from politics; there is no mention of the economic problems affecting the kingdom. In judgement, the answer might suggest that Cade had selfish purpose in writing and distributing the manifesto, but did he do it on his own behalf or was he being used by others, such as propagandists working for York?

Answering AS question 2 and the A level question

The question will be worded as follows:

Using these three sources/four sources in their historical context, assess how far they support the view that …

- Keep a good focus on the question and don't drift off into describing everything the sources say.
- Evaluate the sources – that is, say how valid the evidence they give is. You can do this by looking at their *provenance* – that is, what they are, who wrote them, under what circumstances and why. You can also do this by looking at what they say about the issue and testing it against your own knowledge.

- You have to keep a balance. You should not write an essay on the topic in the question just by using knowledge, but you should not just explain what the sources say about the issue either. You need to apply some knowledge to all the sources to answer the question.

In planning your answer to this question it might be helpful to construct a chart similar to the one below (this can be modified to A, B and C for AS):

Source	View about the issue in the question	Evidence from the source	Provenance	Knowledge that supports the source	Knowledge that challenges the source	Judgement
A						
B						
C						
D						

In the second column you decide whether the source supports or challenges the view in the question, and in third column you should enter evidence from the source which supports your view. The next column considers the provenance, which may affect the reliability of the source. The next two columns bring in your knowledge to support or challenge the view in the source. The final column brings all this together to make a judgement about the source in terms of supporting or challenging the view in the question.

If you complete this chart it should provide you with the material you need to answer the question. Although the mark scheme does not require you to group the sources, it might be more sensible to deal with all the sources that support the view in the question together, and those that challenge the view together, before reaching an overall judgement. However, remember some sources may have parts that both support and challenge the view in the question.

An opening paragraph to the question using all the sources could start as follows:

Source B suggests that monarchs had the right to choose their successors, with Source B putting forward the view 'that because the King had no offspring' 'it should be openly known who should be his heir'. The demand here is for the king to publicly name his successor[1]. However, Source C suggests that the monarch's right to choose his successor is being usurped by the Duke of York, who intends to take the crown from Henry VI. On the other hand, Source A makes no mention of the monarch's right to choose their successors but does make plain the fact that Henry VI was unfit for the office of king and was, therefore, in no position to choose his successor[2].

1 The answer deals with one source that supports the view in the question that the monarchs had the right to choose their successor and provides a brief quotation from the source to support the claim.

2 The answer now considers the views of the other sources and offers the alternative factor that monarchs may have had the right to choose their successors but that in the case of Henry VI this was being usurped because of his feeble kingship. In times of political turmoil when nobles were in conflict with each other for power, the monarch's right to choose their successor was itself a point of conflict. The opening paragraph could be developed further by providing quotations from Sources A and C.

Answers can deal with each source separately and, in considering Source C, an answer might take the following approach:

Source C suggests that Henry VI's right to choose his successor was being taken away from him by the Duke of York[1]. In the period between Source B and Source C, Henry VI's wife, Margaret, had given birth to a son and heir so the question of the succession should have been settled. However, the Duke of York was not prepared to accept this and so opted to take the throne by force, blaming the king's 'evil' advisers such as Suffolk for this turn of events. On the other hand, it should be noted that the identity of the author of Source C is unknown, which raises a question about its credibility and its bias[2]. Nevertheless, the source cannot be entirely dismissed since it is contemporary and written in London, the centre of power and where these events are taking place[3]. It should also be noted that the sources deal with one monarch, which may not be representative of monarchy in general[4].

1 The opening sentence outlines the view of Source C about the issue in the question and there is a brief explanation as to why it takes that view.
2 The answer considers the purpose of the source and this raises questions as to its reliability.
3 Although the purpose of the source raises questions about its reliability, own knowledge is applied to confirm the view in the source.
4 The answer concludes by linking the source back to the question and, although it acknowledges that the source argues the succession was the right of the monarch, it was being usurped illegally by a leading nobleman.

Answers should treat each source in a similar way and then use the judgements reached about each source individually to reach an overall judgement in a concluding paragraph. The conclusion should be based on the evaluation of the sources and not simply own knowledge, as is seen in the following example:

Although Sources B and C support the view that monarchs chose their successors, the purpose of both these sources raises questions about their reliability, as Source B was attempting to justify the right of York to become the successor of the childless Henry VI, who had thus far failed to name his heir, while Source C might be considered to be an attempt to stir up trouble between the two most powerful nobles in the kingdom – York and Suffolk – given that Henry VI had acquired a son and heir and thus denying York's succession[1]. However, Sources A and D do not specifically deal with the monarch's right to choose his successor but they do suggest that Henry VI was not fit to choose his advisers, let alone determine the succession[2]. The reliability of the sources can be questioned, particularly that of Source A since it is a piece of propaganda that is hostile to the king, whereas Sources B, C and D are by anonymous chroniclers whose affiliation can only be surmised. The majority of the sources support York and justify his decision to determine the king's succession though they all imply that it is the monarch's prerogative to choose his successor, although this can be challenged by powerful nobles[3].

1 The opening sentence relates to the issue in the question, namely that monarchs chose their own successors, and summarises the extent to which the sources support it.
2 The second sentence offers the counter view.
3 The concluding sentence reaches an overall judgement based on an evaluation of the sources and a very brief reference to own knowledge to support the argument.

Glossary of terms

Act of Accord   Act of Parliament responsible for determining the line of succession to the throne.

Act of Resumption   Act of Parliament intended to recover Crown lands given away as reward for service.

Artillery   Used to describe wheeled cannons of various sizes.

Attainder   The process by which nobles who broke the law were condemned and then punished. This law enabled the king to seize the law-breaker's estates so that he could benefit from the profits.

Attainted   Accused and declared guilty of treason by a vote of Parliament.

Auditors   Officials who counted and wrote down the figures in an account book.

Benevolence   A type of forced loan which would not be repaid to the loaner.

Black Death   Plague that spread across the British Isles between 1347 and 1351, killing up to half of the population.

Bloody flux   Refers to dysentery, an inflammatory disorder of the intestine that results in severe diarrhoea accompanied by fever and abdominal pain.

Borough   A town with a royal charter granting privileges for services rendered, usually dating well back into the Middle Ages.

Chivalry   Relating to the medieval institution of knighthood. It is usually associated with ideals of knightly virtues, honour and fair play.

Commissioners of 'oyer et terminer'   Literally meaning to 'hear and determine' (also to summon and to dissolve), these commissions were given the power to investigate any crime or disturbance thought serious enough for the Crown to become involved.

Commons   One of the two Houses of Parliament staffed by elected representatives, mainly gentry landowners, to assist in the business of government.

Commonweal   The common good or common wealth of the people and the nation.

Convocation   The clerical equivalent of Parliament in which the upper house of bishops and lower house of ordinary clergy met to discuss Church business.

County   The key unit of administration in England. The kingdom was divided into counties, very much like today, to make the government of England easier. Each county elected representatives to sit in Parliament.

Coup d'état   French term used to describe the overthrow of a monarch or government.

Court   The royal court acted as a public place for people to come and meet the king. The court was attached to whichever palace the king happened to be living in.

Depose   To rid the kingdom of its reigning monarch by forcing him to abdicate or resign.

Distraint of knighthood   The dubbing of a knight based on annual income – more than £40 per annum.

Divine right   Belief that monarchs were chosen by God to rule the kingdom and that their word was law. To challenge their right to rule was the same as challenging God's.

Doctrine   The rules, principles and teachings of the Church.

Dowry   Law by which a father provided his daughter with a sum of money or property to give to her husband on marriage.

Escheat   When a landholder died without heirs, his lands passed by right to the king.

Evil councillors   A useful and often-used contemporary label to brand those around the king as the enemies of sound advice and good government.

Faction   Political groupings that formed around and followed a particular noble leader.

Feudal/feudalism   The medieval social and political system.

Feudatories   Territories with feudal lords who owed allegiance to the king of France.

Field guns   Small cannons mounted on wheels.

Fool of God   Contemporary term used to describe someone who is far too religious for his own good.

French pox   Refers to an outbreak of syphilis (a sexually transmitted disease) that spread through the ranks of the French army and also infected the English.

Gentry   Class of landowners below the nobility. They were divided into three strata: knights, esquires and gentlemen.

Great Chain of Being   The belief that every man was born to a specific place in the strict hierarchy of society and had a duty to remain there. It conveyed the contemporary idea of God punishing those who rebelled against their prince (treason) or who questioned the Church's teachings (heresy).

Hanseatic League   Merchants from the mainly German city ports on the Baltic and North Sea who came together to form a trading union and thus dominate trade in northern Europe.

Hog   Refers to Richard's emblem, the white boar.

Hundred Years' War   Historical term used to describe the intermittent conflict between the kings of England and France for possession or control of the French crown and kingdom of France.

Indenture of retainder   Agreement or contract between a master and his servant where the latter is retained in service.

Indicted   Legal term used to describe those charged with a crime.

Infection-resistant   Constant exposure to infection enabled some people to develop natural immunity.

Justice of the peace (JP)   Local law officer and magistrate at county level. JPs also governed the county by enforcing acts of Parliament and acting on decisions taken by the Crown and central government.

Justices of assize   Senior judges who dealt with serious crimes and dispensed justice in the king's courts, which were held twice a year in each county.

King's council   Elite body of councillors, drawn mainly from the nobility, who met the king regularly to frame policy and govern the country.

King's peace   The idea that, as the king was appointed by God, his law was the highest authority which brought order and protection to the people.

'Live of their own'   A contemporary term meaning monarchs should pay their own way, using money from their own pockets, rather than burden the state with taxes.

Livery   The giving of a uniform or badge to a follower.

Lollards   Followers of John Wycliffe who derived their name from the medieval Dutch word meaning 'to mutter' (probably reflecting their style of worship, which was based on reading the scriptures).

Lord chancellor   The chancellor was a senior government minister who headed the writing office or chancery.

Lord deputy   The effective ruler of Ireland invested with the power and authority to govern the Irish on behalf of the Crown.

Lord lieutenant   In times of peace the office had no function beyond the ceremonial, such as the state opening of the Irish Parliament, but in times of war it was responsible for raising and leading the Crown's forces in Ireland.

Lord privy seal   This official had control of the royal seal, which was used to authenticate legal documents.

Lord treasurer   The treasurer was a senior government minister who was in charge of the kingdom's finances.

Lords spiritual   Senior clergy such as bishops, abbots and the two archbishops who sat in the House of Lords.

Lords temporal   Nobility – barons, viscounts, earls, marquises and dukes – who sat in the House of Lords by hereditary right.

Magnate   A powerful nobleman.

Magnus Intercursus   Latin term used to describe the commercial treaty signed between England and Burgundy.

Maintenance   The protection of a follower's interests.

Marcher   A French word used to describe the border region between Wales and England.

Marriage   The royal right to arrange the marriage, for a fee, of heirs and heiresses.

Mercenaries   Professional soldiers who fight for hire and profit.

Muster of the militia   The muster was a method by which local representatives of the Crown called up fit and able men to serve in the army. The militia was an army of conscripts raised to serve the king for a set period of time.

National assessment   Country-wide system of assessing people's wealth for purposes of taxation.

National debt   Money owed by the Crown to members of the English nobility and continental bankers/financiers. The Crown borrowed the money to help pay for the costs of the court, the royal household and the government.

Necromancy   A form of magic involving communication with the dead – either by summoning their spirit as an apparition or raising them bodily – for the purpose of divination, foretelling future events or discovering hidden knowledge.

'Northern affinity'   Used to describe the noble and gentry supporters of Richard III who came from northern England.

Over-mighty subjects   Used to describe strong nobles who were very wealthy, powerful and often overly ambitious.

Palatine   A territory ruled by a person invested with princely or royal authority.

The Pale   Territory in eastern Ireland occupied and ruled by English kings since the thirteenth century. The capital of this English-controlled region was Dublin.

Parliament   Institution of government representing English landowners, consisting of the Houses of Lords and Commons. It had the power to grant taxes and to pass laws.

Pluralism   The holding of more than one parish by a clergyman.

Privy seal   The king's personal seal was a substitute for his signature and was used to authenticate documents.

Proclamations   Official or public announcements that had the power of law. These were used by the Crown as an alternative to acts of Parliament.

Propaganda   Method by which ideas are spread to support a particular point of view.

Readeption   The restoration of Henry VI as king.

Receivers   Officials who collected and stored money on behalf of the king.

Re-endowment   Reinvestment, or finding other ways of raising money for the Crown.

Regent and Protector   Interchangeable terms used to describe someone who governs the kingdom on behalf of a king.

Regular clergy   Monks and nuns who devoted their lives to prayer and study in monasteries, sheltered from the outside world.

Relief   A payment the king received on the transfer of lands through inheritance.

Retaining   Employing or maintaining armed servants and/or private armies.

Retrenchment   Cutting down on expenditure.

Revisionist historians   Those who revisit historical events and revise earlier historical interpretations.

'Robin of Redesdale' and 'Robin of Holderness'   Pseudonyms used to mask the true identities of the rebel leaders.

Royal household   The retinue and servants who looked after the monarch's personal needs and his financial and political affairs.

Royal patronage   Rewards given by the Crown for faithful service. The rewards were often given in the form of property, money, title or office.

Royal proclamations   Royal commands that had the same authority in law as acts of Parliament.

Sanctuary   A place of safety within the walls of a religious institution such as a monastery or church.

Secular clergy   Parish priests, chaplains and bishops who lived in the outside world. They performed tasks such as marriage, baptism and burial.

Sheriff   Chief law officer in the county who arrested and detained criminals, some of whom were dealt with in the sheriff's court or passed on to the justices of the peace. The sheriff also supervised parliamentary elections.

Simony   The selling of Church appointments and privileges.

Subsidy   Voluntary grants of money to the king by his subjects.

Sweating sickness   A virulent form of influenza.

Treason   Betrayal of one's country and its ruler.

Treasurer of the Chamber   Chief financial official responsible for overseeing the royal finances.

Tripartite Indenture   An agreement signed by Mortimer, Percy and Glyndŵr to partition England and establish an independent Wales.

Under-mighty monarch   Used to describe a weak king.

Usurpation   The seizure of the throne without authority or in opposition to the rightful line of succession.

Viceroy   Title given to a nobleman entrusted with royal authority to rule as the king's deputy in some part of the realm.

Wardship   The practice whereby the king took control of the estates of minors (those who were too young to be legally responsible for their inheritance) and received most of the profits from their estates.

Yorkist Invasion   Used by historians to describe the return of armed Yorkists to England from exile abroad.